The Emerging Chinese Advanced Technology Superstate

by
Ernest H. Preeg

Published Jointly by the
Manufacturers Alliance/MAPI
and
Hudson Institute

It is true India has the advantage in software and China in hardware. If India and China cooperate in the information technology industry, we will be able to lead the world . . . and it will signify the coming of the Asian century of the information technology industry.

Chinese Prime Minister Wen Jiabao
during a visit to India, April 11, 2005

The Emerging Chinese Advanced Technology Superstate

Contents

PART I
THE ANALYTIC ASSESSMENT

Foreword

by
Thomas J. Duesterberg and
Herbert I. London*

Not many years ago, few would have considered China as either an economic or political competitor to the United States. Napoleon's "sleeping giant," after all, was just slowly awakening from its centuries-long slumber. Its economic performance, too, was shackled by the devastation of Mao's "Great Leap Forward" of the 1950s and Cultural Revolution of the 1960s, and by the structural inefficiencies of an authoritarian system so ill adapted to the fast-moving, global market economy. Even as China began to show signs of vibrant economic development, most commentators attributed this to the application of capital and low-cost, low-skilled labor to commodity industries. On the political side, little seemed changed, especially after the violent events at Tiananmen Square in 1989. Military analysts as well judged that Chinese military technology, in line with its industrial economy, was a generation or more behind the West and the new Pacific Rim powerhouses.

This assessment, like most of those attempting to come to terms with the reality of China, was far off the mark. The author of this book, Ernest Preeg, came to understand how far off it was when he started reviewing the balance of trade, for the United States, in advanced technology products. The conventional wisdom about the future of U.S. manufacturing assumed that superiority in such high technology products as telecommunications equipment, microprocessors, biotechnology, and nanotechnology was established and likely to remain the source of strength and growth long into the future. Starting around the turn of the millennium, however, the long-standing U.S. trade surplus in these products quickly became a deficit. As Dr. Preeg shows in this book, the rise of China as a major player in various fields of high technology production is a major factor in this turnabout. Preeg's analysis reveals a systematic effort on the part of China to become

---

* Duesterberg is President and CEO of the Manufacturers Alliance/MAPI and London is President of the Hudson Institute.

v

competitive and even dominant in areas such as information technology and the emerging field of nanotechnology. China has trained the scientists and engineers (many in the United States), devoted resources to basic and applied research, promoted and subsidized foreign investment related to advanced technology, induced technology transfer through various mechanisms, and, in some cases, simply appropriated valuable technology from those who had developed it. The sum of this concerted effort has been the growth of advanced technology industry in China to the point that much is globally competitive, and over half of Chinese exports now fall into these categories of goods.

The rise of China as a high technology powerhouse has not passed unnoticed in the past year among economic and political analysts. Indeed, the momentum has shifted to those worried about China as a competitor. *Foreign Affairs* posted the following summary: "For the last five decades, U.S. scientific innovation and technological entrepreneurship have ensured the country's economic prosperity and military power. . . . Today, however, this technological edge—so long taken for granted—may be slipping, and the most serious challenge is coming from Asia."[1] An article in *Foreign Policy* put the case more directly and identified the challenge squarely with China: "China cannot rise peacefully, and if it continues its dramatic economic growth over the next few decades, the United States and China are likely to engage in an intense security competition with considerable potential for war. Most of China's neighbors, including India, Japan, Singapore, South Korea, Russia, and Vietnam, will likely join with the United States to contain China's power."[2] Futurist Francis Fukuyama has noted that China is rapidly developing a network of economic and political agreements with its Asian neighbors that constitutes a real challenge to the long-standing leadership of the United States in Asia, a matter largely ignored by U.S. policy analysts.[3]

Dr. Preeg's analysis in the first five chapters of this book certainly corroborates—and considerably expands the under-standing of—the emergence of China as a formidable economic competitor to the United States, Japan, and Europe. As the commentary cited above highlights, the harder questions faced by policymakers all revolve around how best to respond to this

---

[1] Adam Segal, "Is America Losing Its Edge: Innovation in a Globalized World," *Foreign Affairs*, 83, No. 6 (November-December 2004), p. 2.

[2] John Mearsheimer, "Better to be Godzilla Than Bambi," *Foreign Policy* 46 (January-February 2005), p. 47.

[3] Francis Fukuyama, "All Quiet on the Eastern Front?" *Wall Street Journal*, March 1, 2005, p. A-18.

challenge. The experience of the 20th Century in accommodating the rise of Germany, and later Japan, onto the global stage informs, broadens, and gives urgency to this challenge. The history of the rise of Germany after full unification in 1871 is most often seen as a cautionary tale, while the reemergence of Japan from the ashes of World War II is generally thought to represent a more successful model for policymakers.

What gives even more urgency to the effort to understand and accommodate the rise of China is the size and scope of the nation and, potentially, its economic and political power. Whereas Germany and Japan were large nation-states, China is more akin to a continental power, and its potential as a competitor surpasses that of Japan and Germany by an order of magnitude.

Dr. Preeg's analysis explicitly follows in the path of Hudson Institute founder Herman Kahn's pioneering work on the rise of Japan.[4] The Japanese analogy with China is sometimes advanced as a means to explain the structure and pace of economic advance in China. Dr. Preeg, however, goes to some length to show the differences between the structure of the Japanese and Chinese economies at similar stages of development. And he asserts that China will not fall into the same trap of economic stagnation—caused by demographic weakness, insularity, and institutional rigidity—as Japan did after 1990. He also usefully explores the differences of scope between the insular (and in many ways closed) Japanese economy and the more globalized economy (in terms of both openness and size) of the Chinese.

Dr. Preeg devotes the second half of his book to a discussion of the economic and geopolitical implications of the entry of China onto the global stage of advanced economies. He explores the efforts by China to become a hegemon—again in both economic and political terms—in Asia; what that means for the United States, Japan, and other economic competitors; and how the United States can and should respond to the Chinese challenge. Preeg rejects the protectionist and alarmist response which often characterized the early American reaction to the rise of Japan. And his constructive suggestions for expanding global networks for free, yet fair, trade and for strengthening the environment for innovation and competitiveness in the United States will be welcomed by all those who remember the disastrous consequences of the descent to protectionism in the 1930s.

---

[4] Herman Kahn, *The Emerging Japanese Superstate: Challenge and Response* (Prentice Hall, 1970).

One of the distinctions drawn by Herman Kahn in his work on Japan was between a "superstate" and a "superpower."[5]   By superstate he meant a country with great size and capabilities, whereas a superpower would use those capabilities to "defend itself, exert political influence on other countries, and initiate and control great events." Kahn was "surprised" but not critical of the fact that Japan hesitated to make the full entry on the global stage that its economic success might permit. China, on the other hand, as Dr. Preeg demonstrates forcefully, has no such hesitation—and indeed clearly has the ambition—to become a "superpower."[6]

Because of China's size, its early success in advanced technology development, and its ambition, the world, as Napoleon predicted, is trembling.[7]   The last chapter of Preeg's book is devoted to an exploration of the implications of having China as a superpower on the world scene. Much of the 21st Century will undoubtedly be dominated by the dispute over, and reality of, the absolute necessity to integrate the new China peacefully in a new world order. Preeg has many constructive ideas about how to accomplish this in a way that avoids the catastrophes of the 20th Century, when the new German superpower was not properly accommodated. Some will disagree with Preeg's analysis and his prescriptions, but certainly he has illuminated the underlying trends that will dominate the debate. And his work will challenge others to take the same constructive approach and to offer a comparable array of creative solutions. We are pleased to offer this work as a major contribution to this crucial debate.

---

[5] Herman Kahn and Thomas Pepper, *The Japanese Challenge: The Success and Failure of Economic Success* (Crowell Publishers, 1979), Introduction, pp. xi-xiv.

[6] One of the ironies of China's rise may be that Japan will be forced to move in the direction of becoming a superpower. Japan, largely in response to China's emergence, has in the last few years become more aggressive in asserting rights to territorial waters disputed by China, building up its military and moving closer to the United States in its support of Taiwan. Japan is also attempting to join other superpowers— or superpower aspirants—on the Security Council of the United Nations.

[7] The quote attributed to Napoleon by Lord Amherst is: "China is a sleeping giant. But when she awakes the world will tremble." See William Safire, *Safire's New Political Dictionary* (Random House, 1993).

Preface

The Chinese challenge to U.S. leadership in advanced technology innovation, production, and exports could well be the most important issue facing U.S. global interests in the decade ahead, and yet it is often downplayed and widely misunderstood. The first objective of this study, therefore, is to shed analytic light on what is happening within the Chinese advanced technology sector and where it is heading over the short to medium term. The point of departure is that a major advance by China to reduce the U.S. leadership role in technology innovation could have substantial adverse impact on U.S. commercial, national security, and foreign policy interests.

The central analytic conclusion is that China, indeed, is on track to become an advanced technology superstate and the principal U.S. rival in the sector. This leads to the second objective of the study which is to develop a forceful and comprehensive policy response in order to maintain the U.S. leadership position for innovation and international competitiveness. Specific recommendations are offered in the fields of international finance, trade and investment, and U.S. domestic economic policies. The principal weakness at this point, however, is the lack of national purpose as to what is at stake, which is prerequisite to an effective U.S. policy response. In this context, the study will hopefully play a catalytic role in raising public awareness and resolve in responding to the *défi chinois*.

I was assisted generously by the advisory group for this study, composed of China experts and representatives of the public and private sectors. We met twice, first to critique the analytic chapters in Part I, and a second time to discuss the recommended policy response in Part II. Additional conversations with, and written comments from, members all contributed to a much more complete and accurate final product. I also wish to thank my colleagues at Manufacturers Alliance/MAPI who assisted me in many ways, especially through their expert current knowledge about what is happening within the U.S. advanced technology sector. My research assistant for the project, Echo Lin, provided superb support throughout, gathering statistical and other material from many sources, in large part Chinese, and assembling much of it into chart and tabular form. Last but not least, Tom Duesterberg, President and CEO of the Manufactures Alliance/MAPI, is an esteemed colleague over many years, and his perspective as a trained historian was invaluable to me at a number of points, as was his sustained encouragement and support for my quest to unveil the emerging Chinese advanced technology superstate.

Chapter 1

Introduction and Principal Conclusions

Introduction

The rapid rise of China as a major producer and exporter of advanced technology products, particularly in the information technology and communications sectors, is generally understood. The inquiry here goes beyond these current trends and addresses the questions of whether the Chinese advanced technology industry will develop more deeply, in terms of technology innovation and new product development, and, more broadly, so as to transform the entire nation into a leading-edge information-based society. In short, is China emerging as an advanced technology superstate, while in the process challenging the long-standing U.S. leadership role as the technology-driven engine for global economic growth?

This Chinese challenge and its importance for U.S. national interests have been recognized by knowledgeable observers. In January 2004, the President's Council of Advisors on Science and Technology (PCAST), comprised of 24 distinguished academic and business leaders, concluded that:

> The loss of U.S. high-tech leadership would have serious detrimental effects on the Nation's economic security and the citizens' standard of living. While not in imminent jeopardy, a continuation of current trends could result in a breakdown in the web of "innovation eco-systems" that drive the successful U.S. innovation system. . . . In particular, the entry of China into the high technology arena has created a new level of nervousness on the part of many industry and academic professionals. In part, this results from China's size and its commitment to a high-tech industrial policy. . . . China also has a flexible, entrepreneurial culture, which some of its neighbors do not. . . . China has an interest in seeing economic benefits accrue to Chinese companies rather than to foreign competitors. . . . It is expected that China's efforts

to develop leading-edge high technology ecosystems will be significant, continue for a long time, and gain extensive assistance from foreign investment.[1]

Unfortunately, the PCAST report received little attention and quickly receded into the depths of the Executive Office website. The point of departure for this study is thus to bring the concerns expressed in the report back into public focus, to analyze the issues raised in greater depth, and to respond to ongoing questions about the nature and sustainability of Chinese performance in advanced technology industries.   There is a widespread view, for example, that China is principally an export platform for advanced technology products, with the truly advanced technology components imported from abroad.   There is also frequent comparison with earlier predictions about the loss of U.S. technological leadership that proved untrue.   In 1970, the futurologist Herman Kahn wrote a book claiming that Japan "almost inevitably will achieve giant economic, technological, and financial stature, that very likely it will become financially and politically powerful in international affairs, and that eventually it is likely to strive to become a military superpower as well."[2] Japan appeared to follow this trajectory during the 1970s and 1980s, but then the emerging Japanese superstate stalled out during the 1990s.   The 2000 Lisbon Agenda of the European Union (EU), which outlined the EU's plan to become the most competitive knowledge-based economy by 2010, has also clearly bogged down.

One objective of this study is to assess how the current Chinese challenge to U.S. advanced technology leadership is distinct from earlier challenges by Japan and Europe.   The conclusion is that the Chinese advanced technology prospect is, indeed, distinct in a number of key respects, that the challenge to U.S. leadership over time is more formidable, and that China will almost certainly become an advanced technology superstate, along similar lines as expressed by Herman Kahn for Japan 35 years ago.   To what extent and over what timeframe a narrowing of U.S. leadership in

---

[1]President's Council of Advisors on Science and Technology, *Sustaining the Nation's Innovation Ecosystems: Report on Information Technology Manufacturing and Competition*, Executive Office of the President, January 30, 2004.

[2]Herman Kahn, *The Emerging Japanese Superstate: Challenge and Response* (Prentice-Hall, 1970), p. vii.

technology innovation and international competitiveness will occur, however, depends on a number of developments, including the policy courses ahead in both countries.

The Chinese historical context for export-led industrial growth began in 1978, when Deng Xiaoping activated the "Four Modernizations," followed in 1980 by the establishment of four Special Economic Zones (SEZs) in coastal cities. Export-oriented foreign investors quickly moved in, but in the initial years they were predominantly in labor-intensive industries, and it was not until 1995 that the "science and technology" modernization was elevated by the Chinese government to top priority. The results for advanced technology industry over the ensuing ten years have been even more dramatic in terms of rapid growth in research and development (R&D), university training, foreign direct investment (FDI), and trade, as described in subsequent chapters.

The Chinese experience can be understood, however, only in the broader context of parallel developments within the global economy. The past 25 years have witnessed an amazing pace of technological change, which has resulted in very large increases in global productivity and economic growth. Two characteristics have largely defined this course of events. The first is the dominant role of the U.S. manufacturing sector as the global engine for growth and technological innovation.[3] Within the U.S. economy, the manufacturing sector accounts for two-thirds of private sector R&D and over 90 percent of new patents, and the result has been an unprecedented surge in technological innovation and new product development. Contributing factors to this engine for growth phenomenon are an innovative management culture, the largest domestic market for new products, a plentiful supply of high-quality scientists and engineers, a flexible and skilled labor force, readily available financing—including venture capital investors—and a generally accommodating infrastructure.

The second characteristic is the rapid pace of market globalization, again with a central role played by technology-intensive manufactured products and related segments of the services sector. Manufactures account for 60 percent of global exports, and this trade has grown more than twice as fast as global gross domestic product (GDP) since 1980. Moreover, within the manufacturing sector, the fastest growth in trade has been in the information

---

[3] This engine for growth role is explained in detail in *U.S. Manufacturing: The Engine for Growth in a Global Economy*, Thomas J. Duesterberg and Ernest H. Preeg, eds. (Praeger Publishers, 2003).

technology and other advanced technology sectors. Foreign direct investment has been growing at an even faster pace since the late 1980s, with a concentration in export-oriented manufacturing with embedded new technologies. All industrialized and newly industrialized nations have been engaged in this rapid globalization process, but China stands out as the fastest globalizer of all.

Within these highly dynamic and fast-moving circumstances, this study is in two parts. The first part is analytic in content, and consists of a comprehensive assessment of Chinese emergence as an advanced technology superstate. Chapter 2 examines internal Chinese indicators, including R&D, university training for scientists and engineers, patent applications, and authorship of articles in technical journals. Chapters 3 and 4 deal with foreign direct investment and trade in advanced technology products. Chapter 5 draws together the analysis in previous chapters to present a net assessment of the current state and future prospects for Chinese advanced technology industry, while Chapter 6 examines related geopolitical and geostrategic implications, including the rise of China as economic hegemon in East Asia and the growing Chinese military capability to develop advanced weapons systems.

The second part of the study presents a recommended U.S. policy response. Chapter 7 contains a general statement of U.S.-China policy under the new circumstances, increasingly related to advanced technology industries. Chapters 8-10 then provide more detailed recommendations for international finance, including the immediate issue of Chinese currency manipulation, international trade and investment (which highlights the mutual U.S.-Chinese interest in multilateral free trade for the manufacturing sector) and the requisite U.S. domestic economic policy agenda. Chapter 11 concludes the study with a broader historical perspective for the evolving U.S.-China policy relationship, which is part of an emerging new world order of advanced technology regional hegemonies dominated by the three-way relationship among the United States, China, and the EU.

A final note concerns terminology: "advanced technology" or "high-tech"? The two adjectives are used, in many instances, interchangeably. There is a specific distinction in trade data, where U.S. "advanced technology" data relates to specific products while Organization for Economic Cooperation and Development (OECD) and some other "high-tech" trade figures cover broader industry sectors. Otherwise, a choice can be made one way or the other, and the practice adopted here is generally to use "advanced technology" as the adjective of choice, principally because "advanced" has a more pointed, action-oriented feel, which is certainly appropriate for the events described in what follows.

Principal Conclusions

Part I. The Analytic Assessment

1. Deng Xiaoping's Four Modernizations in 1978 has led to 25 years of 9 percent annual GDP growth in China, and a fivefold increase in per capita income. This rapid growth, however, has been in two distinct stages. The first stage, from 1980 to 1995, centered on export-led growth in low technology, labor-intensive industries, while only during the past ten years has advanced technology industry development become the top priority.

2. The two principal resource indicators of advanced technology development are R&D expenditures and science and engineering graduates. Chinese R&D expenditures grew by 22 percent per year from 1995 to 2002, compared with 6 percent in the United States. Projected to 2005, Chinese expenditures will be higher than those of Japan, more than 60 percent of the EU level, and about 40 percent of the U.S. level. Chinese R&D is more heavily concentrated in manufacturing than is U.S. R&D, with 60 percent by enterprises, 28 percent by government research institutions, and 10 percent by universities.

3. Chinese science and doctoral degrees increased by 14 percent per year from 1995 to 2001, compared with a 1 percent decrease in the United States. Projected to 2005, Chinese doctoral degrees will be half that of the U.S. level. Chinese doctoral degrees in engineering grew 18 percent per year from 1995 to 2001, compared with -2 percent in the United States. Projected to 2005, the number of Chinese engineering doctorates will be 70 percent higher than the U.S. level.

4. Two performance indicators are patent applications and technical article authorship. Chinese patent applications increased annually by large double-digit percentages from 1995 to 1999, as did technical article authorship from 1995 to 2001, but from very low base levels. More up-to-date figures would be revealing, and the National Science Foundation (NSF) is urged to provide more current figures.

5. FDI in China was relatively low during the first stage of labor-intensive industrial growth, less than $5 billion per year through 1991. FDI then increased sharply, related to wide-ranging

incentives for advanced technology investors, to $38 billion in 1995 and $61 billion in 2004. Seventy percent of FDI is in manufacturing, with heavy concentration in export-oriented companies in advanced technology sectors. In 2004, 57 percent of total Chinese exports was by foreign investors.

6. Taiwan is the largest foreign investor in China, accounting for up to half of total FDI, but there are no precise figures because most Taiwanese investment comes indirectly through Hong Kong and other sources. The United States was the second-largest foreign investor in China through 2002, but, in 2003-2004, South Korea and Japan pulled ahead of the United States. In 2004, South Korea invested $6.2 billion, Japan $5.5 billion, and the United States $3.9 billion.

7. Taiwanese investment is concentrated heavily in the information technology sector, including the semiconductor sector. China plans to build up to 18 semiconductor plants by 2005, and there are now about 400 chip design companies in China, about one-third of which are foreign.

8. American investment in China is broader than that of the East Asians in industry scope, although 70 percent is in manufacturing. China provides tax incentives and exerts coercion on American companies to do R&D and upgrade the technology level of production in China, and many companies are doing so. There is also a trend to work with Chinese suppliers and thus increase value added within China. Ingersoll-Rand employs 20 engineers to train Chinese suppliers to meet quality standards. Cisco CEO John Chambers predicted that "China will be the IT [information technology] center of the world."

9. Chinese exports grew 35 percent in both 2003 and 2004, and will probably come close to that again in 2005. China passed Japan in 2004 to become the third-largest exporter after the United States and Germany, with most of German exports within the EU, and on current course China will be the number one exporter within three years.

10. Chinese high and medium-high technology exports are growing the fastest, and their share of total manufactured exports increased from 33 percent in 1995 to an estimated 52 percent in 2004, while low and medium-low technology exports were down from 67 percent to 48 percent. In 2004, less than 20 percent of Chinese exports were in textiles, apparel, and footwear.

11. The U.S. merchandise trade deficit with China increased from $57 billion in 1998 to $162 billion in 2004. For advanced technology products (ATP), which have the highest R&D and

engineering content, the United States was in rough trade balance with China in 1998, but had a deficit of $36 billion in 2004. The ATP deficit was $39 billion in the information technology and communications sector, offset by small surpluses in semiconductors and commercial jet aircraft.

12. The "export platform" issue involves Chinese exports of advanced technology products with large import content of high technology components. There are no precise figures for the extent of this relationship, and the import content varies widely by plant and industry subsector. The overall degree of export platforming, in terms of value added by imports, is probably less than half and declining steadily as the share of Chinese value added increases. The very large majority of export platforming is by Taiwanese, South Korean, and Japanese companies, and very little is by American companies.

13. The net assessment is that China, indeed, is an emerging advanced technology superstate, in terms of its domestic market size, the resource commitment to R&D, engineering, and infrastructure, the rapidly growing and highly competitive investment sector, and the spectacular export performance.

14. One indicator for final arrival as an advanced technology superstate will be the emergence of internationally competitive Chinese firms, with brand recognition, quality product reputation, and a leading-edge R&D program. A number of large Chinese firms in several sectors are approaching this stage of multinational competitiveness.

15. A blossoming of technology innovation within China will be a decisive factor for China to achieve superstate status. Premier Wen Jiabao, in April 2005, declared that "independent innovation is the national strategy" and, although information is limited, it appears very likely that China will become one of the principal centers of advanced technology innovation.

16. China nevertheless will have to make important structural adjustments to maintain its high rate of growth in advanced technology development. Financial sector reform is most important, and significant steps are under way in this area. A sectoral shift from export-led to domestically generated growth is also necessary, which should include a greater resource commitment within China to health care, infrastructure, energy, and environmental improvements.

17. Political change in China is difficult to predict, but highly disruptive change that would undermine advanced technology industry is most unlikely. A process of democratization within

China, whatever the pace and modalities, is almost inevitable as China progresses toward being an affluent, more educated, information-based society, with a rapidly growing middle class and a highly productive private sector.

18. One geopolitical consequence of the Chinese rise to advanced technology superstate status is that it is becoming the economic hegemon in East Asia. China is or will soon become the principal trading partner of all other East Asian nations, including Japan and South Korea. China is the largest recipient of FDI by far, and an outward flow of Chinese FDI to Southeast Asia is gathering momentum. Once the yuan becomes a convertible, market-based currency, Shanghai, Beijing, and Hong Kong will become the financial centers of Asia. As a result, China will have the dominant economic influence within the region, with corresponding growing policy leverage.

19. One geostrategic consequence of the Chinese rise to advanced technology superstate status is that Chinese internally generated military modernization is moving ahead at a faster pace. A fundamental restructuring of Chinese defense industry in 1997-1999 shifted control of defense enterprises from the military to the civilian government, and integrated their operations with commercial advanced technology enterprises, including competitive bidding for defense contracts. In effect, China shifted from the discredited Soviet model toward the U.S. model for weapons development and production.

20. The result has been a more rapid rate of military system modernization, particularly for the navy and defense electronic systems. During the 1990s, the U.S. Department of Defense (DOD) consistently assessed the Chinese military capability as being at least 20 years behind the United States. The 2004 DOD annual assessment was that China will have uneven success in its goal of catching up with the industrialized nations within five to ten years, and the 2005 assessment will likely indicate an even faster narrowing of the gap.

Part II. The U.S. Policy Response

1. China is now the most important U.S. bilateral relationship. A new relationship, resulting from China's emergence as an advanced technology superstate, centers on a deepening economic engagement of wide-ranging mutual benefit, together with a far less engaged set of mutual national security interests. The most important medium to long-term U.S. interest in play is to maintain

U.S. leadership in advanced technology industries, which is importantly related to relative military force capabilities.

2. The political relationship is currently troubled, but likely to move in a positive direction over time through democratization within China, largely as a result of the intense bilateral economic engagement, which can be helped through targeted U.S. diplomacy. Deepening ethnic and cultural ties between the two countries, including those promoted through study and travel, will also help. Confrontation over Taiwan should be avoided as a mutual interest, but this can become more difficult as Chinese military modernization proceeds at a faster pace.

3. The recommendations here focus on the economic relationship, beginning with the most important immediate problem, Chinese currency manipulation. The Chinese yuan is estimated to be at least 40 percent lower than a market-based exchange rate, as a result of massive purchases of foreign currencies over the past four years by the Chinese central bank. Others, particularly Japan, South Korea, and Taiwan, have followed suit, which has had a substantial overall adverse impact on U.S. trade, particularly the manufacturing sector, including advanced technology industries. The U.S. trade deficit is in the order of $150 billion larger as a result of such currency manipulation, which is in violation of International Monetary Fund (IMF) and World Trade Organization (WTO) obligations. The United States should act vigorously against all four East Asians to cease the practice, initially through direct consultation, but it should also make clear that the United States is prepared to pursue IMF and WTO dispute settlement procedures if necessary.

4. Once China moves to a convertible, market-based exchange rate, which is its stated objective, the international financial system will take on a new structure oriented around three key currencies, the dollar, the euro, and the Chinese yuan. The IMF system will also change fundamentally, with few if any large IMF loans and a greater policy focus on how floating rates are managed. Initiatives for currency unions also may become more important. The most challenging financial relationships will be within Asia and across the Pacific with the dollar. The United States and China will thus take on principal leadership responsibilities and need to structure their bilateral financial collaboration more effectively.

5. The U.S.-China trade and investment policy relationship has bilateral, multilateral, and regional dimensions. The bilateral dimension centers on implementation of Chinese WTO accession

commitments and involves negotiations on a wide range of issues. Protection of intellectual property rights (IPRs) is the biggest problem area, with serious adverse impact on U.S. advanced technology industries. Other issues of particular interest to U.S. advanced technology industries that need to be addressed include investment policy, standards and technical regulations, taxation, subsidies, telecommunications services, and biotechnology regulations.

6. The multilateral dimension currently involves the WTO Doha Round, which is bogged down largely over the issue of nonreciprocity for developing countries. The United States and China could go a long way to breaking the impasse through a jointly supported formula for tariff reductions in the nonagricultural (almost all manufacturing) sector, in which China would make a fully reciprocal offer in view of its strong export competitiveness in manufactures.

7. The regional dimension of trade policy is now focused most importantly on East Asia in view of China's free trade agreement (FTA) negotiations with the Association of Southeast Asian Nations (ASEAN)—with Japan and South Korea following in the wake. Such an East Asian preferential trading bloc would have further adverse impact on the U.S. trade deficit in view of the high tariffs throughout East Asia, and would also have a negative geopolitical consequence as a high-visibility Asian grouping in an adversarial position *vis-à-vis* the United States.

8. The only practical way the United States can head off an East Asian preferential trading bloc that excludes the United States is through initiatives to create an Asia Pacific free trade agreement, as agreed at summit level in Bogor in 1994. The substantive core of such an agreement would be free trade between the United States and China, which although not feasible at this time, should be addressed through the formation of a high-level U.S.-China study group to examine the economic costs and benefits of free trade between the two countries, within the Asia Pacific context.

9. The United States should also undertake or complete FTA negotiations across the Pacific with Thailand (negotiations under way), South Korea (official talks under way), and Taiwan (informal talks under way). This "three spoke" initiative, in addition to existing U.S. FTAs with Singapore and Australia, would definitively move the United States into the transpacific free trade relationship, and would become part of a proposed formal Asia Pacific Economic Cooperation (APEC) review of

progress toward the Bogor objective. Such transpacific FTA initiatives, moreover, could well lead to a multilateral free trade agreement for the nonagricultural sector.

10. A U.S. domestic economic policy response to the Chinese challenge to U.S. leadership in advanced technology industry is essential. In broadest terms, the U.S. manufacturing sector is the engine for technology-driven economic growth and needs to become more competitive internationally. The $552 billion U.S. trade deficit in manufactures in 2004 was one-third the size of U.S. production, which greatly reduces the domestic revenue and employment base for continued innovation and international competitiveness. The trade deficit needs to be greatly reduced or eliminated, which involves two principal domestic policy areas.

11. The first macropolicy area concerns the need to increase domestic savings so as not to have to borrow abroad to finance investment, which, in turn, drives up the trade deficit. Greater incentives for private and business savings, and the reduction or elimination of the federal budget deficit, are the policy vehicles.

12. The second remedial policy area involves various specific policies that place cost or other disadvantages on U.S. manufacturing industries compared to major trading partners, and to China in particular. Specific proposals and conclusions are offered for education, R&D, tax policy, tort reform, health care, regulatory policies, and the Sarbanes-Oxley law.

13. The current U.S. domestic policy response to the Chinese advanced technology challenge is disturbing and points to an increasingly difficult road ahead for American companies. To remedy this, there is a need for better public communication about the relationship between the advanced technology engine for growth phenomenon and U.S. international as well as domestic interests. What is now lacking most of all is a sense of national purpose in responding to a rapidly changing world, driven most importantly by the development and application of wide-ranging new technologies on a global scale.

14. The final conclusions extrapolate from the Chinese advanced technology experience over the past ten years into a broader historical perspective ahead. Prevailing paradigms about the post–Cold War world are found inadequate. A revised and updated new order of international relationships is presented with political, economic, and military power relationships increasingly dominated by three advanced technology superstates—the United States, the EU, and China, each a regional advanced technology hegemon within the North America/Caribbean, European, and

East Asian regions, respectively. The three regions together include 52 percent of global population, 79 percent of GDP, and 85 percent of merchandise exports. India may rise to advanced technology superstate status within 10-20 years, as the South Asian advanced technology hegemon. Relationships among the three advanced technology hegemons are not yet well defined, however, and other regions of the world will face important adjustments as well.

Part I

The Analytic Assessment

Chapter 2

Chinese Advanced Technology Development: The Domestic Indicators

In 1978, Deng Xiaoping activated the Four Modernizations, designed to address, in order of priority—industry, agriculture, science and technology, and national defense/military. In 1980, he introduced the first Special Economic Zones designed to implement market-oriented reforms with emphasis on foreign investment, imported technology, and manufactured exports. This was a truly revolutionary change in economic strategy in the wake of the disastrous consequences of Mao Zedong's "Great Leap Forward" of 1958-1960 and the "Great Proletarian Cultural Revolution" of 1966-1976. The results since 1980 have been extraordinary in terms of annual growth in overall GDP, led by the export-oriented manufacturing sector. The twenty-five year record, however, consists of two distinct stages, largely in keeping with the initial priorities among the Four Modernizations. Industrial development of relatively low technology, labor-intensive industry dominated the first stage, through about 1995, while only during the past ten years have the science and technology and military modernization objectives become top priorities. The modernization of agriculture, meanwhile, earlier slipped from second to fourth priority, although it is now receiving greater political attention, with promising prospects for market-oriented growth.

The subject of this study is the more recent surging role for science and technology as related to advanced technology industry. It is useful, however, to begin with a brief review of the broader export-oriented industrial growth experience so as to understand better the advanced technology restructuring currently under way.

Export-Oriented Industrial Growth Since 1980

The broadest indicator of the successful Chinese economic strategy is the growth path in GDP, both internally and in relation

13

to the advanced industrialized economies of the United States, the EU, and Japan. Internal growth has averaged in the order of 9 percent annually since 1980, resulting in a sevenfold increase in GDP and a fivefold increase in per capita income. The comparison with other industrialized economies requires a critical choice in how the relative size of the output of goods and services is measured. The so-called exchange rate measure values goods and services produced at their internal prices in Chinese yuan,[1] and then converts the aggregate yuan figure into dollars at the official exchange rate. This measure greatly understates the size of the Chinese economy relative to the higher income industrialized economies because a given quantity of comparable goods or services can generally be bought at much lower prices in China. The alternative "purchasing power parity" (ppp) measure adjusts for these purchasing power differentials, and is clearly the more appropriate measure, although it involves judgmental estimates as to the size of the differentials.[2] Official GDP comparisons, such as by the World Bank and the OECD, generally use the ppp measure, but press and other reports often are based on the misleading exchange rate measure. The exchange rate measure is particularly popular for those who still want to believe that Japan has the second-largest national economy.

Table 2-1 presents GDP figures, on a ppp basis, for China, the United States, the EU (15, as used in all references to the EU in this study), and Japan, from 1990 to 2004, with a projection to 2010. Over the period 1990-2004, the Chinese economy grew by 338 percent, compared with 97 percent for the United States, 85 percent for the EU, and 61 percent for Japan, or three to five times faster than the other three.[3] In terms of absolute size, China's economy passed that of Japan in 1995 and was 82 percent larger

---

[1] The Chinese currency is called both the yuan and the renminbi. The term yuan is used here, as it is in the English version of the annual *Chinese Statistical Yearbook*. Renminbi can be difficult to pronounce and easy to misspell, and no other major currency has three syllables. Yuan is often capitalized, but other currencies are not.

[2] The two alternative measures of GDP, as applied to China, are explained in *An Emerging Knowledge-Based Economy in China? Indicators From OECD Databases* (OECD, March 22, 2004), p. 6. The exchange rate measure is assessed as "hardly a plausible measure" for comparing financial data for China with other countries.

[3] These percentage figures are in "current ppp $" and thus do not reflect real growth, but they do demonstrate the relative growth performances.

than Japan's in 2004.[4] Projecting the 2004 ppp figures to 2010, based on estimated annual growth rates of 8 percent for China, 4 percent for the United States, and 3 percent for the EU and Japan, the Chinese economy will reach 73 percent of the size of the U.S. economy, 84 percent of the size of the EU economy, and almost two and a half times that of the Japanese economy. These projections of 2004 ppp levels may overstate Chinese performance in that, as Chinese per capita income grows faster than that of the United States, there is convergence of the ppp and the exchange rate measures of GDP. This impact over only six years, however, is probably small, and China could grow at more than the projected 8 percent, given the 9.5 percent 2004 growth performance.

Table 2-1
Gross Domestic Product
(billions of current ppp$)

	China	United States	EU	Japan
1990	1,512	5,751	5,631	2,264
1995	3,088	7,338	7,255	2,936
2000	4,842	9,762	9,304	3,298
2004	6,626	11,351	10,426	3,638
Percent change 1990-2004	338	97	85	61
2010 projection	10,514	14,362	12,450	4,344
China as a percent of others 2010	—	73	84	242

Source: OECD, *An Emerging Knowledge-Based Economy in China? Indicators From OECD Databases*, March 22, 2004, for 1990-2003, Table SA3; the calculations for 2004 are based on actual growth; projections to 2010 and are based on annual growth of 8 percent for China, 4 percent for the United States, and 3 percent for the EU and Japan

One salient characteristic of this outstanding economic growth performance is the dominant role of the industrial sector, as shown in Table 2-2. The industrial sector share of GDP for China rose steadily from 41.6 percent in 1990 to 51.7 percent in 2002, and this upward trend continues. In 2004, industrial output in China rose 14 percent, compared with about 5 percent for the remainder of the economy.[5] In contrast, the industry shares of GDP in the

---

[4] Based on the exchange rate measure, in sharp and misleading contrast, the Japanese economy in 2004 was more than twice as large as the Chinese economy.

[5] Since the industrial sector comprises over half of total GDP, and total GDP grew 9 percent in 2004, growth for the remainder of the economy was only about 4 percent.

United States, the EU, and Japan declined substantially since 1990, and were all below 30 percent by 2002.

Table 2-2
Share of Industry in GDP*
(percent)

	1990	1995	2000	2002
China	41.6	49.1	50.8	51.7
United States	27.4	25.7	23.6	22.3**
EU	32.8	29.8	27.9	26.9
Japan	38.1	32.8	31.0	29.4**

* Gross value added based on current prices
** 2001
Source: OECD, *An Emerging Knowledge-Based Economy in China? Indicators From OECD Databases*, March 22, 2004, Table SA6

Another salient characteristic is the relatively high percentage of trade as a share of GDP for China, as shown in Table 2-3. The average of imports and exports of goods, as a percent of GDP, more than doubled for China, from 12.2 percent in 1990 to 24.5 percent in 2002. Comparable trade shares of GDP for the United States, the EU, and Japan also rose, but at a far more modest pace. The result is that by 2002, Chinese dependence on trade was more than double that of the EU (excluding intra-EU trade), and almost three times that of the United States and Japan.

Table 2-3
Trade in Goods as a Share of GDP
(Average of imports and exports as a percent of GDP)

	1990	1995	2000	2002
China	12.2	17.0	21.5	24.5
United States	7.6	9.0	10.2	8.9
EU (15)*	7.9	8.7	11.6	11.4**
Japan	8.1	6.9	8.4	8.7

* Excludes intra-EU trade
** 2001
Source: OECD, *An Emerging Knowledge-Based Economy in China? Indicators From OECD Databases*, March 22, 2004, Table SA8

This is a capsule account of the Chinese growth performance over the past 25 years, driven principally by the increasingly trade-oriented industrial sector. It is not clear how long this pattern will continue. At a certain point, growth will have to shift away from the industrial and more strongly toward the services sector, with a corresponding shift in demand from exports and industrial investment to personal consumption. There are also major structural adjustment problems to be confronted, which could alter or slow the overall growth path, as discussed in Chapter 5.

The overall picture, however, projecting the experience of the past 25 years only another five to ten years is of a global economy dominated by three great industrialized economies—the United States, the EU, and China—approaching comparable size, with Japan running a distant fourth. The four together accounted for 57 percent of global GDP in 2003. In terms of trade, all four economies are deeply engaged, together accounting for 60 percent of world exports in 2003, but with China more than twice as dependent on trade as the other three. By 2010, as described in Chapter 4, China will likely surpass the United States and become the largest trading nation.

This emerging predominant trilateral relationship within the global economy in quantitative terms has even more profound implications for geopolitics, national security, and commerce, when the qualitative dimension of the recent rapid development of Chinese advanced technology industry is taken into account. Global economic growth over the past 25 years has been driven by the unprecedented development and application of new technologies, most concentrated in the information technology and communications sector. The United States has maintained a dominant leadership position in this technology innovation process, with close competition from West Europe and Japan. The central question posed in this study involves the extent to which China is now rising to challenge the U.S. advanced technology leadership position and becoming an advanced technology superstate in its own right.

The Rapid Development of Chinese Advanced Technology Industry Since 1995

Deng Xiaoping made labor-intensive industrial growth *primus inter pares* among the Four Modernizations in 1978, but, by about 1995, science and technology (which had been the third priority) had risen to at least coequal status, and it continues to gather momentum as the primary driving force for growth within the Chinese economy. In 1985, the Communist Party Central Committee first took a landmark decision on reform of the science and technology management system, with a strong commercial orientation: "Modern science and technology constitute the most dynamic and decisive factors in the new productive forces . . . Our scientific and technological work must be oriented to economic construction."[6]   The 1988 Torch Program established 53 High Technology Development Zones, emphasizing applied research for commercial application and inviting international partners to collaborate and invest in high technology industries. These initial plans were slow on implementation, however, and in 1995 a more specific and action-oriented "Decision on Accelerating Scientific and Technological Progress" was adopted, in part as an attempt by China's new generation of leaders to assert their influence in advanced technology development.[7] A series of specific goals was adopted, including rapid increases in education and government spending on research and development. Greater incentives, including export credits and tax rebates, were offered to joint ventures with foreign companies in order to attract new technology and management skills. The broad objective was to develop advanced technology to "match those of the advanced countries in some fields," with the information technology sector at the top of the list. Another key step to spur foreign investment, including R&D activities in China, was the 2001 decision to liberalize the establishment of wholly owned foreign enterprises (WOFEs), targeted at advanced technology sectors, and WOFEs quickly expanded in scope. Finally, during the late 1990s, a series of "Golden Projects" were implemented to create an advanced communications infrastructure, including fiberoptic networks in banking services, health and medicines, and tax collection, intended to form China's "information superhighway."

The overall science and technology program since the mid-1990s is ambitious and comprehensive, but the results of the initial years of operations are difficult to measure quantitatively, not to mention assess in qualitative terms. Information can be largely anecdotal, while aggregate indicators can be difficult to interpret and are often two to three years behind in rapidly evolving circumstances. Some observers contend that even the Chinese government does not fully know what is happening, which makes foreign expert opinion even more suspect. The approach adopted here is to begin, in the remainder of this chapter, by laying out the broad trends for five domestic indicators that form the foundation for the

---

[6] This rise of science and technology to political and operational prominence is described in detail in Kathleen Walsh, *Foreign High-Tech R&D in China* (Henry L. Stimson Center, 2003), Chapters 2-3. The information in this paragraph is drawn largely from that work.
[7] China suffered a "lost generation" of university-educated leaders during the Great Proletarian Cultural Revolution, and the older generation of leaders continued to fill the gap until the mid-1990s, when younger scientists and engineers of the post-1976 generation, including many trained abroad, began to come of age.

emerging Chinese advanced technology sector: two "resource" indicators, R&D expenditures and the number of scientists and engineers; two "performance" indicators, patent applications and technical journal authorship; and one composite index of technological competitiveness presented by the National Science Foundation (NSF). This is followed, in Chapters 3 and 4, with more detailed accounts of foreign direct investment (FDI) and trade in advanced technology products, which have constituted the interacting driving forces for the rapid development of advanced technology industry over the past ten years. The findings of all three chapters are then brought together in an overall qualitative assessment of the Chinese advanced technology prospect in Chapter 5.

Resource Indicator #1:
Research and Development

Chinese research and development (R&D) has been growing at a very rapid pace since the mid- to late-1990s, with the greatest concentration in the information technology sector, but until recently there has been very limited data available on the upward trends and detail is still lacking with respect to key aspects of its composition. The authoritative biennial NSF *Scientific and Engineering Indicators* is limited almost exclusively to developments in the major OECD countries.[8] The OECD biennial assessments of the information technology and communications sector have likewise largely ignored China,[9] but in March 2004, the special working paper, *An Emerging Knowledge-Based Economy in China? Indicators From OECD Databases*, provided a comprehensive set of indicators about Chinese advanced technology industry, including R&D expenditures and researchers, which are very revealing.

---

[8] The 2004 edition, released in June, has a 73-page chapter entitled "U.S. and International Research and Development," but the extensive international comparisons are limited to the seven largest industrialized OECD members, and the only reference to China is that in 2000, already four years out of date, Chinese R&D as a percent of GDP was 1.00 compared with 1.88 in the EU, 2.71 in the United States, and 2.98 in Japan. The 2006 NSF report should give China at least comparable treatment with France and Italy.

[9] The December 2004 OECD *Information Technology Outlook* included entries for China in only 4 of the 277 tables and charts presented. The only text on China in the 350-page report is a three-page section on trade and FDI through 2002, already two years behind available Chinese statistics.

Chinese R&D expenditures remained relatively stable at 0.7 percent to 0.8 percent of GDP from 1991 through 1998, and then rose sharply to 1.0 in 2000 and to 1.3 in 2002. The official Chinese target for 2005 is 1.5 percent of GDP, which will likely be met or surpassed. The comparable figures for the United States, the EU, and Japan show an increase of only 0.1 percent from 1998 to 2002, with the net result of a substantial narrowing of the gap between China and the other three. The convergence appears even more rapid when comparing the absolute levels of R&D spending, in view of the much faster rate of GDP growth in China, which magnifies the relative increase based on the rising R&D percentage of GDP. Table 2-4 presents the absolute levels of R&D for the four leading economies, again on a ppp basis as described for GDP levels in Table 2-1. From the takeoff point of 1995 through 2002, Chinese R&D spending grew at 22 percent per year, compared with 6 percent for the United States and 5 percent for the EU and Japan. In relative terms, for China, this translates into an increase over the seven-year period from 10 percent to 25 percent of the U.S. level, from 11 percent to 39 percent of the EU level, and from 19 percent to 55 percent of the Japanese level. It is also noteworthy that, in 2001, the level of Chinese R&D spending surpassed that of Germany, thus putting China in third place after the United States and Japan, on a national basis.

Table 2-4
Gross Domestic Expenditure on R&D
(billions of current dollars)

	China	United States	European Union	Japan
1991	12.5	161.4	114.8	66.9
1995	18.4	184.1	130.8	78.7
2000	48.5	265.2	175.7	98.3
2002	72.1	277.1	187.2*	107.8
Annual percent growth				
1995-2002	+22	+6	+5	+5
Projected				
2005	130.9	330.9	216.7	124.8
2010				
China 22 % growth	353.8	441.7	276.6	159.3
China 15 % growth	220.6	441.7	276.6	159.3

* 2001

Source: OECD, *An Emerging Knowledge-Based Economy in China? Indicators From OECD Databases*, March 22, 2004; for 1991-2002, Table SA20; projections for 2005 and 2010 as explained in the text

Projecting a continuation of R&D growth at the 1995-2002 rates produces striking results, as also shown in Table 2-4. By 2005, based on the 22 percent annual growth recorded in 1995-2002, China surpasses Japan to become second to the United States, while by 2010 China surpasses the EU and reaches 80 percent of the U.S. level. A continued 22 percent annual growth is unlikely, however, since it implies that the Chinese R&D share of GDP will rise to 3.4 percent by 2010,[10] or considerably higher than that of the other three (Japan 3.1 percent, the United States 2.7 percent, and the EU 1.9 percent in 2001). An alternative projection to 2010 is therefore included in the table with a Chinese growth rate of 15 percent, which results in a projected $220.6 billion level, or 2.1 percent of GDP. On this basis, by 2010, Chinese R&D would be about half that of the United States, 80 percent that of the EU, and 40 percent higher than that of Japan.

Another broad quantitative measure of R&D activities is the number of researchers, as shown in Table 2-5. In 2002, there were about 800,000 full-time equivalent researchers in China, compared with 1.3 million in the United States, 1.0 million in the EU, and 700,000 in Japan. In other words, China had already surpassed Japan and was close to 60 percent of the U.S. level. And again, the growth in research workers was highest in China, at 6.5 percent per year, with projections to 2010 indicating China approaching the EU level and at more than 60 percent of the U.S. level.

These aggregate figures on R&D expenditures and researchers indicate a rapidly growing relative position for China compared with the other three advanced industrialized economies. By 2010, the Chinese level would be substantially higher than that of Japan, at least 80 percent of the EU level, and half or more of the U.S. level.

Beyond these aggregate quantitative measures, however, information is sketchy as to the composition and quality of Chinese R&D, which have an important bearing on the ultimate results in terms of innovation and industrial competitiveness. The best that can be offered here are brief observations on Chinese R&D by category, location, and sector, plus a more extensive discussion of R&D by foreign companies in Chapter 3.

By category, Chinese R&D in 2001 was heavily concentrated, with 78 percent in technological development, compared with 17 percent for applied research, and only 5 percent for basic

---

[10] These percentages of GDP projections are calculated based on the GDP projections in Table 2-1.

Table 2-5
Number of Researchers
(thousands of full-time equivalents)

	China	United States	European Union	Japan
1991	471.4	981.7	746.5	491.1
1995	522.0	1,036.0	817.0	552.0
2000	695.1	1,261.2*	965.7	647.6
2002	810.5	N.A.	1,004.6**	675.9*
Annual percent growth 995-2002 ***	+6.5	+5.0	+3.5	+5.0
Projected				
2005	979.0	1,690.1	1,152.8	905.8
2010	1,341.4	2,157.0	1,369.2	1,156.0

*1999

**2001

***1995-2002 for China; 1995-2001 for the EU and Japan; 1995-2002 for the United States. Percentages rounded to nearest one-half percent.

Source: OECD, *An Emerging Knowledge-Based Economy in China? Indicators From OECD Databases*, March 22, 2004, for 1990-2003; the calculations for 2004 are based on actual growth; projections to 2010 are based on annual growth of 8 percent for China, 4 percent for the United States, and 3 percent for the EU and Japan, Table SA17, for 1991-2002; projections for 2005 and 2010 based on actual growth rates in 1995-2002

research.[11]   This is a clear reflection of the central focus on adapting existing technologies to Chinese production for export and domestic sales, including conformity with newly established Chinese technical standards.   The share of research devoted to basic research, however, is expected to grow toward 15 percent to 20 percent based on the 2005-2020 planning period.

The principal locations for Chinese R&D, by percentage in 2004, were state and private enterprises at 60 percent, government research institutes at 30 percent, and universities at 10 percent. This compares with 70 percent private sector, 9 percent federal

---

[11] The three principal categories of R&D are: (1) "basic research" to advance scientific knowledge, but without particular application in view; (2) "applied research" directed toward specific practical or commercial objectives; and (3) "developmental research" which draws on existing knowledge to produce new products, improve current technology, and instill new processes and systems. See Walsh, *op. cit*, p. 10, for more detailed definitions, including some differences between the Chinese and U.S. definitions. The cited percentage figures are from p. 64.

government, and 13 percent universities in the United States. The difficulties in assessing the Chinese relationships among the locations lie in the integrated participation of many R&D projects and the very large and growing number of R&D centers in the country. For example, the United Innovative Research Institute is a joint venture between IBM and the Beijing and Tsinghua Universities, whereby IBM supplies the software, hardware, research technicians, and most of the operating costs, while the universities provide the office space, network connection, and professional staff. The resulting intellectual property rights are shared equally. As for the number of research institutes, the Chinese Academy of Social Sciences identified 124 in 2001,[12] with Chinese news reports estimating foreign-invested R&D centers in China ranging from 120 to 400, with one reporting an increase in Shanghai alone from 40 in 2001 to 80 in 2003.[13] By 2005, foreign-invested R&D centers are estimated to be more than 700 and will employ more than 500,000 researchers and engineers when fully operational.[14]

The allocation of R&D by sector is especially difficult to quantify, but the broad orientation is heavily toward manufacturing, especially for enterprise R&D, with particular concentration in the information technology sector. Almost all sectors, however, are engaged in expanding R&D activities. The chemicals and pharmaceutical sector, where production has been concentrated on generic drugs, is noteworthy for recently expanding R&D work in clinical trials, including late-stage trials for new products, with at least 20 of the 25 largest global companies now with operating facilities in China.[15] Agricultural R&D, in contrast, is almost entirely public sector, amounting to $500 million per year, with a heavy focus on an internally generated program for the early launch of genetically modified crops.[16]

---

[12] See Charles W. McMillion, "China's Very Rapid Economic Industrial and Technological Emergence" (paper presented to the U.S.-China Security and Economic Review Commission, Palo Alto, April 22, 2005). This paper is the source of the IBM example and Chinese Academy of Social Sciences figures on research centers by category.

[13] Walsh, *op. cit.,* p. 91.

[14] See Gary Edward Rieschel, "China's Global Technology Competitiveness" (paper presented before the U.S.-China Economic and Security Review Commission, Palo Alto, April 22, 2005), p. 4.

[15] McMillion, *op. cit.,* p. 12.

[16] The heavily technology and market-oriented Chinese agricultural strategy is described in Daniel H. Rosen, Scott Rozelle, and Jikun Huang, *Roots of Competitiveness: China's Evolving Agricultural Interests* (Institute for International Economics, July 2004). The $500 million figure, ppp adjusted, was given by Rozelle in response to a question by the author at the IIE book launch on July 29, 2004.

These are the broad lines of the rapid and comprehensive growth in Chinese R&D activities. A more detailed and up-to-date compilation would be very useful for understanding the likely competitive relationships ahead among China, other East Asian countries, the United States, and West Europe. This could best be done by the OECD Science, Technology and Industry Directorate, through its ongoing relationship with the Chinese Ministry of Science and Technology,[17] or bilaterally by the NSF through the long-standing U.S.-China Science and Technology Cooperation Agreement, as recommended in detail by Kathleen Walsh.[18]

Resource Indicator #2:
Scientists and Engineers

The second principal resource indicator for advanced technology industry development is the number of scientists and engineers coming into the labor force, and in this respect Chinese performance since the mid-1990s has been at least as dramatic as for R&D growth. China has rapidly expanded its overall university program with the total number of graduates more than tripling from 800,000 in 1995 to an estimated 2.8 million in 2004.[19] This compares with 2.3 million U.S. graduates in 2000, where college enrollment is increasing at only about 2 percent per year. Thus, the total number of university graduates at all levels in China surpassed the U.S. level by 2004, and continues on a strong upward path.

For science and engineering (S&E) doctoral degrees, which comprise a more directly targeted indicator for advanced technology industry, graduates from Chinese universities, as shown in Table 2-6, rose at an annual rate of 14 percent from 1995 to 2001, compared with 6 percent in Japan, 4 percent in the three largest West European countries, and -1 percent in the United States. As a result, Chinese doctoral graduates had surpassed Japanese graduates and were more than 25 percent of the U.S. and European levels by 2001. Projecting the 1995-2001 growth rates to 2005, China reaches half the U.S. level, and by 2010, there is a rough parity between China and the United States, although both are still about 40 percent below the European grouping.

---

[17] Chinese Deputy Minister of Science and Technology Liu Yanhua attended the January 2004 OECD Technology Ministerial Meeting, one of only four nonmember participants.
[18] Walsh, *op. cit.,* pp. 133-134.
[19] *The Economist*, June 12, 2004, p. 42.

Table 2-6
Science and Engineering (S&E) Doctoral Degrees

	China	United States	France Germany United Kingdom	Japan
A. All S&E Doctorates				
1990	1,069	22,868	22,127	3,704
1995	3,417	26,536	23,050	5,205
2000	7,304	25,951	27,571	7,089
2001	7,601	25,509	28,378*	7,401
Annual percent growth				
1995-2001	+14	-1	+4	+6
Projected				
2005	12,838	24,504	33,198	9,344
2010	24,718	23,303	40,391	12,504
B. Engineer Doctorates				
1990	715	4,894	4,920	1,967
1995	1,659	6,008	4,864	2,791
2000	4,484	5,320	5,983	3,800
2001	4,432	5,502	5,832	3,964
Annual percent growth				
1995-2001	+18	-2	+3	+6
Projected				
2005	8,593	5,075	6,564	5,005
2010	19,658	4,587	7,609	6,697

*2000 for France

Sources: NSF, *Science and Engineering Indicators 2004*, Appendix Tables 2-38–2-39, for 1990-2001; projections for 2005 and 2010 based on actual growth rates in 1995-2001

Doctoral degrees in engineering, as shown in Part B of Table 2-6, present an even starker picture of Chinese ascendancy. A more than doubling of Chinese graduates from 1995 to 2001 put China well ahead of Japan—and at about 80 percent of the U.S. and European levels in 2001. The growth projections for 2005 and 2010, this time with 18 percent annual growth in China in contrast to -2 percent growth in the United States, puts China well into the lead by 2005, and with four times as many engineering doctorates per year as in the United States by 2010.

Undergraduate degrees in engineering present the most dominant position of all for China. Already in 2001, there were 220,000 graduates in China, compared with 104,000 in Japan, 90,000 in the three West European countries, and only 60,000 in the United States.[20]   By 2005, Chinese engineering graduates will be more than 300,000.

Another significant dimension of the relative growth in Chinese scientists and engineers is the large number of Chinese students in American universities, many of whom return home, either immediately upon graduation or after several years' work experience in the United States, which greatly enhances their job opportunities upon return to China. The number of U.S. science and engineering doctorates by Chinese students peaked at almost 3,000 in 1996, and then leveled off through 2001, reflecting, in part, the rapid growth in higher quality educational opportunities in Chinese universities. U.S. doctorates by Chinese students are highly concentrated in physical sciences and mathematics (31 percent of total S&E doctorates) and engineering (27 percent), while disproportionately low in social sciences (6 percent) and agricultural sciences (3 percent).[21]   Another several thousand undergraduate degrees in science and engineering are granted to Chinese students each year. Of all these Chinese graduates, approximately 18,000 were estimated in 2003 to return to China each year,[22] which, while a relatively small number compared with the current output of Chinese universities, raises significantly the quality and experience of the advanced technology industry professional workforce. The 18,000 U.S. level is declining rapidly as the number of student visas for Chinese dropped sharply after September 11, but this is being compensated for by a comparable rise in Chinese students in European universities, particularly in the United Kingdom.

Performance Indicator #1:
Patent Applications

One standard indicator of performance for technology innovation is the number of patent applications. Table 2-7, which presents data on applications in China, the United States, and Europe, shows the large increase in applications in all three economies from 1990 to 1999. This reflects, in large part, the rapid pace of new technology development and application in all industrialized economies. The rise in applications, however, was relatively even throughout the decade in the United States and Europe, while in China there was an initial surge from the very

---

[20] NSF, *Science and Engineering Indicators 2004*, Appendix Table 2-33.
[21] *Ibid*, p. 2-30–2-31, Appendix Table 2-19. The percentage figures by field are for 1985-2000.
[22] *The Economist*, November 8, 2003, p. 59.

low level in 1990 to 1995, from 9,000 to 26,000—when aggregating the four columns in the table—followed by a continued though more moderate upward movement through the remainder of the decade. In 1999, there were 41,000 applications in China, compared with 99,000 in Europe, and 155,000 in the United States, a clear indication that China is coming of age as an advanced industrialized economy. This also has important implications for Chinese interests in the protection of intellectual property rights, as discussed in Chapter 9.

Table 2-7
Patent Applications by Residence of Inventor

	China	United States	European Union	Japan
A. In China				
1990	5,323	1,562	1,153	840
1995	9,877	5,010	5,306	5,747
1999	15,943	7,334	8,376	9,813
Annual percent growth				
1995-1999	+13	+10	+12	+14
Projected				
2005	33,193	12,993	16,553	21,539
2010	61,555	20,925	29,136	41.472
B. In the United States				
1990	75	55,727	17,990	25,096
1995	75	76,711	22,885	29,512
1999	282	92,349	27,220	35,443
Annual percent growth				
1995-1999	+39	+5	+4	+5
Projected				
2005	2,034	123,757	34,442	47,497
2010	10,554	157,948	41,904	60,620
C. In Europe*				
1990	29	17,443	26,923	13,000
1995	52	21,194	30,840	12,326
1999	301	28,668	49,353	20,676
Annual percent growth				
1995-1999	+55	+8	+13	+14
Projected				
2005	4,174	45,493	102,751	45,383
2010	37,344	66,843	189,311	87,382

*As reported to the European Patent Office

Source: OECD, *An Emerging Knowledge-Based Economy in China? Indicators From OECD Databases*, March 22, 2004, Tables SA22–24; the projections for 2005 and 2010 are based on the actual growth in 1995-1999

Two distinct developments are apparent in the table. The first is that, within China (Section A), the share of applications by residents remained large throughout the decade, and continued to grow at a rapid rate, 13 percent per year, during 1995-1999. Many of these patents, of course, were filed by resident foreign companies, and their rapid increase in R&D in China since 1999 could well lead to accelerated growth in patent applications. Some of these patents, however, derive from joint R&D with Chinese universities, companies, and government research centers, with shared intellectual property rights. Independent R&D by the government and Chinese companies has also been growing rapidly since 1999. The pattern of high growth in patent applications in China, strongly oriented toward Chinese residents, is therefore likely to continue, as suggested by the projections to 2005 and 2010.

The second development is the beginning of Chinese patent applications in the United States and Europe (Sections B and C), from the miniscule levels of 1990 and 1995 to somewhat higher levels in 1999. The numbers remained relatively very small in 1999, and there is clearly a lengthy time lag between Chinese growth in resource expenditures—R&D and scientists/engineers—and performance in terms of patent applications abroad. Unfortunately, the five year time lag in available data on patent applications prevents a clear assessment as to whether the 40 percent to 50 percent annual growth in Chinese applications in the United States and Europe during the late 1990s has continued through 2004.

Performance Indicator #2:
Technical Article Authorship

Another closely tracked performance indicator is the number of authored articles in key science and engineering journals, as shown in Table 2-8. Such authorship has long been dominated by the United States and West Europe, which together accounted for 70 percent of the global total from 1988 to 1995. Since 1995, however, this dual concentration has declined somewhat, down to 65 percent of the global total in 2001, as the result of a substantial increase in publications by East Asians—by South Koreans, Taiwanese, and Chinese most rapidly of all. As shown in the table, Chinese articles doubled from 4,600 in 1988 to 9,300 in 1995, and then more than doubled again to 21,000 in 2001. For 1995-2001, annual growth in publications by Chinese authors was 15 percent, compared with 3 percent by Japanese, 2 percent by West Europeans, and no change by Americans.

Table 2-8
Science and Engineering Articles
by Country/Region
(thousands)

	China	United States	West Europe	Japan
1988	4.6	177.7	143.9	34.4
1995	9.3	202.9	200.0	47.6
1998	13.8	197.9	221.7	54.7
2001	21.0	200.9	229.2	57.4
Annual percent growth				
1995-2001	+15	0	+2	+3
Projected				
2005	36.7	200.9	248.1	64.6
2010	73.9	200.9	273.9	74.9

Source: NSF, *Science and Engineering Indicators 2004*, Appendix Table 5-35 for 1988-2001; projections for 2005 and 2010 are based on the annual growth in 1995-2001

Projecting the 1995-2001 growth rates to 2005 and 2010, the number of Chinese articles rises to 73,900 by 2010, in rough parity with Japan, although still less than half the U.S. and one-third the European levels. This performance indicator thus also lags far behind the resource indicators, which may reflect a number of factors, cultural and technical in nature, not to mention the strong orientation of Chinese advanced technology strategy toward production and exports rather than more theoretical and basic research.

Another significant qualitative dimension of professional journal authorship is the sharp contrast in fields of concentration, as shown in Table 2-9. In almost all categories, the United States and China are at the two extremes, with West Europe and Japan somewhere in the middle. U.S. authorship is most heavily concentrated in the biomedical fields, accounting for 54.8 percent of total articles, compared with 22.5 percent for China. In contrast, for the physical sciences of chemistry and physics as well as mathematics, China is the most concentrated with 53.6 percent of the total compared with 17.6 percent for the United States. Likewise, for engineering/technology, China has a much higher share, at 16.3 percent, compared with 6.9 percent for the United States. And finally, for social sciences/psychology, the United States is far more prominent, with 8.6 percent of total articles, compared with an almost negligible 0.6 percent for China. The

Chinese orientation by fields of concentration is thus highly supportive of the development of advanced technology industry, and also consistent with the lower priority given to health care at this stage of Chinese development. The polar extremes of intellectual interest between the United States and China in the social sciences and psychology is a curious subject worthy of journal articles by social scientists who, apparently, will almost all be American.

Table 2-9
Science and Engineering Articles, by Field
(2001 percentage)

	China	United States	West Europe	Japan
All fields	100.0	100.0	100.0	100.0
Engineering/technology	16.3	6.9	8.1	11.6
Physical sciences/math	53.6	17.6	26.6	35.4
Chemistry	26.3	7.1	11.5	14.9
Physics	23.4	8.7	12.7	19.1
Mathematics	3.9	1.8	2.4	1.4
Biomedical	22.5	54.8	52.6	48.7
Clinical medicine	10.7	31.7	32.0	28.7
Biomedical research	8.0	16.9	14.0	14.0
Biology	3.8	6.2	6.6	6.1
Social sciences/ psychology	0.6	8.6	4.6	1.0
Other	7.0	12.1	8.1	3.3

Source: NSF, *Science and Engineering Indicators 2004*, Appendix Table 5-38

A Composite of Leading Indicators of Technological Competitiveness

The NSF has presented a composite of leading indicators for a selected group of countries with the "potential to become more important exporters of high technology products during the next 15 years." The composite index, based on published data and surveys of expert opinion, has four components: (1) national orientation, as indicated by national strategies involving cooperation between the public and private sectors; (2) socioeconomic infrastructure, including characteristics of capital markets, levels of foreign investment, and investment in education; (3) technological infrastructure, including protection of IPRs, the relationship of R&D to industrial application, competency in high technology manufacturing, and the qualitative capability of scientists and engineers; and (4) productive capacity, including the level of high technology production, the quality and productivity of the labor force, and innovative management practices.[23]

The indices were calculated for 1999 and 2002, as shown in Table 2-10, for major potential high technology exporters and for the United States, Japan, and Germany. For 2002, the three advanced industrialized countries, led by the United States, posted the highest scores, followed by the three East Asians—Taiwan, South Korea, and China—with the remainder trailing down to lowest scoring Thailand and Indonesia.

Table 2-10
Leading Indicators of Technological Competitiveness

Country/Economy	1999	2002	Percent Change 1999-2002	Projected 2005
United States	350.0	341.2	-3	331.0
Japan	300.0	298.1	-1	295.1
Germany	275.0	284.3	+3	292.8
Taiwan	262.2	272.2	+4	283.1
South Korea	241.8	259.0	+7	277.1
China	206.0	222.7	+8	240.5
Poland	210.5	211.1	0	211.1
Malaysia	204.4	205.9	+1	208.0
India	214.2	196.6	-8	180.9
Brazil	190.6	174.2	-9	158.5
Mexico	128.8	168.2	+31	220.3
Argentina	153.1	160.7	+5	168.7
Thailand	148.3	156.7	+6	166.1
Indonesia	140.6	132.6	-6	124.6

Source: NSF, *Science and Engineering Indicators 2004*, p. 6-18 and Appendix Tables 6-5–6-6, for 1999-2002; projections for 2005 based on the percentage change from 1999-2002

The percent changes in the indices from 1999 to 2002 are especially noteworthy. The United States and Japan had declines of 3 percent and 1 percent, respectively, while the three East Asians all showed sizeable increases, led by China with an 8

---

[23] NSF, *Science and Engineering Indicators 2004*, pp. 6-15–6-18, Appendix Tables 6-5–6-6.

percent increase. Others, such as India, Brazil, and Indonesia, recorded sizeable declines, while Mexico surged by an exceptional 31 percent, which is worthy of some further examination by the compilers of the index.

The figures for 2002 are projected ahead to 2005, which indicates a further closing of the gap between the three advanced industrialized countries and East Asians, and a further falling behind for most of the others. It will be particularly interesting to compare these projections with the next NSF survey, presumably for 2005. Since the survey is targeted at potential for high-tech exports, the results can also be compared with actual exports, as done for China in Chapter 4, with the conclusion that Chinese export potential has already largely become reality.

※ ※ ※

The various indicators presented in this chapter permit a partial assessment of the overall path of Chinese development of advanced technology industry. Clearly, the two principal resource indicators—R&D expenditures and the number of scientists and engineers—are on track for China to become an advanced technology superstate of comparable order of magnitude with the United States and West Europe within a decade or less. The two standard performance indicators, patent applications and technical article authorship show, in contrast, a major time lag in Chinese performance, although the beginnings of sharp upward movement took place in the late 1990s, and more recent data should be revealing. The NSF composite of leading indicators confirms China's rapid advance in technological competitiveness for exports, with a significant narrowing of the gap with the United States and other advanced industrialized countries from 1999 to 2002.

A fuller assessment, however, needs to delve more deeply into the very dynamic and unique characteristics of Chinese advanced technology industry development, which center on highly open international investment and trade, in the context of increasingly fierce competition from within and without. Such competitive international investment and trade relationships are the basic driving forces for Chinese success in stimulating technological innovation and growth, to which the study now turns.

Chapter 3

The Decisive Catalyst: Foreign Direct Investment

There is no parallel with the central role played by foreign direct investment in the export-oriented industrial development that has taken place in China since the early 1990s. It is, in fact, the opposite of what happened in the prior two decades, first in Japan and then in Taiwan and South Korea, where FDI was shunned and thus inconsequential. The familiar analogy of the earlier period of East Asian export-led growth was that of flying geese, with Japan as the lead goose. The more recently airborne Chinese goose, in contrast, has been on a radically different flight path, with FDI as the decisive catalyst for the rapid development of both labor-intensive and advanced technology industries.

The Chinese experience began with Deng's Four Moderni-zations in 1978 and the establishment of the first Special Economic Zones in 1980, which encouraged export-oriented foreign investment. The ensuing course of events is summarized in Charts 3-1 and 3-2. Chart 3-1 presents the trajectory of FDI inflows from 1980 through 2004, and shows modest levels during the 1980s leading to a dramatic surge in 1992-1993 that has been maintained, as China surpassed the United States to become the single largest importer of direct investment at $53.5 billion in 2003, and then rose further to $60.6 billion in 2004.

Chart 3-2 shows the closely related linkage of FDI to the growth of Chinese exports. Again the relationship was slow to develop during the 1980s, then took off in the mid-1990s, and continues to strengthen in the 2000 decade. The percentage of total Chinese exports generated by foreign invested enterprises rose from 1 percent in 1985 to 13 percent in 1990 to 32 percent in 1995 to an extraordinary 57 percent in 2004.

The story of how this came about is fascinating in its own right, but also critical for assessing the likely course ahead. It has involved both political and economic forces in play, and is clouded by the limited and sometimes unreliable sources of available information. The definition of FDI is itself a problem and can vary by data source. The distinction between FDI and other portfolio investment is arbitrary, depending on what minimum

Chart 3-1
FDI Flows Into China*
1980-2004

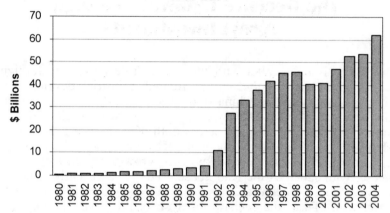

Source: Chinese Ministry of Commerce
* Capital actually disbursed or "used," as distinct from "signed agreements"
The figures for signed agreements are usually larger because some
agreements do not reach the disbursement stage.

Chart 3-2
Exports of Foreign Invested Enterprises
and Total Chinese Exports
1985-2004

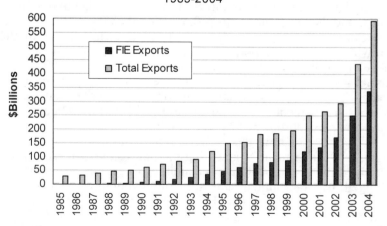

Source: Chinese Ministry of Commerce

share of ownership is necessary to qualify as a "direct invest-ment." It is often but not always defined as a minimum 10 percent ownership by the foreign parent company, which can become more complicated in consortium arrangements or joint ventures with Chinese partners. U.S. figures on FDI in China by American companies are much lower than Chinese data on inflows from the United States, which reflects differences in the classification of foreign direct investment. The data presented here is from official Chinese sources, unless specified otherwise. In any event, the point of departure for the presentation is the evolution of the Chinese policy framework for FDI, which can be summarized as the triumph of free trade and investment policy by demonstration effect, although the triumph remains far from complete.

The Chinese Path to Open Trade and Investment

The establishment of four SEZs in coastal provinces in 1980 was designed to attract export-oriented foreign investment, while at the same time keeping the foreign companies isolated so as not to compete directly with the state-owned enterprises (SOEs) that dominated the Chinese economy, or contaminate the socialist society in broader terms. The initiative was thus a political compromise between the ideological hard-liners opposed to FDI in principle, and the pragmatists, led by Deng, who sought the job- and export-creating benefits derived from foreign investment and market forces. Some economists criticized the targeted SEZ approach, compared with opening the entire Chinese economy to FDI, as having impeded Chinese development, but their valid theoretical arguments ignore the political forces in play in 1980.[1]

The pragmatists' position was progressively strengthened by the demonstration effect of actual job creation and export growth within the SEZs. Other cities and provinces were eager to attract the jobs and wealth generated by FDI, which led to the creation of numerous other SEZ-like zones, which offered similar benefits to foreign investors, such as duty-free imports of raw material and intermediate goods and export credits. In 1984, 14 coastal cities

---

[1] The political and economic factors involved in the SEZ "building block" approach are explained in Edward M. Graham, "Do Export Processing Zones Attract FDI and Its Benefits: The Experience From China," *International Economics and Economic Policy* (Spring 2004), pp. 87-103. Graham chooses not to identify the analysts who believe the SEZs impeded Chinese development, while noting that "this view is quite prevalent at certain organizations, e.g., the World Bank," p. 94.

were designated "Economic and Technical Development Zones," and by the end of the decade there were more than 100 such zones of one form or another. Finally, in 1991, the entire Chinese economy was opened to foreign investors on the same terms. The building block pragmatists thus won the day in terms of geographic scope of access.

The regulatory terms of approval for foreign investment also went through a process of progressive liberalization. The central government regulations for approval of foreign investments were subject to interpretation, which was administered largely on a decentralized basis, with strong competition among provinces and cities to offer more liberal interpretations of the law and other incentives in order to attract new investment. This decentralized and investment-friendly competitive process for project approval continues to strengthen. In July 2004, the minimum level of an investment requiring central government approval was raised from $30 million to $100 million.[2]

At the national level, the political momentum was also in the direction of broadening the scope of FDI participation, not only in geographic terms but in productive content. Export-oriented investment continues to have priority, but production for the domestic Chinese market has become more acceptable and, as a consequence, many investments are now developed to serve both the export and domestic Chinese markets. The more explicit targeting of advanced technology industry in the mid-1990s, in parallel with the large increases in resources devoted to R&D and advanced training for scientists and engineers (described in Chapter 2), was critical for transforming the FDI role from a limited export-oriented objective, centered on labor intensive industry, to that of engine for growth by advanced technology industries to modernize the entire Chinese economy. A decisive step for unleashing these dynamic forces for change through FDI was the 2001 decision to greatly liberalize the approval of WOFEs, directly linked to advanced technology production and export. As a result, the WOFE share of total realized FDI rose from 39 percent in 1999 to 68 percent in 2004,[3] which largely accounts for the surge in FDI in 2001-2004 after the somewhat down years of 1999-2000.

---

[2] Reported in *China Watch Weekly,* Briefing, July 30, 2004.
[3] The share of contracted FDI in WOFEs, which is an indicator of future realized FDI, was even higher, at 75percent.

Another important step for completing the policy framework was the opening of the Chinese economy to fierce, market-oriented competition, both from within the Chinese economy and from abroad, through a substantial reduction in import barriers. Internally, two or more foreign investors are often approved to compete against one another, which contrasts with the practice in many developing countries of inducing a foreign investor by offering a monopoly position behind high import protection. Chinese "national champion" companies are, in parallel, being nurtured to compete against the foreign firms, often with extra incentives that can be considered unfair. Even the financially beleaguered and overstaffed SOEs are being progressively opened to competitive pressures and threatened with cutbacks in financial subsidies or privatization.

On the import liberalization front, China reduced import barriers substantially on a unilateral basis during the 1990s, and foreign investors were given duty-free privileges. In 1996, China joined the WTO multilateral free trade agreement for the information technology sector. Chinese accession to WTO membership in 2001 involved further across-the-board reductions in tariffs and other import barriers, which are still in the process of implementation.

This is the broad and comprehensive policy framework that has evolved in China over the past 25 years with respect to FDI. The current circumstances are still far from a totally free and open market economy.[4] Import barriers remain high in certain sectors. Foreign investors, particularly large advanced technology companies, can be subject to severe pressure to bring in their more advanced technologies and to undertake targeted R&D activities before receiving approval to invest. Chinese companies receive many forms of preference, including the way new technology standards are developed and implemented. These issues are addressed at various points in subsequent chapters. The fact nevertheless remains that in a relatively short period of time China has skyrocketed to become the largest recipient of FDI and the third-largest trading nation, after the United States and Germany (over half of German trade is internal-EU), with a heavy orientation toward the rapid development of advanced technology industry, and all within a policy framework of open trade and investment on a highly competitive, market-oriented basis.

---

[4] The current legal and institutional framework for FDI in China is summarized in K. C. Fung, Lawrence J. Lau, and Joseph S. Lee, *U.S. Direct Investment in China* (American Enterprise Institute, 2004), pp. 24-41.

Chinese foreign investment policy is officially summed up in the June 14, 2004, "Overview of FDI in China."[5] It opens by stating that "China's absorption of foreign investment is an important component of China's fundamental principle of opening up to the outside world." The modalities of joint ventures, co-operative businesses, joint exploitation, and WOFEs are described, with the qualification that WOFEs are subject to one or both of the criteria that they "must adopt international advanced technology" and that "most of the products must be export-oriented."

The overview goes on to elaborate six directions to further absorb foreign investment, including: (1) energetically improve the political and legal environment for foreign investment; (2) maintain and improve an open and fair market environment; (3) further open the field of service industry; (4) attract actively more multilateral companies to invest; and (5) further promote foreign investment in the central and western provinces.

The sixth direction, actually listed as number four, relates to advanced technology industry and is the most detailed, as follows:

> Encourage foreign businessmen to invest in the new high-tech industry, the basic industry, and supporting industry. The ability of technology innovation and sustainable development directly reflect the competitiveness advantages of a country. We will continue to encourage foreign investors to introduce, develop, and innovate technology and to invest in technology-intensive projects, and projects with advanced technology and to guide in enterprise registered capital proportion limitation and funding conditions. The relevant stipulations of setting pioneering investment enterprise should also be consummated in order to facilitate the conditions of setting and developing high-tech corporations. We should attract foreigners to invest in supporting industry and encourage the localization of new materials, push domestic small and medium-sized enterprises to enforce cooperation with foreign companies and introduce the advanced and applicable technology to match the large foreign-funded enterprises, thus to enter the production and sales network of multinational companies.

---

[5] Chinese Ministry of Commerce, in English, www.mofcom.gov.com.

FDI Inflows by Source and Sector

When moving beyond the aggregate FDI flows into China to greater detail by country source and sectoral orientation, daunting problems of data availability quickly emerge. FDI by source, as reported by the Chinese government, is presented in Table 3-1 for the 15 largest sources in 2001-2004. The two largest sources of investment in 2004 were Hong Kong, $19.0 billion, and the Virgin Islands, $6.7 billion. These are clearly not the actual sources of all of this investment, but largely conduit locations to conceal the true identity of the investing company. Add to this the recorded investment from the Cayman Islands, of $2.0 billion, West Samoa of $1.1 billion, and lesser amounts from Macao, Bermuda, Mauritius, and elsewhere, and roughly half of the global total of $60.6 billion came from these largely veiled conduit sources.

Table 3-1
Foreign Direct Investment
In China: Top 15 Country Source
(billions of dollars)

	2001	2002	2003	2004
Total	46.9	52.7	53.5	60.6
Hong Kong	16.7	17.9	17.7	19.0
Virgin Islands	5.0	6.1	5.8	6.7
South Korea	2.2	2.7	4.5	6.2
Japan	4.3	4.2	5.1	5.5
United States	4.4	5.4	4.2	3.9
Taiwan	3.0	4.0	3.4	3.1
Cayman Islands	1.1	1.2	0.9	2.0
Singapore	2.1	2.3	2.1	2.0
West Samoa	0.5	0.9	1.0	1.1
Germany	1.2	0.9	0.9	1.0
United Kingdom	1.1	0.9	0.7	NA
Netherlands	0.8	0.6	0.7	NA
France	0.5	0.6	0.6	NA
Australia	0.3	0.4	0.6	NA
Canada	0.4	0.6	0.6	NA
Other	3.3	4.0	4.9	10.1

Sources: *China Statistical Yearbook*, 2003, Table 17-15 for 2001 and 2002; Foreign Investment Administration, Ministry of Foreign Commerce (MOFCOM), for 2003 and 2004

The two principal actual sources of this veiled investment are Taiwan and so-called "round-tripping" by Chinese investors, including SOEs, back into China in order to obtain tax benefits as foreign investors. The officially reported figure in 2004 for Taiwan is $3.1 billion, but all observers agree that it is much larger, and that Taiwan is the largest investor in China. How much larger, however, is a matter of partially informed guesswork, with estimates ranging from $10 billion to $30 billion per year. The order of magnitude adopted here is that Taiwanese investment in China is about $20 billion per year, plus or minus $5 billion. In the early 1990s, round-tripping was estimated to be 25 percent to 40 percent of total FDI, but it is likely much lower than 25 percent since 1998.[6]

After Taiwan, the largest reported investor in 2001 and 2002 was the United States, followed by Japan and South Korea, but in 2003 and 2004 the United States fell back into fourth place, down to $3.9 billion in 2004, while South Korea and Japan moved up with $6.2 billion and $5.5 billion, respectively. This upward trend in Japanese and South Korean investment in China will likely continue, in keeping with the deepening East Asian regional economic integration discussed in Chapter 6. Indeed, the dominant characteristic of the sourcing of foreign investment in China is the primacy of East Asian investors, amounting to at least 60 percent of the total, based on an estimate of $20 billion for Taiwan, compared with about 10 percent or less for the United States and West Europe.

The sectoral breakdown of FDI is presented in Table 3-2 for all sectors of reported investment that were at least $0.5 billion in 2003. The manufacturing sector dominates with $37.5 billion, or 70 percent of the total. In qualitative terms, this investment is very different from transatlantic FDI between the United States and West Europe, which consists principally of mergers and acquisitions, with relatively small amounts of newly constructed manufacturing facilities and, if anything, a reduction in employ-ment through consolidation. In China, in extremely important contrast, most of the manufacturing investment is for new plant construction, largely in advanced technology industries, and in-volving job creation in the order of 400,000 manufacturing jobs each year.[7]

---

[6] See Fung, *et al., op. cit.,* p. 46.

[7] This estimate is based on the standard rule of thumb that $1 billion of production relates to about 10,000 jobs; if anything, this rule of thumb could be on the low side for China in view of the relatively low cost of labor.

This rapid growth by export-oriented foreign investors and by Chinese private companies is obscured by Chinese labor statistics for the manufacturing sector. The data are dominated by the grossly overstaffed and noncompetitive SOEs which have been progressively cut back with large losses of jobs. The official figures for total manufacturing employment rose from 105 million in 1990 to 130 million in 1996, and then declined to a low of 108 million in 2000 before recovering slightly to 109 million in 2002. Meanwhile, employment in private companies within these aggregate figures rose steadily from 1.4 million in 1990 to 15.8 million in 2002, and a separate small business category rose from 1 million in 1990 to 8.2 million in 2002.[8] This compares, incidentally, with U.S. manufacturing employment which declined from 17 million in 2000 to 14 million in 2004.

Table 3-2
Foreign Direct Investment
In China by Sector
(billions of dollars)

	2001	2002	2003	Percent of Total 2003
Total	**46.9**	**52.7**	**53.5**	**100**
Manufacturing	30.1	36.8	37.5	70
Real estate Management	5.1	5.7	5.2	10
Social Services	2.6	2.9	3.2	6
Electric power, gas and water	2.3	1.4	1.3	2
Farming, forestry, and fishery	0.9	1.0	1.0	2
Wholesale and retail trade	1.2	0.9	1.1	2
Transport and Telecommunications	0.9	0.9	0.9	2
Other	3.8	3.1	3.3	6

Sources: *China Statistical Yearbook*, 2003, Table 17-18; Foreign Investment Administration, Ministry of Foreign Commerce (MOFCOM) for 2003 Statistics

[8] See Judith Banister, "Manufacturing Employment and Compensation in China" (draft report), prepared for the U.S. Department of Labor (November 2004), pp. 66-67.

Other sectors have much lower levels of investment, led by real estate management, $5.2 billion, social services, $3.2 billion, and electric power, gas, and water, $1.3 billion. Noteworthy for not making the $0.5 billion cut is the banking and insurance sector, at only $107 million. The transport and telecommunications sector, which figures prominently in FDI in other newly industrialized countries, is also very low in China, at $0.9 billion. The reason is that both the financial services and the telecommunications sectors are reserved almost exclusively for the public sector and Chinese companies, although some increased foreign participation in financial services will take place as Chinese WTO commitments are implemented.

Further detail on the sectoral orientation of Taiwanese and U.S. investment is contained in the following section.   As for Japanese investment in China, the trend has been toward increasing concentration in manufacturing, from about 80 percent of the total in 1996-1998 to 90 percent in 2001-2002.[9] The sectoral breakdown within the manufacturing sector is shown in Table 3-3 for 2001. The electronics sector is the largest, at 40 percent, followed by transport at 16 percent and chemicals at 12 percent. In contrast, the textiles sector, once substantial, is down to only 3 percent. Japanese investment is principally for export, accounting for 65 percent of production in 2002, and ranging as high as 80 percent for industrial machinery and 70 percent for electronic machinery. Moreover, about half of these exports are shipped back to Japan, either as final products or as intermediate inputs for Japanese companies. Particularly noteworthy, Japanese investment in China, unlike that in ASEAN, where investment initially focuses on labor-intensive production, is increasingly high-tech oriented. One observer concludes that "many Japanese firms started to produce high-tech products at the initial stage of their investment."[10]   He cites the examples of Fuji/Xerox's developing and producing digital copy machines for export to Japan, the United States, and Europe, and Toshiba's producing 70,000 notebook computers per month for export.

---

[9] These figures, plus most of the information in this paragraph, are from Yuqing Xing, "Japanese FDI in China: Trend, Structure, and the Role of Exchange Rates," International University of Japan, March 2004, Xing@iuj.ac.jp.

[10] *Ibid*, p. 11.

Table 3-3
**Japanese FDI in China by
Manufacturing Sector**
(2001 percentage)

Electrical	40.2
Transportation	16.2
Chemicals	11.7
Metals	10.2
Machinery	10.2
Textiles	2.7
Lumber and pulp	1.7
Food	0.8
Other	6.3

Source: Japanese Ministry of Finance, *Monthly Statistics*

South Korean investors in China were mostly small and medium-sized firms through 2001, but with Chinese WTO accession in that year, the larger Korean firms moved in quickly, resulting in almost a tripling of FDI from $2.2 billion in 2001 to $6.4 billion in 2004. About 80 percent of the investment is in manufacturing, led by the electronics and telecommunications sector. Samsung alone has invested nearly $3 billion in China, with 26 factories producing electronic products, including notebook computers, flat panel displays, and cellular phones.[11]

Taiwanese and U.S. Investment in China:
A Study in Contrasts

Taiwan and the United States, over time, have been the largest foreign investors in China, and together they account for about half of total foreign investment. Each is also making a substantial contribution to the rapid development of Chinese advanced technology industry. Beyond this, however, their participation in the Chinese economy is a study in contrasts. This is most evident in their relative sizes, with Taiwanese investment in the order of four times larger than U.S. investment. The contrast then carries over to most aspects of investment composition and operations, although documenting the differences is exceedingly difficult.

---

[11] For further detail, see Yao Shame, *Korea's FDI in China: Status and Perspectives* (Korea Institute for International Economic Policy, December 2003).

Taiwanese Investment in China

Taiwanese investors in China have tended to be small- and medium-sized firms that blend into the Chinese industrial countryside aided by the common language and culture, and with at least one million Taiwanese residents in China, many with family ties. The average investment by Chinese officially recorded Taiwanese projects in 2003 was $1.4 million, compared with $3.1 million per U.S. project. This gap would be wider if the unrecorded Taiwanese investments were included, which are likely to be smaller in average size because small investors do not need authorization to invest in China.

Taiwanese investment by sector was widely dispersed in the initial period of high investment in the 1990s. The percentage distribution by sector for 1991-1998, based on Taiwanese sources, was electronics 21 percent, food and beverages 9 percent, basic metals 9 percent, plastic products 8 percent, chemicals 7 percent, minerals 6 percent, textiles 6 percent, precision instruments 6 percent, transport equipment 5 percent, rubber products 3 percent, and others 20 percent.[12]

Toward the end of the decade, however, Taiwanese investors in China were changing strategy. One observer concluded that Taiwanese direct investment (TDI) "tends to be larger, newer (in technology), and slightly more capital intensive (e.g., Acer computers). In addition, besides export orientation, some TDI started to aim at China's domestic market."[13] Since 2000, the primary position of the electronics sector and related information technology (IT) products has grown rapidly in relative importance in view of the top priority given this area of foreign investment by the Chinese government, the market complementarities between the Taiwanese and Chinese sectors, and the Chinese burgeoning IT export performance described in Chapter 4.

The most comprehensive assessment of the rapidly evolving China-Taiwan relationship in the IT sector is the July 2004 study issued by the Rand National Defense Research Institute.[14] It concludes that "the scope and scale of trade and investment flows across the Taiwan Strait has increased dramatically in recent years,

---

[12] Jack W. Hou, "China's FDI Policy and Taiwanese Direct Investment (TDI) in China," working paper, California State University, 2003, pp. 22-23, with reference to the *Taiwan-China Economic Statistics Yearbook*.
[13] *Ibid*, p. 13.
[14] Michael S. Chase, Kevin L. Pollpeter, and James C. Mulvenon, *Shanghaied? The Economic and Political Implications of the Flow of Information Technology and Investment Across the Taiwan Strait* (Rand National Defense Research Institute, July 2004).

driven in large part by the increasing integration of the information technology sectors. . . . In 2002, more than 49 percent of Taiwan's IT hardware was made in China, and Taiwanese-invested companies produced more than 70 percent of the electronics made in China. . . . The share of Taiwan's IT hardware production in mainland China reached 60 percent in 2003."[15]

Anecdotal reports reinforce the picture of a deepening sectoral integration, with the Taiwanese providing more advanced R&D and training for engineers and managers within a rapidly expanding Chinese industrial sector. One report in February 2004 notes that Taiwan's IT companies have recently "begun to shift their research and development over to China, tapping into the country's large pool of engineering resources."[16] The trend is largely a training process. A manager of Taiwanese PC maker MiTAC International Corp. explains, "We set up an R&D center in Shanghai in 2000, in which Chinese engineers worked on the designs of our mainboards, PCs, servers and information appliances. . . . While our Shanghai team works on mature products or specific products for the China market, our R&D engineers focus on high-end, high-profit, or advanced products, or products for the global market. . . . Basically all tasks could be done in China with the support of our R&D team. . . . The biggest hurdle with our Chinese engineers is that they have to learn to adjust to the Taiwanese work ethic. They are coming from a government-run business model; while we are very market-oriented. . . . We teach them how to work in a market-oriented company where time-to-market is a very critical factor." A manager of the Taiwanese integrated-circuit design house VIA Technologies comments along the same lines: "We have three R&D centers that we have opened in the past two years. . . . The key difference is design experience, particularly in a commercially driven environment. Our Chinese R&D staff concentrates mainly on DGA and BIOS software development as Chinese engineers have particularly strong skills in software and on the communications side."

One striking indicator of strong qualitative complementarities in the IT sector between the more advanced R&D and innovation capability of Taiwanese firms and the rapidly growing Chinese human resources and domestic market was provided by *Business Week*, in June 2004, in its annual selection of the "Top 100 Info-

---

[15] *Ibid*, p. xiii.
[16] "China special firms shift R&D to China," http://neasia.nikkeibp.com/nea/200204/srep_178979.html. The two quotations from Taiwanese managers are from this report.

Tech Firms."[17] The selection is from a global survey based on four criteria: return on equity, revenue growth, shareholder return, and total revenues. The country breakdown has the United States in a substantial lead position, with 46 firms, followed by Taiwan with 15, Japan with 13, the EU with 8, and China/Hong Kong with 4. The strong showing of Taiwan is even more prominent among the top 25 firms in the survey: Taiwan moves to first place with eight firms, followed by the United States with six, three each from China/Hong Kong and South Korea, one from the EU, and none from Japan. The 15 Taiwanese firms in the top 100 are listed in Table 3-4, with information on revenues, profits, and product orientation. Company information on investment in China is not available, but it is generally believed that all or almost all of the Taiwanese firms are well engaged in the China market.

The semiconductor industry, in particular, is an important area of growing China-Taiwan integration through Taiwanese investment in China. The rapid development of this industry is a high priority for China, while Taiwan is the global leader in the foundry production process, with strong related positions for packaging and testing and for design.   Each of the three components of the semiconductor industry is engaged across the Taiwan Straits, although in different ways and with differing time frames.[18]

Taiwan dominates the global foundry industry for semi-conductors with the two largest companies, Taiwan Semiconductor Manufacturing Co. (TSMC) and United Microelectronics Corp., which together had revenues of $8.6 billion in 2003, compared with only $2.8 billion by the six next largest producers scattered in Singapore, the United States, Japan, China, and South Korea.   In 2004, for the first time, the Taiwanese government approved the construction of a semiconductor foundry in China by TSMC. The TSMC Chairman, Morris Chang, called it "a land-mark decision,"[19] with the implication that other foundry investments in China would follow. Another important event in 2004

---

[17] *Business Week*, June 21, 2004. The top 100 listing was especially newsworthy in the context of the accompanying special report, entitled "Big Bang: Digital Convergence is Finally Happening," which claimed that digital convergence is "likely to produce the biggest explosion of innovation since the dawn of the Internet."

[18] The information presented about the semiconductor sector is drawn principally from Chase *et al., op. cit.*, and US-Taiwan Business Council, *Semiconductor Report*, second quarter 2004.

[19] US-Taiwan Business Council, *op. cit.*, p. 7.

Table 3-4
The Info Tech Top 100
Taiwanese Companies

Rank	Company Country	Revenue* $millions	Profits* $millions	Comments
3	Quanta Computer	8,742	389	The world's biggest producer of notebook PCs counts Dell and HP among its customers. And it's diversifying into cell phones and LCD TVs.
4	Hon Hai Precision Ind.	10,899	670	This powerful producer of PCs and parts is closing in on Flextronics as the world's top electronics contract manufacturer.
15	Compal Technology	5,195	332	One of the leading producers of notebook PCs. Compal will make hay out of Toshiba's decision to outsource more production.
16	Asustek Computer	5,747	339	The producer of PC motherboards has diversified, racking up impressive sales of its notebook PCs in Asia.
17	AU Optronics	3,085	461	Formerly a joint venture of PC maker ACER and chip company UMC, AU is now one of the biggest producers of flat-panel displays.
20	Novatek Microelectronics	320	62	As the leading designer of semiconductors for LCD panels, the company is seeing sales take off with rising consumer demand.
21	Lite-On Technology	4,246	214	This Taiwanese manufacturer of PC components expects revenues to increase 40% this year thanks to strong LCD monitor sales.
25	ACER	4,626	215	Spinning off divisions and narrowing ACER's focus has paid off. But with Chairman Stan Shih retiring, will the good times continue?
35	Mediatek Taiwan	1,118	485	This chip-design company is the leader in one of the industry's hottest segments: DVD players. But low-cost rivals are attacking its profits.
36	Chi Mei Optoelectronics Taiwan	2,423	210	Taiwan tycoon Shi Wen-long took this unit of his Chi Mei Group public to fund expansion of thin-display manufacturing. His bet is paying off.
55	Taiwan Semiconductor Mfg. Taiwan	5,972	1390	With the chip cycle on an upswing, profits at the world's top contract manufacturer are soaring.
70	Synnex Technology Intl. Taiwan	3,174	70	Surging demand for PCs in China has bolstered the fortunes of this Taiwan-based computer distributor.
77	BENQ Taiwan	3,762	220	This spin-off from PC maker ACER has become Taiwan's premier name-brand consumer electronics brand.
85	Adv. Semicond. Engineering Taiwan	1,908	143	The world's second-biggest chip packager has profited from the upswing in demand for semiconductors.
96	United Microelectronics Taiwan	2,816	412	Surging tech and consumer electronics demand has this Taiwanese chipmaker's fabs operating at 100% capacity.

* Latest 12-month period, ranging from December 2003 to April 2004.

Source: Excerpted from *Business Week*, June 21, 2004, pp. 94-101. The top 100 firms were listed in the *Business Week* article; only Taiwanese firms were selected for this table. Reprinted with permission.

for Chinese semiconductor production was the delivery to the largest Chinese company, Semiconductor Manufacturing International Corp. (SMIC), of 12-inch chip production equipment, the most advanced production technology, from German partner Infineon Technologies.

The combination of further Taiwanese investments and further joint ventures with 12-inch chip production could thus draw China and Taiwan together as the dominant center of global chip foundry production. The whole process, moreover, is being driven by generous Chinese financial incentives for new investment, centered on fierce competition between Shanghai and Beijing. Shanghai has a "5+5" policy of a five-year tax holiday plus an additional five years at half the tax rate, while Beijing offers a "Shanghai +1" plan of one additional year of tax benefits beyond whatever Shanghai offers. The two cities together plan to build 15 to 18 foundry plants by 2005, although this pace will likely be reduced in the face of a projected global over-capacity and intensified competition from the larger producers abroad.[20]

China has a significant cost advantage in the labor-intensive packaging and testing phase of semiconductor production, and foreign firms have been moving into China for this processing. Taiwanese firms have been prohibited from doing so by the Taiwanese government, but under pressure from Taiwanese industry, the government will likely begin approving such investments in 2005, which will further integrate the two semiconductor industries.

For semiconductor design, which is critical to advanced technology innovation, the United States has a strong leadership position, but Taiwan has a respectable second-place position. Of the 20 largest design firms, 14 are American, 5 are Taiwanese, and 1 is Canadian. China has also recently placed high priority on expanding semiconductor design work, and there are now about 400 chip design firms in China, most only a few years old, of which about one-third are foreign companies. The growing Taiwanese role in the process of expanding and upgrading design capability in China is summarized by industry analyst Nancy Wu: "The Taiwanese are all aware that China is catching up in semiconductor design, and they certainly don't want to see that happen. But the problem is they love to invest in China. The advantage of the same language, favorable tax rates, large end market, lower operational costs and good quality of design engineers are very attractive." The United States is still number

---

[20] Chase *et al.*, *op. cit.*, p. xix.

one for semiconductor design, with about 50 percent of the global market, but the Chinese share is expected to increase.[21]

An outstanding example of how rapidly the Chinese semiconductor industry is developing—and of the Taiwanese connection—is Shanghai-based SMIC. It was founded in 2000 as a Cayman Islands company by Chairman Richard Chang, Taiwanese born, who was an executive with Texas Instruments and ran a semiconductor company in Taiwan before moving to China. By 2004, SMIC had five plants in operation, was gearing up the 12-inch chip production noted above, and had sales of $408 million. In 2005, SMIC will begin producing 90-nanometer integrated circuits, the most advanced manufacturing available, on communications chips for Texas Instruments.[22] SMIC still has weak profits, but this has not yet slowed down its growth.

There is finally the political dimension of the developing China-Taiwan integration in advanced technology industry. The conflict over Taiwanese sovereignty, including threats of military action by China, contrasts with the ever growing mutual economic interests from trade and especially Taiwanese investment in China. China benefits greatly from the very large investment by technologically advanced Taiwanese firms, while the latter are able to reduce costs and gain access to the rapidly growing Chinese market.

The immediate issue in play concerns on-again, off-again discussion about an agreement on the "three links"—direct trade, transport, and postal service—between Taiwan and China, which would have high visibility psychological impact in terms of drawing the two economies together, as well as commercial benefits for both sides.[23] Taiwanese business interests are pressing strongly for an agreement, while Taiwan independence advocates oppose it. Y.C. Wang, Chairman of Formosa Plastics, warned that if the three links are not opened, "all our businesses in China will lose their competitiveness in three years."[24] The president of the American Chamber of Commerce in Taipei, Andrea Wu, agreed that "with each passing day, Taiwan is losing competitiveness as a

---

[21] *Ibid*, p. 12. The figures on design firms are also from this source. Ms. Wu is an analyst for Gartner Dataquest, where she is part of the design and engineering group.

[22] See US-Taiwan Business Council, *Semiconductor Report*, third quarter 2004, pp. 9-14, for the full SMIC story.

[23] The "three links" under discussion are distinct from the "mini three links," approved by the Taiwanese government in January 2000, for very limited direct travel and trade.

[24] Cited in Chase *et al.*, *op. cit.*, p. 14.

regional business center because the lack of direct links is marginalizing its role."[25]   The *Taiwan News*, in opposition, countered that the three links would "totally undermine Taiwan's national security, . . . leaving it fewer and fewer cards to play in its attempt to resist China's ever-mounting pressure and blackmail."[26] Agreement on the three links has been at an impasse in part over Chinese insistence that the trade be referred to as "domestic." China has also been seeking, with some success, to drive a wedge between Taiwanese business leaders and their government.[27] It is likely that at some point relatively soon the two sides will reach an agreement on the three links.   Where the China/Taiwan relationship is headed longer term cannot be predicted, but it is clear that the economic component of the equation is steadily growing in importance.

U.S. Investment in China

American direct investors in China are distinguished from most Taiwanese counterparts by their high public visibility and name recognition, which brings certain advantages.   Product recognition can be a plus for sales within the Chinese market. American corporate culture has the deserved reputation for top-level treatment of employees, with emphasis on career training, promotion based on merit rather than personal connections, and generally higher wages and benefits.[28]   This enables American companies to hire the best-qualified people and develop their skills over time, which is particularly important for advanced technology industry.   Another advantage is that American companies, for the most part, integrate their Chinese operations into a global strategy of supply chain management and marketing at home and abroad, while Taiwanese production is far more concentrated on the bilateral China relationship, with a very limited home market.

China is nevertheless an extremely complex and difficult market for American companies.   They often face on-the-ground competition from European and Japanese rivals in addition to

---

[25] "American Chamber Chief Tells Taiwan Direct Transport Links To China Essential," *Daily Report for Executives*, June 3, 2004, p. A3.

[26] Cited in Chase *et al.*, *op. cit.*, p. 16.

[27] "China Raises Economic Heat on Taiwan," *Wall Street Journal*, July 27, 2004.

[28] Ernest H. Preeg, *U.S. Manufacturing Industry's Impact on Ethical, Labor and Environmental Standards in Developing Countries: A Survey of Current Practices* (MAPI 2001).   This survey contains more than 300 examples of specific "good practices," including 18 by U.S. companies in China.

well-entrenched and well-connected Chinese firms, including the Taiwanese. At the same time, however, the cost advantages for production in China can be substantial, and the Chinese market, now and as projected ahead, is simply too large to ignore. As summed up by senior members of the Boston Consulting Group, "China is a must-play place for any global company. . . . It also means that inevitably you will be competing with Chinese companies, or with others who are leveraging China better than you are. . . . If you don't have a China strategy, you're missing the biggest single business opportunity today."[29]

Despite the actual and potential importance of China for all U.S. companies, the available information about direct investment in China is relatively sparse, particularly that of broad analytical content. There is little, for example, that compares with the studies of the Taiwan-China relationship in the semiconductor industry recounted above. The problem begins with the massive discrepancy between the U.S. figures on outward investment to China and the Chinese figures on U.S. investment into China. The U.S. Department of Commerce (DOC) reported direct investment capital outflow to China at $1.9 billion in 2001 and $0.9 billion in 2002; the Chinese Ministry of Commerce, for the same years, reported capital inflows of direct investment from the United States of $4.7 billion and $5.3 billion. For the two years together, the Chinese figures were thus almost four times larger than the U.S. figures. Apparently, the difference is primarily accounted for by the normal U.S. accounting procedure of recording only financial flows out of the United States, while much if not most of direct investment by U.S. firms in China is financed out of their subsidiaries in Asia or from banks in Asia. In this context, the larger Chinese figures would be a more accurate reflection of what American companies are actually doing in China, and the DOC should consider collecting an alternative set of figures more in line with the Chinese approach.

As for a breakdown by sector, China provides no detail on American investment, while the DOC, based on the much smaller U.S. figures, reports a very broad breakdown, as shown in Table 3-5. The figures in the table are for the composite 2000-2003 period in order to even out sharp year-to-year fluctuations in some sectors. These figures indicate that the manufacturing sector dominates with 69 percent, although this is lower than the 80

---

[29] The Boston Consulting Group, *China and the New Rules for Global Business*, http://knowledge.wharton.upenn.edu, June 2004. The quotes are from BCG Vice President David Michael and Senior Vice President George Stalk, p. 1.

percent to 90 percent by Japanese and South Korean firms noted earlier, and with mining and wholesale trade significantly represented with 15 percent and 14 percent of the total. Other service industries, including financial services and professional, scientific and technical services, which are included in the DOC report, were very small in China in 2000-2003, but they could be rising as China progressively opens its services sector to foreign investors. Within manufacturing, the information technology sector—as represented by computers and electrical equipment—is clearly the largest, with 42 percent of total investment, followed by transportation equipment with 9 percent and food and chemicals with smaller shares.

Table 3-5
U.S. Direct Investment in China: Capital Outflows
(percentage, 2000-2003)

All industries	100	
Mining	15	
Manufacturing	69	
Computers and electronic products		26
Electrical equipment, appliances, and components		16
Transportation equipment		9
Food		7
Chemicals		5
Other manufactures		6
Wholesale trade	14	
Other industries	2	

Source: U.S. Department of Commerce

The next step in assessing the degree of participation by American firms and their qualitative impact for the development of Chinese advanced technology industry should be more in-depth surveys of key sectors and subsectors. Unfortunately, there is little such analysis available for American participation in China, and a procedural recommendation offered here is that such sector-specific assessments be undertaken. Survey work would not need to get into specific detail about R&D programs and new product development, but could focus on broader questions of the scope of R&D activities, the numbers and qualities of Chinese engineers and managers, the relationship of imported components to final products for the domestic and export markets, the extent of product competition from other foreign investors and Chinese companies, and, most importantly, a qualitative assessment of the degree to and pace at which China is closing the U.S. leadership position in advanced technology innovation and production.

Such survey work could be undertaken both within the U.S. government and by the private sector. The new Assistant Secretary of Commerce for Manufacturing could be the focal point for government surveys, while the NSF could undertake parallel work for the more scientific and technologically complex dimensions of international competition. In the private sector, industry associations could survey their members in coordination with the American Chamber of Commerce in China. The US-China Business Council might also initiate targeted assessments, as the US-Taiwan Business Council does for the semiconductor industry. As for sectoral priorities, the information technology and telecommunications sectors should be the initial primary focus in view of the current concentration in these sectors by American and other multinational companies in China, and the top priority placed on them by the Chinese government. Looking ahead, pharmaceuticals and biotechnology should be priorities.

The presentation here is limited to selected examples of U.S. investment in key sectors and related quotes from senior managers. At a minimum, these examples indicate the scope and intensity of American interests in play and thus serve as a catalyst for the recommended in-depth sectoral assessments.

Computers.—IBM and Hewlett-Packard (HP) began operations in China in 1985 and have been steadily expanding and upgrading their R&D programs there. HP established the first foreign-sponsored high-tech research center in China in the mid-1990s, and IBM created its China Research Lab in Beijing in 1995, "to focus initially on creating software and applications that are especially relevant to China . . . [including] digital libraries, speech recognition for Mandarin, machine translation, Chinese language processing, multimedia and the Internet."[30] Dell's large Chinese plant makes computers almost exclusively for the domestic market and neighboring countries. In the face of increased competition from Chinese competitors for lower-cost desktop PCs, however, Dell decided in 2004 to move up to higher price bands, which, according to one analyst, creates the risk "that Dell could end up sitting on the sidelines in a key segment of China's fast growing PC market."[31] The $80 million Microsoft advanced technology center outside Beijing employs 500 engineers, Ph.D. students, and visiting professors. Microsoft Vice President Richard Rashid explained that one of the reasons for the

---

[30] Walsh, *op. cit.*, pp. 73-74.
[31] *Financial Times*, August 17, 2004.

lab was "to tap into a great pool of talent."[32] Cisco announced in September 2004 a five-year, $32 million investment in a research center in Shanghai to investigate new voice technologies. CEO John Chambers said that this is just one of many steps Cisco will take in research and development in China, explaining that over the next decade, half of Cisco's top 12 business partners and half of its main competitors will come from China. He told a Beijing news conference: "China will be the IT [information technology] center of the world."[33]

Telecoms.—The Chinese telecoms industry has grown rapidly since the mid-1990s and now serves about 300 million cellular subscribers and 300 million fixed-line users. Telecoms service providers are large Chinese firms competing against one another and purchasing equipment both from abroad and from multinational and domestic producers within China. Chinese producer Huawei had $3.8 billion in sales in 2003, including $1 billion of exports, and its leaders want it to become a broadly based, research-intensive telecoms company. In 2004, Huawei had a $500 million R&D program, with 10,000 engineers developing next-generation networking equipment for telecom operators and third-generation (3G) mobile phones for consumers. In response, Lucent Technologies plans to invest $70 million in an R&D center for 3G cellular phones in Nanging, and Motorola said it would spend $90 million on an R&D center in Beijing. David McCurdy, President of the U.S. Electronic Industries Alliance, contends that in China, "the Chinese haven't created a culture of innovation. . . . Foreign-owned enterprises in China will be the centers of innovation."[34] As for cell phones, Motorola initially took a dominant lead position, but it quickly drew strong competition from other multinationals, including Nokia, Siemans, Samsung, and Sony Ericsson. In 2000, Chinese regulators licensed over 30 domestic manufacturers who gained close to a 50 percent market share by 2003, but then lost some of it in 2004 as the multinationals introduced new advanced technology features, such as cameras and hard disc drives. Some Chinese companies, in response, are increasing R&D, such as number two TCL, with an R&D staff of 1,000.[35] The sector will remain hyper-competitive with a risk of over-capacity and sharp price cutting.

---

[32] *Business Week*, October 11, 2004, p. 100.

[33] Http://story.news.yahoo.com/news?tmpl=story&cid, September 23, 2004.

[34] For the references to Huawei and the McCurdy quote, see "Huawei: More than a local hero," *Business Week,* October 11, 2004, pp. 180-184.

[35] Ted Dean, "The Fights for China's Handset Market," *China Business Review*, November-December 2003, pp. 28-31.

The possibility of China introducing its own 3G standard in 2005, perhaps as a way to favor Chinese companies, further complicates the market outlook. Nevertheless, Ray Yam of Motorola China remained optimistic: "We believe we are neck-and-neck in terms of units with Nokia and ahead in value. . . . We believe we can hold on to our number one position in China in both."[36]

Automobiles.—The Chinese automotive sector has experienced extremely rapid domestic growth, with automobile sales up 80 percent in 2003 to over 2 million vehicles. Growth was down sharply in 2004, but looking ahead, China will soon pass Germany and Japan to become the second largest national market. Initial growth and production centered on foreign investors, first Volkswagen and later General Motors (GM), who together captured half of the market in 2003, with 700,000 and 400,000 vehicles respectively. GM is increasing engineering design work in China, and announced it will build and test its first hybrid bus in China, together with its partner Shanghai Automotive Industrial Corp. Ford entered the Chinese market more recently, with plans to invest $1 billion, and other multinationals are also expanding production. In parallel, there are over 100 Chinese vehicle producers, mostly of much smaller size. Unlike the information technology and other sectors, where WOFEs now predominate, China limits foreign participation in the automotive sector to 50 percent in joint ventures with Chinese firms. The Chinese market is also highly protected from imports with a 25 percent tariff, even after WTO entry. A new set of rules in June 2004 pointed in the direction of consolidation, with an emphasis on advanced technology application. GM China Group Chairman Phil Murtaugh praised the new regulations that would "further the consolidation of the fragmented industry into a few globally competitive companies, assure long-term customer satisfaction, and promote the sustainable development of the industry."[37] Independent observers offer a more cautionary note for foreign investors: "The Chinese government's eventual goal is to have innovative homegrown vehicles makers that can export a sizeable number of cars and parts. Beijing has made it clear it wants to develop 'state controlled' firms into globally competitive firms, and the auto sector is stated as a key strategic industry."[38] The automotive sector in China is highly competitive, and the outlook uncertain. In early 2005, Volkswagen experienced a sharp decline

---

[36] *Financial Times*, August 24, 2004.
[37] "China Issues New Rules for Automakers, Aims at Consolidating, Assists Foreign Firms," *Daily Report for Executives*, June 3, 2004.
[38] *Ibid.* The observers are Andrew Yeh (Beijing) and Toshio Ariteki (Tokyo).

in market share while several joint ventures announced plans to begin exporting cars to Europe and the United States by 2007 or sooner.

Machinery.—This is a wide-ranging sector for supplying the full range of machinery to the rapidly growing Chinese market and for export, from relatively simple pumps and sewing machines to advanced automation equipment and robotic machine tools. General Electric (GE) has been assembling medical diagnostic machines in China since the early 1990s, and in 2003 won a $900 million contract to build 13 advanced, 300-megawatt electricity turbines, which included a commitment to share sophisticated technology with two Chinese companies that intend eventually to make the equipment themselves.[39]   This technology-sharing agreement was negotiated in the context of competing offers from Mitsubishi and Siemans.   The GE China Learning Center in Shanghai has many of the features of GE's training facilities in Crotonville, New York, with classrooms for up to 178 people.[40] The Ingersoll-Rand compressor division plant in Shanghai uses 18 local suppliers to supply about half of the parts, and the plant operations manager explains: "Roughly half are top class and the rest are coming up to speed. . . . We employ 20 engineers to work with the suppliers to train them to meet our quality standards."[41] Cummins produces 700,000 to 800,000 diesel engines for the domestic Chinese market each year in two joint venture plants. Fewer than 5 percent of the engines currently meet U.S. and European environmental standards, but Cummins is studying how to move some Chinese production up-market, which would require an investment of a "few tens of millions of dollars."[42]   A Caterpillar joint venture in the 1990s for construction machinery failed, but the company is confident that conditions have changed for the better as it attempts to quadruple its $500 million annual sales to China by 2010. Asia-Pacific Operations Manager Jack Nichols says: "We're very optimistic. . . . State-owned companies in China have been through a huge shift, in terms of both technology and commercial attitudes."[43]

Pharmaceutical and biotechnology.—At least 20 of the largest 25 pharmaceutical companies have operations in China, and these operations are changing rapidly toward cost-effective clinical trials. Pfizer, Merck, and Bristol-Myers Squibb are now

---

[39] *Wall Street Journal*, February 26, 2004.
[40] *Business Week*, October 11, 2004.
[41] *Financial Times*, June 24, 2004.
[42] *Ibid.*
[43] *Ibid.*

investing heavily in later stage clinical trials. Outsourcing is also developing, such as the San Diego-based Targe Gen contract with the Wuxi Pharmatech Co. in Shanghai to do research on components related to cardiovascular disease. Novartis Chief Executive Daniel Vasella believes that Chinese biotechnology companies are rapidly adopting Western research standards and knowledge, and that it is only a matter of time before China catches up.[44] For the pharmaceutical sector, one investigator concluded that "China now seems poised for an even more dramatic 'take off' in advances over the next four years. Those advances could very greatly widen its current pockets of excellence, slash its technological lag time, and even push China to the lead in some key technologies."[45]

Venture capital.—This financial vehicle for advanced technology development played a central role in Silicon Valley development and is now gathering momentum in the high-risk, high-return Chinese market. Patrick McGovern was the first American venture capitalist in China in 1992, and he has built his IDG Technology Investment Inc. fund from $1.7 million to $37 million, for small, largely high-tech investments averaging just over $1 million, typically startups.[46] It was not until after 2000, however, that foreign venture capitalists began to arrive in larger numbers, and by 2004 there were 253 deals totaling $1.3 billion in China, about 80 percent by foreign venture capitalists.[47] In April 2004, the Carlyle Group announced plans for $1 billion of investment in China, mostly smaller investments of $20 million to $30 million, with a focus on start-up companies and corporate buyouts, including in pharmaceuticals, financial services, and manufacturing.[48] In June 2004, Silicon Valley Bancshares organized a week-long China tour for 24 West Coast venture capitalists, which was quickly over-subscribed. One of the participants commented that people in Silicon Valley "have decided they have to do something in China, but very few have figured out what they want to do."[49] In the investment banking field, Goldman Sachs reached agreement in

---

[44] "Drug Companies Look to China for Cheap R&D," *Wall Street Journal*, November 22, 2004.

[45] Charles W. McMillion, "China's Very Rapid Economic, Industrial and Technological Emergence" (paper prepared for the U.S.-China Economic and Security Review Commission, June 5, 2002), p. 12.

[46] *Business Week*, January 24, 2005.

[47] *Zero2IPO–China Venture Capital Annual Report 2004*; and Pieter Bottelier, "Venture Capital and Innovation in China," presented at SCID Conference on "China's Policy Reforms: Progress and Challenges" (Palo Alto, October 14-16, 2004).

[48] *Wall Street Journal*, April 21, 2004.

[49] *Business Week*, June 14, 2004.

July 2004 to become the first foreign investment bank to offer the same full range of banking services as Chinese banks, through a joint venture arrangement that involved a $200 million investment by Goldman Sachs, including a $62 million "donation" to a troubled Chinese brokerage firm.[50] In sum, the venture capital market is off and running in a Wild West (or East) Chinese market, with strong U.S. participation, and will play an increasingly important role in nurturing innovative start-up companies.

The Uncertain Course Ahead

FDI is currently the central driving force for the rapid development of Chinese advanced technology industry. The $50 billion to $60 billion of annual investment inflow is 70 percent in manufacturing industry, with concentration in the information technology and telecommunications sectors, and the large majority of this investment consists of new plant construction with a heavy R&D orientation. Foreign investors hire roughly half a million new Chinese employees each year, which includes tens of thousands of engineers, scientists, and managers. The accumulated work experience of these professional employees over the past ten years in the most modern multinational companies is creating the critical human resource base for the rapid expansion of Chinese advanced technology companies and related public sector R&D. Chinese exports tripled from $149 billion in 1995 to $438 billion in 2003, with 57 percent of total exports in the latter year attributed to foreign invested companies. All of these developments, together, have produced an extraordinary record of creative accomplishments and mutual economic benefits.

The course ahead for FDI in China is nevertheless uncertain. Can it continue on its current manufacturing sector, export-oriented, high-growth trajectory? And if not, how will it change? The answer to the first question is almost certainly "no." As for the second question, some changes in direction are reasonably clear, others not so.

The clearest change in direction ahead is for a relative decline in the FDI concentration in manufacturing and exports. The Chinese economy will inevitably shift toward a relatively higher share of GDP in services and a greater relative role for domestic demand compared with exports for achieving the desired path of overall economic growth. This will require a restructuring of Chinese economic policies and involve policy interaction with the United States and other trading partners, issues which are

---

[50] *Financial Times*, August 6 and August 10, 2004.

addressed in subsequent chapters. The direction of change is not in doubt, however, and foreign investors are already redirecting their production strategies more heavily toward the Chinese domestic market, including the services sector.

Another question about the course ahead relates to the level of FDI. Is the $50 billion to $60 billion level of 2002-2004 sustainable, or might it rise even higher? In January 2003, Chinese experts predicted a $100 billion level of FDI during 2006-2010, and the inflow did rise from $54 billion in 2003 to $61 billion in 2004.[51] In 2003 and 2004, China surpassed the United States as the most attractive country to invest in, according to the FDI Confidence Index.[52] The level might also trend downward, however, if competitive Chinese companies proliferate at a faster rate, related to Chinese banking sector reform to eliminate the financial disadvantages to private Chinese companies compared with multinationals financed from abroad.[53] The uncertainty is compounded by the enormity of internal Chinese savings, at over 40 percent of GDP in 2004, which relegates FDI, in quantitative terms, to only about 10 percent of total investment within China. In any event, a moderate upward or downward movement in the level of FDI in the next several years should not greatly alter the current central role of FDI for the development of advanced technology industries, or the mutual interest of the Chinese government and the multinationals to continue their rapidly growing and mutually rewarding engagement.

A more fundamental and medium to long-term question concerns the qualitative relationship between multinational and Chinese firms competing in advanced technologies industries. A steady strengthening and more technologically confident Chinese industry could alter the attitudes within China about the desirability of a continued lead role for foreign companies in various advanced industries. The relationship could be influenced by the policy direction of the Chinese government, to the degree it favors and nurtures national champions, as well as by the policy

---

[51] Http://english.people.com.cn, January 2, 2003. The experts were from the Chinese Development Research Centre under the State Counsel.

[52] The index is conducted by the A.T. Kearney Global Business Policy Council in Alexandria, Virginia, and is based on a worldwide survey of 1,000 executives.

[53] This relationship is developed in Yashen Huang, *Selling China: Foreign Direct Investment During the Reform Era* (Cambridge University Press, 2003). Huang concludes that if privatization of SOEs had been politically feasible, or if Chinese private entrepreneurs could have obtained financing to fulfill export contracts, many of the benefits currently associated with FDI could have been realized with a lower level of FDI.

reaction of the United States and other nations with heavy FDI participation in China. There is no reason why broadening and deepening competition between foreign and Chinese companies cannot continue to be of mutual benefit, within the likely context of a growing relative role for Chinese companies and continued high growth in the overall Chinese economy. The multinationals would simply have a diminishing slice within an ever-expanding pie. But politics, nationalist sentiments, and exogenous foreign policy developments all lurk in the shadows.

The final and most critical uncertainty for this study is the degree to which FDI raises Chinese capability for technological innovation, new product design, and commercial application, leading to a reduction in the U.S. global advanced technology leadership position.   This is not a matter of multinational companies versus Chinese companies and public sector R&D, but rather a matter of how all three interact and mutually reinforce one another toward the ultimate result of technological innovation and new product development and production within China.   The likely prospect for the technology leadership relationship is that the U.S. lead over China will progressively decline in relative terms. This vital subject is discussed in Chapter 5, but first one further key dimension of the overall U.S.-China advanced technology relationship needs to be examined, namely, international trade competitiveness in advanced technology products.

Chapter 4

The Leading-Edge Bottom Line: Trade

International trade in high technology or advanced technology products is the most revealing indicator of advanced technology performance in three respects: (1) trade data is the most detailed, by sector and product, on a comparative basis among nations; (2) trade data is the most current available indicator; and (3) trade performance is the bottom-line measure of international competitiveness. Each of the three requires a brief introduction.

(1) *Trade data.*—The presentation of trade data raises the question of how to define high technology or advanced technology products. Long-standing practice has been to define high technology in terms of selected sectors or industries, usually beginning with the information technology and telecommunications sectors, and then relating this selection to available sources of trade data, based on the Standard International Trade Classification (SITC), as collected by the World Trade Organization and the United Nations (UN). One criticism of this approach is that within the selected industries there are not only advanced-design, technology-intensive products but also mass-produced "commodity" products, and that trade in these latter products should not be considered high-tech trade. A counter argument is that a broadly based production capability in a given sector, be it semiconductors or computers, is a relevant measure of high-tech resource allocation and trade performance. The alternative approach for defining high-tech trade is to select the individual products that have the highest levels of embedded R&D and engineering resources, which is the basis for the U.S. "advanced technology products" or ATP trade category. In any event, the availability of trade data at the industry and product levels, on a reasonably comparable basis among nations, is far more detailed and reliable than it is for the internal indicators and foreign direct investment figures discussed in the previous two chapters.

(2) *The most current data.*—There was frequent lamentation in Chapter 2 about the two-to-four year time lags for key domestic indicators related to advanced technology development, such as

R&D, engineering graduates, and patent applications. Trade data, in contrast, has minimal time lags. Both the United States and China release detailed trade statistics within six or seven weeks after the fact, and the WTO annual *International Trade Statistics* is scheduled for public release in September of the following year, although this can slip by a month or two. UN and OECD trade statistics have longer delays, but this does not prevent a reasonably detailed current tracking of trade performance. Such up-to-date availability of data is, of course, especially important for the fast-moving course of events addressed in this study, wherein Chinese exports grew by 22 percent in 2002, and 35 percent in both 2003 and 2004.

(3) *The trade competitiveness bottom line.*—The trade balance shifts, to a certain degree, on annual and cyclical bases, but the underlying trends are, by definition, the measure of international competitiveness. This, in fact, is the disturbing reality in the U.S. ATP trade account in recent years, where the sustained large trade surpluses of the 1990s deteriorated sharply into deficit since 2002, led by a surging bilateral deficit with China, which, in 2004, equaled the global U.S. ATP deficit.

The remainder of this chapter is divided into five parts: (1) the high technology restructuring of Chinese trade; (2) sectoral trends in manufactures trade; (3) recent Chinese advanced technology trade performance; (4) recent U.S. advanced technology trade performance; and (5) the export platform issue.

High Technology Restructuring
of Chinese Trade

Chinese exports and imports of manufactures have both shifted steadily from low technology to high technology products since the early 1990s, as shown in Table 4-1. These OECD figures are divided into four categories of manufactures: high, medium-high, medium-low, and low technology. All categories grew rapidly during the nine-year period 1992-2001: total Chinese imports tripled and total exports more than tripled. Within this overall rapid growth in trade, the technology-based upward shift for exports, shown in the percentage distributions in the bottom half of the table, is most striking in the high technology share, which more than doubled, from 12.3 percent in 1992 to 25.3 percent in 2001, and the corresponding decline in the low technology share from 60.8 percent to 41.2 percent. The medium-high technology category showed a smaller but still substantial increase from 14.3 percent to 20.3 percent, while the medium-low technology category was up by less than 1 percent. Combining the two higher and the two lower tech categories, the higher tech export share increased from 26.6 percent in 1992 to 45.5 percent in 2001, while the lower tech export share was down from 73.4 percent to 54.5 percent.

Unfortunately, this highly revealing OECD series, which appeared in March 2004, went only as far as 2001 trade, and thus does not include the very high Chinese export growth years of 2002-2004. The bottom line in the table therefore projects the sectoral shares of exports to 2004, based on the rate of change during 1995-2001, when the Chinese advanced technology economic strategy was shifting into high gear. The 2004 projected shares show a further increase of the two higher technology categories to 52 percent of the total and a corresponding decline of the lower technology shares to 48 percent. Thus, by 2004, China likely crossed the 50 percent divide to become a primarily high-tech exporter of manufactures. This estimated 52 percent figure may experience a slight decline in 2005, with the elimination of multilateral textile and apparel quotas, giving highly competitive Chinese producers expanded access to industrialized country markets, but the reversal should be temporary and relatively small, in view of the growth in manufactures trade oriented heavily toward higher tech products.[1]

The restructuring of Chinese exports toward high-tech products is closely related to the rising share of total exports by foreign invested enterprises, from 32 percent in 1995 to 57 percent in 2004, shown earlier in Table 3-2. The declining share of low-tech exports, such as apparel, footwear, and toys, is primarily produced by Chinese companies, often on contract to indus-trialized country distributors or retailers, while the high-tech exports are principally by the foreign investors. In other words, the share of high-tech exports by foreign enterprises is higher than 57 percent, and probably much higher.

The technology-based upward shift for Chinese imports is substantial, but not as sharp or clear cut as for exports. The percentage of imports in the high-tech category increased greatly, from 17.3 percent in 1992 to 33.1 percent in 2001, while the percentage for low-tech imports was down more modestly, from 21.9 percent to 15.1 percent. In fact, a large part of the increase for the high-tech category was at the expense of the medium-high category, which was down from 45.0 percent to 36.4 percent, while there was little change in the medium-low tech category. The

---

[1] In 2004, only 15 percent of Chinese exports consisted of textiles and apparel.

Table 4-1
Chinese Trade in Manufactures by Technology Intensity
($ billions)

	High Technology		Medium-high Technology		Medium-low Technology		Low Technology		Total Trade	
	Exports	Imports	Exports	Imports	Exports	Imports	Exports	Imports	Exports	Imports
1992	9.3	12.5	10.8	32.5	9.5	11.4	45.8	15.8	75.4	72.2
1993	10.7	15.9	12.4	41.1	9.5	22.4	49.9	16.3	82.5	95.7
1994	15.6	20.1	16.6	46.3	13.4	19.6	65.4	21.0	111.0	107.0
1995	21.5	21.6	23.6	52.4	21.5	18.9	72.2	26.1	138.8	119.0
1996	24.3	22.7	24.4	55.3	20.5	19.8	72.1	27.1	141.3	124.9
1997	30.0	26.4	29.0	50.7	26.3	21.3	86.1	27.9	171.4	126.3
1998	34.7	32.6	31.4	48.8	25.7	21.4	83.4	26.0	175.2	128.8
1999	40.2	42.8	35.3	55.2	25.8	24.2	85.4	27.6	186.7	149.8
2000	55.8	59.4	47.3	69.3	33.3	31.8	101.9	32.6	238.3	193.1
2001	64.4	70.2	51.5	77.4	33.8	32.8	105.0	32.0	254.7	212.4
Percentage Distribution										
1992	12.3	17.3	14.3	45.0	12.6	15.8	60.8	21.9	100.0	100.0
1995	15.5	18.2	17.0	44.0	15.5	15.9	52.0	21.9	100.0	100.0
2001	25.3	33.1	20.2	36.4	13.3	15.4	41.2	15.1	100.0	100.0
2004*	30.2	40.6	21.8	32.6	12.2	15.1	35.8	11.7	100.0	100.0

Source: OECD, *An Emerging Knowledge-Based Economy in China? Indicators from OECD Databases*, March 22, 2004, Tables SA10–SA11.

*Estimated, based on the rate of change during 1995-2001

shift from medium-high to high technology probably reflects the upward movement of Chinese advanced technology production, whereby more medium-high technology products are being sourced domestically, and imports are becoming more concentrated in the high-tech products, not available in China, and needed either to equip new plant construction and infrastructure or for inputs in final products for the domestic or export markets.

Combining the two high-tech and the two low-tech categories for imports, the higher tech share increased from 62.3 percent in 1992 to 69.5 percent in 2001, with a corresponding decline from 37.7 percent to 30.5 percent for the lower tech categories. The 2004 projection shows some further shift to 73.2 percent for higher tech imports and 26.8 percent for lower tech imports.

The overall picture is strikingly clear. China has rapidly shifted the structure of its trade in manufactures from low to high technology products, and this upward trend is likely to continue, as both the level of applied technology and wage rates trend steadily upward in China. This upward technological shift in the structure of Chinese exports, together with the exceptionally high growth in total Chinese exports, leads, in turn, to a steady upward movement of the level of Chinese high-tech exports compared with the other major exporters, shown in Table 4-2. Again, the actual figures for high-tech exports from 1992 to 2001, provided by the OECD, are projected to 2004, based on actual growth in total exports in 2002 through 2004.

Table 4-2
High Technology Manufactured Exports
($ billions)

	1992	1995	2001	Percent Growth 1992-2001	2004*
United States	120.7	146.8	251.0	108	280.2
EU**	96.1	140.1	217.0	127	322.6
Japan	100.7	137.9	118.4	18	155.8
China	9.3	21.5	64.4	592	143.2
Taiwan	21.1	37.4	55.1	161	80.6
Greater China	30.4	58.9	119.5	293	223.8
South Korea	26.7***	36.9	48.4	81***	72.5

*Estimated, based on actual growth in total exports in 2002-2004
**Excludes intra-EU trade
***1994, the earliest year in the source table; percentage growth 1994-2001

Source: OECD, *An Emerging Knowledge-Based Economy in China? Indicators From OECD Databases*, March 22, 2004, Table SA12

The percentage growth in high-tech manufactured exports from 1992 to 2001 varies greatly among the listed exporters in Table 4-2. China was far out in front with 592 percent growth, followed by Taiwan with 293 percent growth, while EU, excluding intra-EU trade, grew 127 percent, the United States 108 percent, and Japan only 18 percent. As a result, the Chinese level, in relative terms, rose from less than 10 percent of the Japanese level in 1992 to 54 percent in 2001 and from 8 percent to 26 percent of the U.S. level. The estimated figures for 2004 show Chinese high-tech exports rising to 92 percent of the Japanese level, 44 percent of the EU level, and 51 percent of the U.S. level. Clearly, Chinese high-tech export performance is moving China into the top four advanced technology exporters, and is on track, within ten years, to reach parity with the United States and the EU, and to double the Japanese level.

The other significant feature in Table 4-2 is the inclusion of the line for Greater China, which combines the high-tech exports of China and Taiwan. This is a relevant measure in view of the two already deeply integrated advanced technology sectors, particularly in information technology, described in Chapter 3. The consolidation also factors out the effects of Taiwanese companies using China as an "export platform," whereby Taiwanese higher tech components are combined with lower tech Chinese components to form a final product exported out of China. In any event, this has not dampened Taiwanese high-tech exports, which rose by 161 percent from 1992 to 2001. The Greater China high-tech export level rose from $30.4 billion in 1992 to $119.5 billion in 2001, reaching parity with the Japanese level and roughly half of the U.S. and the EU levels in the latter year. The projection to 2004 shows a further relative gain, with Greater Chinese exports at 144 percent of the Japanese level, 80 percent of the U.S. level, and 69 percent of the EU level. Hong Kong high-tech exports of $67.5 billion in 2001 are not included in the Greater China figures because most of these exports are reexports from China, which would be double counting; to the extent Hong Kong exports are produced in Hong Kong, however, the Greater China figures are even higher.

The broad conclusions of this section are stark. Chinese trade in manufactures, particularly exports, is moving steadily upward in terms of higher versus lower technology products, with the high technology categories already above 50 percent. This upward restructuring, together with the much faster growth in total manufactured exports, is catapulting China toward parity with the United States and the EU in high-tech exports within five to ten years, with Japan dropping back to a somewhat distant fourth place.   The extension of Chinese exports to Greater China, including Taiwan, accelerates this scenario significantly.

Sectoral Composition of Trade in Manufactures

The heavy orientation of trade in manufactures is also evident in global trade accounts, although data collection related to technology intensity is limited. There is no specific breakdown between high- and low-tech sectors in the global trade statistics reported by the WTO and the UN. The available WTO reporting by sector, however, does give a rough idea of how trade is heavily concentrated in the more advanced technology industries, as shown in Table 4-3.

Table 4-3
World Exports of Manufactures by Sector

	Percent Share	
	1995	*2003*
Total manufactures	100	100
Higher tech	65	68
Office and telecommunications equipment	16	17
Other machinery and equipment	24	23
Automotive products	12	13
Chemicals, including pharmaceuticals	13	15
Mixed tech	15	13
Iron and steel	4	3
Other semimanufactures	11	10
Lower tech	20	19
Textiles	4	3
Apparel	4	4
Other consumer goods	12	12

Source: WTO, *International Trade Statistics 2004*, Chart IV.I

The percentage distribution among the nine reported sectors of manufactures trade has been regrouped by the author in the table in terms of being "higher," "mixed," or "lower" tech in composition. The four higher tech sectors—office and telecommunications equipment, other machinery and equipment, automotive products, and chemicals, including pharmaceuticals—accounted for 65 percent of total manufactured exports in 1995, rising to 68 percent in 2003. This upward trend is probably understated because of the bursting of the telecommunications bubble in 2001, when world exports of the very high growth office and telecommunications equipment sector plunged by 13 percent and recorded only a 1 percent positive growth in 2002, before resuming the upward trend with 10 percent growth in 2003, which is continuing in 2004-2005. The other two groupings of mixed and lower tech industries experienced loss of market share between 1995 and 2003, with iron and steel down from 4 percent to 3 percent, textiles down from 4 percent to 3 percent, and apparel holding steady at 4 percent. It is noteworthy that these three latter sectors, which receive considerable public attention because of their political sensitivities, together account for only 10 percent of global manufactures trade, and are on a downward trend line as a share of global trade.

Table 4-4 presents the value of manufactured exports in 2003, as available by sector, for the "Big Four" largest exporters: the EU (15), the United States, Japan, and China. The next-largest exporters are listed in the footnote to the table, with South Korea in fifth place with $177 billion, or less than half the Chinese level. A judgment has to be made as to whether to include in the country comparison internal trade among the 15 EU members, which amounted to 59 percent of total EU manufactured exports of $2,358 billion in 2003. The EU figures in Table 4-4 are limited to the extra-EU exports of $957 billion, in view of the unified EU trade policy, which excludes this trade, among other things, from WTO dispute procedures, and in view of monetary union among most of the members. On this basis, the Big Four accounted for 59 percent of total manufactured exports, which would have risen to 70 percent if intra-EU trade were included, with above average shares for the higher tech sectors of automotive products and chemicals, and well below average shares for iron and steel, textiles, and apparel. The below average Big Four share of 53 percent for office and telecommunications equipment reflects the strong exports of other East Asians, including Malaysia, Singapore, South Korea, and Taiwan. The total East Asian export share in this sector approached 60 percent in 2003, again excluding intra-EU trade.

The most striking feature of Table 4-4 is the emergence in 2003 of China as a full member of the Big Four exporters of manufactures, especially following Chinese export growth of 22 percent in 2002 and 35 percent in 2003. In 2004, China, again with export growth of about 35 percent, passed Japan to become number three, at roughly two-thirds the U.S. level of exports and one-half the EU level. On current course, Chinese manufactured exports will surpass the U.S. level within three to five years. The relative Chinese performance, however, varies greatly by sector. China was already number one in 2003 for office and telecommunications equipment, and far ahead for apparel. Chinese exports in the automotive sector, in contrast, were only $4 billion in 2003, although Chinese companies are increasing exports to Southeast Asia and plan to begin exporting to Europe and North America by 2007.

Table 4-4
Big Four Exporters of Manufactures by Sector, 2003
($ billions)

	EU (15) (Extra)	United States	Japan	China	Big Four as percent of World*
Total Manufactures	957	587	439	397	59
Higher tech					
Office and telecommunications equipment	91	113	90	118	53
Other machinery and equipment	NA	NA	NA	NA	NA
Automotive products	125	69	103	4	63
Chemicals, including pharmaceuticals	175	92	39	20	62
Mixed-tech					
Iron and steel	24	7	18	5	42
Other semimanufactures	NA	NA	NA	NA	NA
Lower tech					
Textiles	26	11	6	27	51
Apparel	19	6	NEG	52	42
Other consumer goods	NA	NA	NA	NA	NA

Source: WTO, *International Trade Statistics*, 2004, Table IV (Various)

*After the Big Four, the next biggest exporters were South Korea ($177 billion), Canada ($165 billion), Taiwan ($141 billion), Mexico ($135 billion), Switzerland ($93 billion), Malaysia ($77 billion), Singapore ($66 billion, domestic exports), and Thailand ($60 billion). Noteworthy countries with smaller exports of manufactures were Russia ($38 billion), Brazil ($37 billion), and India ($37 billion in 2002).

One obvious conclusion that can be drawn from the discussion in this section is that more detailed trade data by sector is needed for the rapidly expanding advanced technology industries, which together with related foreign direct investment are the engine for global economic growth. The recommendation here is that the WTO and the OECD develop a common definition of high technology industries, starting with the information technology and telecommunications industries, which would become part of the annual WTO *International Trade Statistics* report, and thus provide more up-to-date trade data for the public and for the biennial and other assessments of these sectors by the OECD Science and Technology Directorate. China already participates in this OECD analytic work, and other East Asians, not members of the OECD, including Malaysia, Singapore, and Taiwan, should be invited to participate as well. Once properly defined by sector, such timely trade data for high technology or advanced technology trade could be provided at minimal additional cost from the existing WTO database.

Recent Chinese Advanced
Technology Trade Performance

Chinese trade data for advanced technology products are more current than the OECD data and more targeted on specific industries than the WTO data presented in the previous sections. *China's Customs Statistics Monthly, Exports & Imports* has, in recent years, provided two overlapping industry groupings—mechanical and electrical products and high-tech products—which have a similar scope to the OECD high and medium-high categories, and provides considerably more detail on individual industries. This data is presented in Table 4-5 for 2000, 2002, 2003, and 2004 for global exports and imports.

The two most striking characteristics of this recent trade performance are the high growth in both exports and imports and the especially rapid rise in the higher technology share of trade, particularly for exports. From 2000 to 2004, total exports of goods rose by 139 percent, compared with 207 percent for mechanical and electrical products, and 337 percent for high-tech products; total imports rose 149 percent, compared with 193 percent for mechanical and electrical products and 207 percent for high-tech products. As for the rising share of higher technology products in overall Chinese trade, the percentage distribution in the bottom section of Table 4-5 shows the shares for both higher tech categories rising sharply from 2000 to 2004: from 42 percent to 54 percent for the first category and from 15 percent to 28 percent for the "high-tech" category; and from 46 percent to 54 percent, and from 23 percent to 29 percent for the corresponding import categories. Since the two categories overlap, however, the percentage figures for the two categories cannot be added together.

These rapid increases in the shares of higher tech trade are an important indicator of how fast Chinese advanced technology industry is developing. These figures also confirm the 2004 projections of the OECD export figures in Table 4-1 that Chinese exports are now predominantly higher rather than lower tech. This restructuring of Chinese trade is confirmed by the declining export shares for textiles, apparel, and footwear, down sharply from 24 percent in 2000 to 18 percent in 2004. It is also noteworthy that

Table 4-5
Chinese Trade in Higher Technology Products
($ billions)

	Exports				Imports				Trade Balance 2004
	2000	2002	2003	2004	2000	2002	2003	2004	
(A) Total trade	249.2	325.6	438.4	593.4	225.1	295.2	412.8	561.4	+32.0
(B) Mechanical and electrical products	105.3	157.1	227.5	323.4	102.9	155.6	225.0	301.9	+21.5
Metal products	9.3	12.6	15.9	22.4	2.4	3.2	4.5	6.1	+16.3
Machinery	26.8	50.8	83.5	118.1	34.4	52.2	71.5	91.6	+26.5
Electric and electronic products	46.1	65.1	89.0	129.7	50.7	73.3	103.9	142.1	-12.4
Transport equipment	9.3	10.5	15.6	21.0	6.4	11.5	17.5	19.5	+1.5
Instrument and apparatus	6.3	7.4	10.6	16.2	7.3	13.5	25.1	40.2	-24.0
Other	7.5	10.7	13.0	15.9	1.7	2.0	2.4	2.5	+13.4
(C) High-tech products	37.0	67.9	110.3	165.5	52.5	82.8	119.3	161.4	+4.1
Biotechnology	0.1	0.2	0.2	0.2	0.1	0.1	0.1	0.1	+0.1
Life science	1.4	2.0	2.5	3.2	1.7	2.3	3.1	3.8	-0.6
Opto-electronics	1.0	1.3	1.8	3.8	0.9	1.5	2.2	3.2	+0.6
Computer and telecommunications	27.0	54.5	91.9	136.4	20.6	28.3	40.3	50.7	+85.7
Electronics	5.8	7.9	11.4	18.4	19.3	35.3	53.6	77.2	-58.8
Computer-integrated manufacturing	0.5	0.7	1.0	1.5	5.6	8.3	11.4	17.4	-15.9
Materials	0.3	0.2	0.4	0.7	0.8	1.6	2.4	2.3	-1.6
Aerospace	0.7	0.7	0.8	1.0	2.7	5.0	5.5	6.4	-5.4
Other technology	0.2	0.3	0.3	0.3	0.9	0.5	0.8	0.3	0
(D) Labor-intensive products	59.2	69.0	86.4	104.2	16.9	17.3	19.6	23.2	+81.0
Textile yarn, fabrics, and make-up articles	13.6	16.9	21.4	26.4	15.4	15.7	17.8	21.3	+5.1
Garments and clothing accessories	35.7	41.0	52.0	62.6	1.2	1.3	1.4	1.4	+61.2
Footwear and parts thereof	9.9	11.1	13.0	15.2	0.3	0.3	0.4	0.5	+14.7
Percentage distribution									
B / A	42	48	52	54	46	53	55	54	
C / A	15	21	25	28	23	28	29	29	
D / A	24	21	20	18	8	6	5	4	

Source: China's Customs Statistics, *Monthly Exports & Imports*

the shares of higher tech imports also increased sharply, reflecting the rapid growth of foreign direct investment in advanced technology industries, the large investment in more advanced technology infrastructure, and the use of China as an advanced technology export platform.

Tables 4-6 (A) and (B) present the Chinese trade figures for bilateral trade with the United States in selected higher technology industries. This data on bilateral trade does not match the higher tech categories in Table 4-5, which are provided only for global trade, but the industrial scope is largely the same. This higher tech bilateral trade, along with trade in apparel and footwear, is tracked back to 1996, when Chinese advanced technology production was just beginning to gather momentum.[2] These Chinese figures are lower than corresponding U.S. bilateral trade data, mainly because a substantial amount of Chinese exports reported by China as going to Hong Kong and other destinations ultimately goes to the United States, but this should not change greatly the sectoral shifts in Chinese trade with the United States presented in the table.

The U.S.-China bilateral trade figures confirm the trends for global Chinese trade in Table 4-5. Total Chinese exports to the United States grew from $26.7 billion in 1996 to $124.9 billion in 2004, or by 368 percent, while the higher tech exports (section B of the table) are up from $8.0 billion to $64.5 billion, or 706 percent. In contrast, exports of apparel and footwear (section C of the table) were up from $7.1 billion to $16.1 billion, or by only 127 percent. By sector, machinery and electronics, B2 and B3 in the table, were dominant, together accounting for 88 percent of the high-tech sector's total in 2004, which is consistent with the earlier WTO figures.

Total Chinese imports from the United States were up from $16.2 billion in 1996 to $44.7 billion in 2004, or by 176 percent. By sector, however, the aircraft and optical, etc., sectors were prominent, along with machinery and electronics.

The trade balance figures in the last column of Table 4-6(b) show a total surplus with the United States of $80.3 billion in 2004, of which $42.3 billion, or 53 percent, was in the higher tech category, and $13.8 billion, or 17 percent, was in apparel and footwear. Again, the Chinese trade surplus figures are considerably smaller than the corresponding U.S. figures on the trade deficit with China, to which the discussion turns shortly.

---

[2] The higher tech categorization for global trade figures in Table 4-5 is available only for more recent years, reflecting the more recent focus of the Chinese government on high technology trade performance.

Finally, the bottom two lines of the tables show the percentage shares of the higher and lower tech categories, with the familiar pattern of the higher tech export category rising steadily from 30 percent in 1996 to 52 percent in 2004. The import share for higher-tech sectors was stable, however, rising only 1 percent, from 49 percent to 50 percent, while the apparel and footwear sectors were predictably small throughout.

Recent U.S. Advanced Technology Trade Performance

U.S. trade data for advanced technology products is the most detailed and up-to-date indicator related to the growing U.S.-China rivalry in advanced technology industries. It is also the most disturbing indicator of an apparent decline in U.S. international competitiveness, both *vis-à-vis* China and on a global basis. U.S. trade in ATP was in substantial surplus during most of the 1990s and then swung sharply down into deficit beginning in 1999, as shown in Chart 4-1. A surplus of $29.9 billion in 1998 declined steadily to deficits of $16.6 billion in 2002, $26.8 billion in 2003, and $37.0 billion in 2004.

Chart 4-1

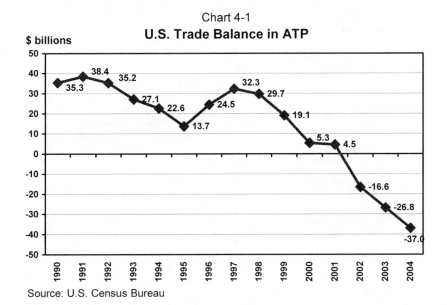

U.S. Trade Balance in ATP

Source: U.S. Census Bureau

Table 4-6 (A)
Chinese Exports to the United States
in Higher Technology Products
($ millions)

| | Chinese Exports | | | | |
	1996	2000	2002	2003	2004
(A) Total	26,685.5	52,103.8	69,950.5	92,473.6	124,947.7
(B) High-tech sectors	7,958.7	19,957.2	30,227.4	44,922.3	65,544.9
1. Pharmaceutical products	105.5	166.0	144.7	176.8	240.8
2. Nuclear reactors, boilers, machinery and mechanical appliances; parts thereof	2,439.4	6,855.1	12,056.5	21,361.0	30,000.1
3. Electrical machinery and equipment and parts thereof; sound recorders and reproducers, television image and sound recorders and reproducers, and parts and accessories of such articles	4,082.5	9,538.5	14,178.3	18,006.0	26,670.1
4. Railway or tramway locomotives, rolling-stock and parts thereof; railway or tramway track fixtures and fittings and parts thereof; mechanical (including electro-mechanical) traffic signaling equipment of all kinds	174.3	466.4	425.8	1,026.3	1,556.4
5. Vehicles other than railway or tramway rolling-stock, and parts and accessories thereof	483.9	1,182.5	1,726.6	2,458.7	3,688.4
6. Aircraft, spacecraft, and parts thereof	30.4	88.9	67.2	114.1	92.3
7. Ships, boats, and floating structures	1.2	33.7	36.6	22.7	29.6
8. Optical, photographic, cinematographic, measuring, checking, precision, medical or surgical instruments and apparatus; parts and accessories thereof	641.5	1,626.1	1,591.7	1,756.7	2,267.2
(C) Labor-intensive sectors	7,103.4	10,183.8	11,322.2	13,505.6	16,131.5
1. Apparel	3,231.5	4,557.2	5,427.6	7,192.7	9,060.0
2. Footwear	3,871.9	5,626.6	5,904.6	6,312.9	7,071.5
Percentage distribution					
B / A	30	38	43	49	52
C / A	27	20	16	15	13

Source: China's Customs Statistics, *Monthly Exports & Imports*

Table 4-6 (B)
Chinese Imports From the United States and Trade Balance in Higher Technology Products
($ millions)

| | Chinese Imports | | | | | Trade Balance |
	1996	2000	2002	2003	2004	2004
(A) Total	16,155.2	22,363.2	27,230.1	33,860.8	44,678.6	+80,269.1
(B) High-tech sectors	7,876.7	12,508.7	16,002.4	17,159.1	22,248.5	+42,296.4
1. Pharmaceutical products	36.6	68.0	103.1	116.5	139.2	+101.6
2. Nuclear reactors, boilers, machinery and mechanical appliances; parts thereof	3,755.5	4,503.2	5,515.2	6,017.8	7,836.9	+22,163.2
3. Electrical machinery and equipment and parts thereof; sound recorders and reproducers, television image and sound recorders and reproducers, and parts and accessories of such articles	1,818.0	4,699.7	5,654.4	5,398.0	7,626.6	+19,043.5
4. Railway or tramway locomotives, rolling-stock and parts thereof; railway or tramway track fixtures and fittings and parts thereof; mechanical (including electro-mechanical) traffic signaling equipment of all kinds	8.0	6.2	10.8	10.1	16.6	+1,539.8
5. Vehicles other than railway or tramway rolling-stock, and parts and accessories thereof	218.0	189.6	228.3	470.5	587.7	3,100.7
6. Aircraft, spacecraft, and parts thereof	1,269.5	1,454.3	2,329.5	2,312.2	2,521.7	-2,429.4
7. Ships, boats, and floating structures	3.3	9.6	37.8	25.8	45.2	-15.6
8. Optical, photographic, cinematographic, measuring, checking, precision, medical or surgical instruments and apparatus; parts and accessories thereof	767.8	1,578.1	2,123.3	2,808.2	3,474.6	-1,207.4
(C) Labor-intensive sectors	1,166.0	380.5	483.6	1,140.9	2,377.8	+13,753.7
1. Apparel	1,126.3	309.9	437.1	1,075.5	2,308.3	+6,751.7
2. Footwear	39.7	70.6	46.5	65.4	69.5	+7,002.0
Percentage distribution						
B / A	49	56	59	51	50	
C / A	7	2	2	3	5	

Source: China's Customs Statistics, *Monthly Exports & Imports*

China has been the largest source of the growing ATP deficit, but before examining the overall trends in ATP trade and the China relationship in particular, a definition of the ATP category of trade statistics, used by the United States, and the circumstances of its creation, are in order.[3] As noted earlier, "high-tech" trade was long defined in terms of broad industry sectors, such as the OECD four-sector grouping of aerospace, computers, electronics, and pharmaceuticals, and a similar "DOC3" categorization used by the U.S. Department of Commerce. This definitional approach was criticized because the aggregate industry data included a mixture of high-tech and low-tech products, with varying production processes, including the degree of R&D and engineering content. It also excluded truly high-tech products in other industry sectors. This issue came to a head when the aggregate DOC3 "high-tech" trade account shifted from a surplus of $24 billion in 1982 to a deficit of $3 billion in 1986. The negative shift was believed to reflect low-tech products within the aggregate industry data rather than a decline in the trade balance for truly high-tech products. To clarify this contention, the Census Bureau adopted a disaggregated approach of individual product selection, at the ten-digit commodity code level, where, based on the judgment of bureau industry analysts, the concentration of R&D and scientists/engineers/technical personnel was judged to be exceptionally high. Approximately 600 products were selected, which account for about one-third of U.S. manufactured exports and one-quarter of U.S. manufactured imports.[4] A subsequent comparison of the ATP with the aggregate DOC3 data for the years 1982, 1986, and 1987 confirmed the view that the deterioration of the high-tech trade account was due to low-tech products being included within high-tech industries. The Bureau of the Census report concluded that "at the level of individual products (i.e., the ATP grouping), the high technology sectors of the economy continue to enjoy a strong competitive advantage and are surprisingly healthy."[5]

---

[3] The ATP origins, as well as a full assessment of U.S. trade by sector and region, is contained in Ernest H. Preeg, *The Threatened U.S. Competitive Lead in Advanced Technology Products (ATP)* (Manufacturers Alliance/MAPI, March 2004).

[4] The creation of the ATP listing is described in Thomas Abbott, Robert McGuckin, Paul Herrick, and Leroy Norfolk, "Measuring the Trade Balance in Advanced Technology Products" (Bureau of the Census, Center for Economic Studies, January 1989). An example given of an overly broad "high-tech" industry is "Office and Computing Machines," which included low-tech calculators and adding machines together with high-tech computers.

[5] *Ibid,* p. 3.

The irony of this historical account is that the ATP grouping itself has now turned sharply negative, raising doubts as to whether the earlier "strong competitive advantage" assessment still prevails. Until recently, however, it was difficult to understand what was happening, because the Bureau of the Census trade reports provided only aggregate export and import figures for ATP. This was rectified in February 2004, when the report was expanded to include ATP trade by country and broken down into ten sectors, back through annual figures for 2002 and 2003. ATP trade thus now can be tracked in considerable detail.

Table 4-7 presents global U.S. trade in ATP by sector for the years 1998 and 2002-2004.[6] The three largest export sectors are information and communications (largely computers and telecommunications equipment), electronics (largely advanced design semiconductors), and aerospace (mainly Boeing). The three together accounted for 80 percent of the $201 billion of total U.S. ATP exports in 2004. On the import side, the information and communications sector dominates, with 56 percent of the $238 billion of total imports in 2004, followed by life science technology (including pharmaceuticals), and aerospace (mainly Airbus). The trade deficit of $37 billion in 2004 was likewise dominated by the $73 billion deficit for information and communications, offset in part by smaller surpluses for aerospace and electronics.

The regional composition of the trade balance is presented in Table 4-8 for total ATP trade ("All Technologies"), and in Table 4-9 for the information and communications sector. For total ATP trade in 2004, the United States had a $1 billion surplus with North American Free Trade Agreement (NAFTA) partners and a $6 billion surplus with the EU (15), although this was down from much larger surpluses in 1998. The "all other" category in the bottom line represents all parts of the world except North America, West Europe, and East Asia, which have relatively small capacity for advanced technology production and are thus large net importers of ATP. It is therefore no surprise that the United States continues to have an ATP surplus with these other parts of the world, although again the surplus is down from $23 billion in 1998 to $17 billion in 2004. And then there is East Asia, where the eight listed trading partners registered a very large deficit, rising from $23 billion in 1998 to $61 billion in 2004. The deficit

---

[6] The 1998 figures are from an earlier analysis by the National Science Foundation, which included only figures through 1999 and thus did not pick up the rapid decline which began in 1999.

Table 4-7
U.S. ATP Trade, World Total
($ millions)

	Exports				Imports				Trade Balance			
	1998	2002	2003	2004	1998	2002	2003	2004	1998	2002	2003	2004
All Technologies	186,553	178,567	179,787	201,452	156,673	195,151	207,196	238,478	+29,880	-16,584	-27,409	-37,026
Biotechnology	1,469	2,136	2,863	3,743	748	1,869	2,184	1,967	+721	+267	+679	+1,776
Life Science Technology	10,173	11,828	13,002	14,516	12,426	25,416	30,937	32,799	-2,253	-13,588	-17,935	-18,283
Opto-Electronics	1,944	2,430	2,467	3,506	3,952	5,443	5,255	7,795	-2,008	-3,013	-2,788	-4,289
Information & Communications	61,527	53,296	53,128	59,210	74,875	100,660	110,089	132,539	-13,348	-47,364	-56,961	-73,329
Electronics	38,156	42,747	46,597	48,564	33,923	26,592	25,135	27,454	+4,235	+16,155	+21,462	+21,110
Flexible Manufacturing	7,295	8,580	8,320	13,044	6,576	6,550	6,262	7,587	+719	+2,030	+2,058	+5,457
Advanced Materials	1,290	1,088	1,036	1,137	1,137	1,468	1,511	1,794	+153	-380	-475	-657
Aerospace	61,269	53,233	49,433	54,377	21,984	25,005	22,773	23,833	+39,285	+28,228	+26,660	+30,544
Weapons	2,177	1,558	1,452	1,852	288	406	461	540	+1,889	+1,152	+991	+1,312
Nuclear Technology	1,251	1,671	1,489	1,503	765	1,738	2,589	2,170	+486	-67	-1,100	-667

Source: National Science Foundation, *Science & Engineering Indicators 2002*, for 1998; Bureau of the Census for 2002-2004.

is spread widely among most of East Asia, but the deficit has grown most rapidly with China, where a bilateral trade balance in 1998 moved to deficits of $12 billion in 2002, $21 billion in 2003, and $36 billion in 2004. Thus, in 2004, for the first time, the bilateral ATP deficit with China roughly equaled the global deficit.   In parallel, Japan dropped back from being the source of the largest bilateral deficit, at $10 billion, in 1998, to $6 billion, or one-sixth of the Chinese deficit, in 2004. The one surplus account with Hong Kong, at $5 billion in 2004, reflects U.S. exports through Hong Kong to China, principally advanced-design semi-conductors, which reduces the combined China-Hong Kong deficit accordingly.[7]

Table 4-8
U.S. ATP Trade Balance by Region
All Technologies
($ billions)

	1998	2002	2003	2004
(1) World total	+29.9	-16.6	-27.4	-37.0
(2) NAFTA (Canada & Mexico)	+8.2	+0.1	NEG	+1.0
(3) EU (15)	+20.4	+2.3	+0.5	+5.7
(4) East Asia (4a – 4h)	-23.4	-34.5	-42.6	-60.5
(a) China		-0.1	-11.8	-21.1	-36.3
(b) Hong Kong	+3.0	+3.6	+4.1	+5.3
(c) Japan	-9.6	-6.8	-5.4	-5.7
(d) Malaysia	-5.0	-7.9	-8.6	-10.6
(e) Singapore	-5.7	-1.9	-2.0	-0.6
(f) South Korea	-1.9	-4.2	-4.8	-7.7
(g) Taiwan	-3.2	-4.2	-3.8	-2.8
(h) Thailand	-0.9	-1.3	-1.0	-2.1
(5) All other (world total minus 2-4)	+22.7	+15.5	+14.7	+16.8

Sources: NSF, *Science & Engineering Indicators 2002*, for 1998; Bureau of Census for 2002-2004

The U.S. deficit picture for the information and communi-cations sector is even bleaker, with the global deficit deteriorating from $13 billion in 1998 to $73 billion in 2004. In 2004, trade was in $2 billion deficit with NAFTA and in $7 billion surplus with the EU, the latter reflecting exports of computers and telecommunications equipment. The surplus with "all other" is down from $9 billion in 1998 to $8 billion in 2004, as a result of increasing competition from the East Asians, who in this sector

---

[7] In 2004, $3.6 billion out of the $5.3 billion U.S. ATP surplus with Hong Kong was in electronics, principally semiconductors. See Preeg, *op. cit.,* Table A14.

registered a bilateral U.S. deficit of $37 billion in 1998, rising to $87 billion in 2004. The rise of China to the largest bilateral deficit position is even more striking. In 1998 China accounted for only 8 percent of the $37 billion East Asian deficit, while in 2004, it was 45 percent of the $87 billion total deficit. By 2004, the U.S. sectoral deficit with China was triple that of second-place Malaysia.

Table 4-9
U.S. ATP Trade Balance by Region
Information and Communications Sector
($ billions)

	1998	2002	2003	2004
(1) World total	-13.3	-47.4	-57.0	-73.3
(2) NAFTA (Canada & Mexico)	+1.7	-1.9	-1.3	-1.6
(3) EU (15)	+12.7	+7.0	+7.3	+7.2
(4) East Asia (4a – 4h)	-36.7	-55.6	-66.2	-86.7
(a) China	-3.1	-14.7	-24.2	-39.2
(b) Hong Kong	+1.5	+1.1	+0.9	+0.8
(c) Japan	-9.2	-8.6	-8.1	-7.9
(d) Malaysia	-5.9	-9.6	-11.7	-13.4
(e) Singapore	-8.9	-5.8	-5.3	-5.6
(f) South Korea	-2.4	-7.8	-8.8	-11.5
(g) Taiwan	-6.8	-8.4	-7.1	-6.9
(h) Thailand	-1.9	-1.8	-1.9	-3.0
(5) All other (world total minus 2-4)	+9.0	+3.1	+3.2	+7.8

Sources: NSF, *Science & Engineering Indicators 2002*, for 1998; Bureau of Census for 2002-2004

Table 4-10 presents the bilateral ATP trade account with China for exports, imports, and trade balance, broken down by sector. For 2004, U.S. ATP exports to China were concentrated in the electronics ($3.1 billion), information and communications ($2.2 billion), and aerospace ($2.0 billion) sectors, reflecting the strong performance of Intel and Boeing in the first and third instances. The three sectors together accounted for 78 percent of total ATP exports to China. On the import side, information and communications dominated, with $41.4 billion, or 91 percent of total ATP imports, while opto-electronics was at $1.7 billion and electronics at $1.4 billion. The trade deficit of $36.3 billion in 2004 was likewise dominated by the $39.2 billion deficit for information and communications, offset modestly by surpluses for aerospace ($1.8 billion), and electronics ($1.6 billion).

Table 4-10
U.S. ATP Trade with China
($ millions)

	Exports				Imports				Trade Balance			
	1998	2002	2003	2004	1998	2002	2003	2004	1998	2002	2003	2004
All technologies	6,056	8,289	8,290	9,401	6,125	20,097	29,345	45,698	-69	-11,808	-21,055	-36,297
Biotechnology	6	11	15	12	12	13	17	16	-6	-2	-2	-4
Life science technology	197	461	654	725	231	433	481	577	-34	+28	+173	+148
Opto-electronics	45	108	98	179	677	1,857	1,257	1,653	-632	-1,749	-1,159	-1,474
Information & communications	1,494	1,857	1,921	2,156	4,603	16,582	26,149	41,380	-3,109	-14,725	-24,228	-39,224
Electronics	510	1,664	2,553	3,050	553	810	917	1,421	-43	+854	+1,636	+1,629
Flexible manufacturing	188	618	523	1,188	37	131	170	250	+151	+487	+353	+938
Advanced materials	34	27	39	47	18	40	74	97	+16	-13	-35	-50
Aerospace	3,556	3,499	2,434	1,987	64	99	124	172	+3,492	+3,400	+2,310	+1,815
Weapons	17	36	49	48	31	37	55	58	-14	-1	-6	-10
Nuclear technology	9	8	8	9	1	95	100	74	+8	-87	-92	-65

Source: National Science Foundation, *Science & Engineering Indicators 2002*, for 1998; Bureau of the Census for 2002-2004

These are the sobering figures of the U.S. trade account in ATP over the past six years. If international competitiveness is defined in terms of exports versus imports, there has been a dramatic deterioration in U.S. competitiveness for advanced technology products since 1998, predominantly with East Asia, and with a growing central deficit relationship with China. The fact that these trade figures are released with only a seven-week time lag, compared with one to three years for other measures of Chinese advanced technology development, makes them an important leading indicator for what lies ahead elsewhere. The United States still has a substantial lead in terms of innovation in leading-edge technologies, as evidenced in the performance of a number of American companies. There should be no question, however, that the sharp deterioration in the U.S. trade balance for ATP is a warning signal of great consequence that should not go unheeded. The recommended policy response to this warning signal is contained in Chapters 7-10.

One technical issue about the U.S. policy response which merits discussion at this point is the need for greater knowledge about the product mix within the overall ATP trade account. A listing of the 600 individual ATP items, scattered throughout various sectors, is available for a fee from the Census Bureau, but the content is difficult to evaluate in view of the technically drawn product definitions. For example, the import items with the largest imports from China in 2003 were: (1) Port Dgtl ADP Mach, <10kg, at least CPU, KBRD, DSPL ($4.2 billion); (2) Display Units, NESOI, without CRT ($2.9 billion); (3) PTS & Accessories of Mach of Heading of 8471; and (4) NESOI facsimile machines ($2.7 billion). Only 37 of the 600 items had imports from China of over $100 million in 2003, and such a select listing could be assessed by industry trade analysts to confirm the degree and intensity of advanced technology content. The Census Bureau industry experts, who update ATP selection from time to time, could undertake this task, perhaps together with NSF expert staff. An alternative would be a more independent assessment by the International Trade Commission (ITC), triggered by a request from the Congress.

More broadly, the ATP sectoral presentation could be broken down further, particularly for the dominant information and communications sector. The NSF survey of the 1990s, for example, broke out software, which amounted to $3.4 billion of exports and $0.7 billion of imports in 1999. A targeted breakout into several subsectors, linked to the prospect for technology innovation, could be revealing.

One response to avoid, however, and which is already being heard, is to dismiss the ATP categorization as technically flawed, citing a couple of examples of "commodity" type products, and thereby to ignore the sharp turn into deficit on overall ATP trade account. This amounts to shooting the messenger, which, from a policy perspective, would be derelict.

The Export Platform Issue

A frequent question is whether China is not principally an export platform, whereby high-tech components are imported, particularly by the export-oriented foreign firms in China, and then assembled with lower tech Chinese components into final products for export. If this were the principal formula for Chinese advanced technology exports, China could be considered the assembly vehicle for advanced technology development and production elsewhere, without having an advanced technology capability of its own. Some such importation of advanced technology com-ponents as input for exported products undoubtedly is taking place, and the more specific and relevant questions become the extent of such export platform operations, and the likely course ahead.

One fairly clear observation is that there is relatively little use of advanced technology imports from the United States for assembly and export back to the United States. U.S. ATP exports to China of $9 billion in 2004 were principally aircraft and semiconductors. Boeing aircraft are already final products, while advanced-design semiconductors by Intel and AMD, although key inputs in information technology products throughout the world, are not sufficient in themselves to justify export platform status. Other U.S. advanced technology exports of machinery and automotive parts are for sale in the Chinese market, while even where some products with U.S. components are exported, the East Asian market can be the principal destination. Finally, the fact that only 10 percent or less of foreign direct investment in China is by American companies limits the scope of U.S. generated export platform operations.

In contrast, to the extent export platforming is taking place, it is principally by the more technologically advanced East Asian investors in China—Taiwan, Japan, and South Korea, in particular—through their dominant foreign investment position in China, largely for export. Japanese investment in China, prin-cipally in electronics and other technology-intensive industries, was cited earlier as 65 percent export oriented, with half of the exports shipped back to Japan. There is thus a significant bilateral export platform relationship between Japan and China. The South Korean citation for Samsung, with wide-ranging production of electronic products in 26 Chinese plants, is another example that probably involves significant export platforming, with broadly targeted exports, including to the United States.

The largest export platform relationship is undoubtedly with Taiwan, based on its primary position as foreign investor in China. The discussion in Chapter 3 contained examples of how the more advanced R&D and engineering capabilities in Taiwan were being integrated with production operations in China, presumably in large part for export. Moreover, this relationship appears to have grown rapidly since 2001, based on Taiwanese exports by destination, shown in Table 4-11. Taiwanese exports to China, presumably through third-country ports, plus those to Hong Kong, increased from $31.7 billion in 2001 to $40.7 billion in 2002, $49.8 billion in 2003, and $63.8 billion in 2004. For some reason, most of this growth is in exports to China, up from $4.7 billion in 2001 to $34 billion in 2004, while exports to Hong Kong leveled off at about $30 billion. Some of these exports are for the internal Chinese market and a large proportion is semiconductors, but there is also likely to be a considerable export platform relationship in play. It is noteworthy that Taiwanese exports to the United States were of comparable magnitude to exports to China/Hong Kong through 2001, while by 2004, Taiwanese exports to China/Hong Kong were more than double exports to the United States.

Table 4-11
Taiwanese Exports by Destination
($ billions)

	World	China	Hong Kong	China Plus Hong Kong	United States	Japan
2000	148.3	4.2	31.3	35.5	34.8	16.6
2001	122.9	4.7	27.0	31.7	27.7	12.8
2002	130.6	9.9	30.8	40.7	26.8	12.0
2003	144.2	21.4	28.4	49.8	25.9	11.9
2004	174.0	34.0	29.8	63.8	28.1	13.2

Source: Directorate General of Customs, Ministry of Finance, ROC

The big question is how large is the export platform relationship or, more precisely, how much import content is there in Chinese high or advanced technology exports? Unfortunately, there are no precise figures, which can only be obtained from surveys of Japanese, Korean, and Taiwanese plants in China with respect to the domestic and import content shares of value added.

A rough idea of the likely magnitudes, however, can be derived from Table 4-12, which presents Chinese trade figures for 2002-2004 for the information technology and telecommunications sector, the predominant high technology sector where export platforming is concentrated. The three subsectors listed show a big export surplus in computer and telecommunications, $85.7 billion in 2004, in contrast to deficits of $58.8 billion and $15.9 billion in the other two subsectors. The export platforming presumably involves imports largely in the latter two subsectors reexported in the first subsector. Many, and probably most, imports, however, are for the domestic market rather than as components for export, as final products such as computers and telecommunications equipment, or as components for domestic products ranging from cell phones to PCs, consumer electronics, automobiles, and machinery. If, for example, half of the imports were for the domestic market, the average import content for exports in 2004 would have been 47 percent (i.e., $72.7 billion out of $156.3 billion). If three quarters of imports were for the domestic market, the import content share of exports would decline to 23 percent. This 23 percent to 47 percent span could be considered a reasonable range of likely import content, subject to confirmation or revision based on plant surveys.

Table 4-12
Chinese Trade in the Information Technology and Telecommunications Sector
($ billions)

	2002	2003	2004
(A) Exports			
Computer and telecommunications	54.5	91.9	136.4
Electronics	7.9	11.4	18.4
Computer-integrated manufacturing	0.7	1.0	1.5
Total	63.1	104.3	156.3
(B) Imports			
Computer and telecommunications	28.3	40.3	50.7
Electronics	35.3	53.6	77.2
Computer-integrated manufacturing	8.3	11.4	17.4
Total	71.9	105.3	145.3
(C) Trade balance			
Computer and telecommunications	+26.2	+51.7	+85.7
Electronics	-27.4	-42.2	-58.8
Computer-integrated manufacturing	-7.6	-10.4	-15.9
Total	-8.8	-1.0	+11.0

Source: China's Customs Statistics, *Monthly Exports & Imports*

The final question is whether export platforming in China will expand or contract over time, and the assessment here is that it will diminish, at least in relative terms, as Chinese productive capability moves up the technology ladder, both in production by foreign companies sourcing more extensively within China, and by Chinese companies investing heavily in R&D and higher technology product development. This is confirmed by the bottom line of Table 4-12, where the trade balance for the overall information technology and telecommunications sector shifted from a deficit of $8.8 billion in 2002 to a surplus of $11.0 billion in 2004. This question, in fact, goes to the heart of the central inquiry of this study: Is China an emerging advanced technology superstate in its own right?

Chapter 5

The Chinese Advanced Technology Prospect: A Net Assessment

The previous chapters have examined in considerable detail three principal dimensions of the rapid development of Chinese advanced technology industry over the past ten years: the internal resource commitments, most importantly for R&D and university training for scientists and engineers; the central, catalytic role of FDI; and the very rapid growth and restructuring into advanced technology products of Chinese trade. Together, these three dimensions, assessed in both quantitative and qualitative terms, constitute the foundation for concluding that China, indeed, is an emerging advanced technology superstate.

This conclusion requires, first, specificity as to the definition of a superstate and the projected timeframe for China's reaching a full-fledged superstate status. The superstate definition can be taken from Herman Kahn's rendering in 1970 for Japan, quoted in Chapter 1, with only minor modification: China almost inevitably will achieve giant economic, technological, and financial stature, will likewise become financially and politically powerful in international affairs, and, in the not too distant future, will become a military superpower as well. As for the timeframe for reaching advanced technology superstate status, the assessment here is that it will be reached within ten years, or by 2015. China has already come a long way since placing top priority on advanced technology industrial development in 1995, and the strong momentum on all fronts to continue the rapid upward trajectory for a second ten-year period provides ample scope to achieve superstate status as here defined.

This superstate outcome is not, of course, certain, and is contingent on a number of evolving developments within a very dynamic Chinese economy and polity. A highly disruptive turn of events could derail the whole process, such as a military conflict with the United States over Taiwan, or a civil war within China. Such events over the coming ten years are most unlikely, however, and are subsumed here within the "almost inevitable" quali-fication. The principal developments that will surely influence the outcome and require careful consideration relate to the course ahead within the advanced technology sector, the structural adjustment that will take place within the overall Chinese economy, and the directions of social and political change under way within China.

The Course Ahead Within the Advanced Technology Sector

The course ahead within the Chinese advanced technology sector will be determined essentially by the outcome for three interacting developments currently in progress: the continuing momentum of the basic indicators presented in Chapters 2-4; the relative rise of Chinese company participation; and the blossoming of technology innovation within China.

Continuing Momentum of the Basic Indicators

Assuming that China continues a high 7 percent to 9 percent annual rate of GDP growth, which is assessed positively at the conclusion of this chapter, the current rapid pace of broadening and deepening of the advanced technology sector, in terms of internal resource commitments, private sector investment, and trade, should continue as well, with China reaching parity with the United States and the EU, in almost all respects, by 2015, while pulling far ahead of fourth-place Japan.

The internal resource commitments, primarily for R&D and education, even at a somewhat reduced rate of growth, are firmly on course toward quantitative parity with the United States and the EU by 2015.   Chinese growth in R&D expenditures was 22 percent per year in 1995-2002, compared with 6 percent in the United States and 5 percent in the EU and Japan.   Projected to 2015, even at a lower 15 percent rate of growth, these figures show the Chinese level at three-quarters the U.S. level, more than 25 percent higher that the EU level, and well over double the Japanese level. These projections, based on relative GDP projections as presented in Table 2-1, result in Chinese R&D at 2.9 percent of GDP in 2015, compared with 3.4 percent in the United States, 2.4 percent in the EU, and 4.1 percent in Japan. The 2.9 percent for China appears reasonable, in view of the rapid rise from 1 percent in 2000 to at least 1.5 percent in 2005. As for the education of scientists and engineers, China is already well ahead of the other three for domestic engineering graduates, not to mention the reflow of Chinese graduates from U.S. and European universities, and it is rapidly closing the gap for science and engineering doctoral degrees. There is little doubt that, by 2015, China will be *primus inter pares* with the United States and the EU in terms of the number of scientists and engineers.

The levels of FDI are more difficult to project. FDI into China could continue to grow from its $61 billion level in 2004, or it could level off or even decline somewhat. In any event, however, the central driving force of foreign investors for manufacturing sector R&D, already with over 700 R&D centers, advanced technology exports, and the provision of experience and training for tens of thousands of Chinese engineers and managers, will continue to grow in absolute terms, probably at a strong, double-digit annual rate.

There is little question that China will pass by the United States to become the number one trading nation within three to five years, and that it will overtake the EU (excluding intra-EU trade) well before 2015. Moreover, the share of Chinese exports in high technology industries, already above 50 percent, will continue to rise, probably to the 70 percent to 80 percent range by 2015, driven in large part by the inevitable upward adjustment of the yuan exchange rate, as discussed below.

There will thus be rough parity, by 2015 and probably before, among China, the United States, and the EU, in all of the basic quantitative indicators of advanced technology superstate status.

The Relative Rise of Chinese
Company Participation

A major qualitative dimension as to how the Chinese superstate will evolve concerns the relative role of Chinese company participation in the advanced technology sector, both as a supplier of inputs to foreign investors and as competitive multinational companies in their own right. On both counts, all indicators are for a major increase in participation by Chinese companies, even likely dominance in some industries. Virtually all foreign companies producing in China are seeking to expand supplier relationships within China and thereby increase the degree of Chinese value added in the final product. Cost incentives abound and quality control is improving, often with technical assistance from the foreign firms, while the Chinese government offers financial incentives and applies political pressures to speed up the process.

A more fundamental development is the emergence of Chinese companies as multinational competitors. This is already beginning to happen, and participation will likely broaden over the next several years in many advanced technology industries. Front-runners include Huawei for telecommunications equipment,

Lenovo in computers, TCL for televisions, Haier for consumer white goods, SMIC for semiconductors, and Chery and Shanghai Automotive Industry Corp. for automobiles. The common strategy is to establish brand-name recognition, develop quality product reputation, and build a major, leading-edge R&D program. There is likewise a common marketing approach of starting within the Chinese market, then moving abroad to developing countries, particularly in Southeast Asia, and finally penetrating the industrial country markets. Chinese automobile companies have announced stage-three marketing initiatives in Europe and the United States, and others, such as Huawei and Lenovo, are not far behind. Chinese companies in the petroleum and mining sectors, mostly state-owned, are also rapidly expanding their overseas direct investment in Asia, Africa, and Latin America, often with official financial support.

The outlook is therefore for a major relative expansion of Chinese company participation with the overall Chinese advanced technology sector, although this should take place together with continued expansion of foreign company production, in view of the very high overall growth of Chinese GDP and exports. There is also a risk, however, that Chinese government actions to favor its "national champions" over foreign investors, through various discriminatory policy measures (described in Chapter 9) fueled by nationalist if not xenophobic pressures, could have substantial adverse impact on the investment climate for foreign companies, and thereby decrease the momentum for continued expansion toward higher levels of technology and innovation. Such a nationalist turn against multinational companies is, in fact, the most serious potential economic threat to Chinese superstate status by 2015.

The Blossoming of Technology Innovation Within China

This is the decisive factor, not only for ensuring Chinese status as an advanced technology superstate, but also for the central challenge posed to long-standing U.S. leadership in technology innovation, with major economic and national security implications for the future U.S. role in international affairs. It is also the most controversial area, with many observers expressing skepticism that China will become a serious, leading-edge innovator, at least over the coming ten years. Hard information, one way or the other, is still limited, but the assessment here is that China is developing the capacity for such innovation, within the public and private sectors, by both foreign and Chinese companies, and that China will very likely become one of the three principal technology innovation centers, along with the United States and the EU, by 2015.

The Chinese top priority commitment to technology innovation was emphasized in a speech by Premier Wen Jiabao in Beijing on April 1, 2005: "Science and technology are the decisive factors in the competition of comprehensive national strength. . . . We must introduce and learn from the world's achievements in advanced science and technology, but what is more important is to base ourselves on independent innovations because it is impossible to buy core technology . . . independent innovation is the national strategy."[1] The Chinese government is pursuing this strategy in the public sector through its projected increase in basic research and public sector R&D in areas ranging from nanotechnology to genetically modified agricultural products to a manned space program.

The priority on innovation in the Chinese private sector is evident in the results of company surveys in China and the United States in the first half of 2004.[2] There were 406 Chinese respondents—41 percent private Chinese companies, 25 percent joint ventures, 25 percent state-owned enterprises, and 9 percent foreign companies—and 681 American respondents. Related to technology innovation, the companies were asked to choose their three most important corporate objectives out of a listing of eight such objectives, and the results are presented in Table 5-1. "High quality" received the highest scores from both the Chinese and American respondents, with 72.9 percent and 69.6 percent, respectively, listing it as among the three top objectives. The rankings for "innovation," in contrast, show a wide divergence. Innovation has the second-highest score for the Chinese companies, at 54.2 percent, while U.S companies scored it next to last, at only 26.3 percent. These survey results may not be statistically significant, but they are at least a potent signal of the high priority placed on innovation in the Chinese managerial mindset.

A February 2005 report by the task force on the future of American innovation concluded that U. S. leadership in research and discovery "is eroding rapidly as other countries commit significant resources to enhance their own innovative capabilities,"

---

[1] Cited in Michael Pillsbury, "China's Progress in Technological Competitiveness: The Need for a New Assessment" (paper presented to the U.S.-China Economic and Security Review Commission, Palo Alto, April 21, 2005), p. 5.

[2] David Drickhamer, "Manufacturers Like Us," November 1, 2004, pp. 1-5, at www.industryweek.com/currentarticles.

and that China "has been investing heavily in nanotechnology and already leads the U.S. in some areas ... and is making rapid progress in biotechnology."[3]

Table 5-1
Top Objectives of Chinese and U.S. Manufacturers
(percent ranked as one of the top three objectives)

Chinese Manufacturers		U.S. Manufacturers	
1. High quality	72.9	1. High quality	69.6
2. *Innovation*	54.2	2. Service and support	53.4
3. Service and support	40.9	3. Total value	36.9
4. Low cost	27.6	4. Fast delivery	34.7
5. Product variety	24.9	5. Low cost	28.3
6. Fast delivery	20.2	6. Customization	26.7
7. Total value	16.5	7. *Innovation*	26.3
8. Customization	11.8	8. Product variety	15.4

Source: www.industryweek.com. Current articles, November 1, 2004, pp.4-5. Reprinted with permission.

Examples of Chinese innovation and new technology applications include the following: [4]

• The planned launch of more than 100 satellites by 2020 to form a global earth observation system;

• Seven projects sponsored by the National Astronomical Observatories, including the "Giant Eye" telescope that will have the highest spectrum acquiring rate in the world, the SST spatial telescope for international solar space research, and an infrared vacuum solar tower for solar physics;

• The Dawning 4,000A Shanghai supercomputer that can operate at ten trillion calculations per second, putting it in third place behind U.S. and Japanese supercomputers; and

• The Godson II central processing unit (CPU) computing chip to support the 64-bit Linux operating system, the first high-performance CPU chip for which China has proprietary intellectual property rights.

---

[3] "The Knowledge Economy: Is the United States Losing Its Competitive Edge?" February 16, 2005, at www.futureofinnovation.org. The task force was comprised of 21 academic and private sector organizations and companies, such as the American Electronics Association, the American Physical Society, the Material Research Society, Intel, Lucent, and Microsoft.

[4] Pillsbury, *op. cit.*, pp. 10-14. He presents a total of 17 examples of recent Chinese programs in science and technology.

These observations lead to the assessment that China will very likely become one of the principal centers of advanced technology innovation, but more detailed information is needed to draw a more definitive conclusion. The lack of interest in or resources devoted to collecting such information by the U.S. government is dismaying, and stands in extraordinary contrast to the intensive tracking of Soviet advanced technology capabilities by U.S. intelligence agencies during the Cold War. This lack of official U.S. interest in Chinese advanced technology innovation is addressed more fully in Chapters 7 and 10.

In conclusion, the prospective developments within the Chinese advanced technology sector strongly support the conclusion that China is on track to become an advanced technology superstate by 2015, if not sooner.

Structural Adjustments in the Overall Chinese Economy

Major structural changes will inevitably occur in the Chinese economy over the coming ten years, which may be painful or disruptive to certain sectors or regions, but unless there is serious policy mismanagement, all of the economic fundamentals are in place to continue a very high annual rate of GDP growth of 7 percent to 9 percent, which would support continued forward momentum in the advanced technology sector along the lines described in the previous section. Indeed, if the structural changes are managed in a reasonably competent manner, the resulting restructured economy should be even more conducive to further broadening and deepening of the advanced technology sector.

The direction of inevitable structural change, in broadest terms, will be a relatively smaller role for the industrial sector and manufactured exports as the engine for growth in the overall Chinese economy, and a progressively larger growth role for other sectors, including expanded economic infrastructure construction, social services, and consumer demand. As shown in Table 2-2, the industrial share of Chinese GDP in 2002 was 52 percent, roughly double that of the United States and the EU, and industrial production grew about 15 percent in 2004. Exports grew 35 percent per year in 2003 and 2004, and should come close to that again in 2005. Putting these very high growth figures in the context of recent overall Chinese growth of 9 percent, it is evident that the other half of Chinese GDP has been growing at rates well below 9 percent. This cannot be sustained, and at some point soon there will be a shift to more balanced growth. The change will be driven largely by market forces, which should be reinforced by policies of the Chinese government and its major trading partners. Higher growth rates for health and education services, infrastructure, domestic energy supply, environmental improvements, and the full range of consumer products would offset lower rates of growth for industrial production and manufactured exports. The adjustment would involve a shift in national savings, currently at the extraordinary level of more than 40 percent of GDP, away from investment in industry, heavily oriented toward exports, and related large purchases of foreign exchange by the Central Bank, and toward investment in other sectors and personal consumption. The process would include an appreciation of the yuan and substantial growth in real personal incomes. A very consumer-oriented middle class, already about 300 million strong and growing steadily throughout the country, would be a critical catalyst for this structural adjustment to more broadly based growth, just as foreign direct investment has been the catalyst for the initial phase of industrial and export-led growth.

In many respects, this scenario would be a dream world for any politician running for reelection, and even for a Communist Central Committee that needs a broad base of public acquiescence if not formal approval: improved health care and education, environmental improvements, and more adequate roads and bridges; and lower prices for gasoline and imported products and cheaper foreign vacations, as a result of an appreciated yuan. There will also be painful adjustment costs from such structural adjustment, however, involving the phase-out of noncompetitive or insolvent industrial enterprises, principally state-owned enterprises, with deeply embedded political interests. These, however, can be addressed through targeted adjustment assistance programs.

How the whole process will play out, by sector and region, is beyond the scope of this study. There is a growth industry of studies about Chinese health care, the environment, agriculture, and the labor force more broadly.[5] The commentary here is limited to the central and most important area of policy reform, which will largely drive the outcome in the other sectors, and which has direct links to international trade and investment

---

[5] For a primer on the challenges ahead for the Chinese health care sector and the environment, see *The Economist*, August 21, 2004, pp. 20-24 and 55-57; a full assessment of an increasingly efficient and market-oriented agriculture sector is provided in Rosen, *et. al, op. cit.*, 2004; a detailed analysis of Chinese employment in the manufacturing sector is contained in Banister, *op. cit.*, 2004.

relationships: financial sector reform. The increasingly complex and technologically advanced Chinese economy is vitally in need of a more responsive and efficient financial services sector if it is to achieve its full potential.

Financial sector reform involves both the banking sector within China and international financial relationships. Reform of the banking systems within China is moving forward at a rapid though uneven pace.[6] The China Banking Regulatory Commission, established in 2003, requires all banks to meet global capital adequacy standards by 2007, and 19 Chinese banks met global standards by the end of 2004. Twelve foreign banks have been approved to buy strategic stakes in Chinese banks, and nine more are headed toward approval. In October 2004, banks were allowed full freedom to set their lending rates, and thus for the first time can price their loans to reflect the risk profile of the borrower. The Bank of China, one of the largest state banks, is undergoing a thorough restructuring and plans to list on the Hong Kong stock market. The largest state-owned banks, however, are for the most part still saddled with massive amounts of non-performing loans and bloated management prone to corrupt practices. The overall transformation to a market-based competitive banking sector may require a very large bailout from the $660 billion Central Bank reserve account, but a successful result will work to allocate financial resources to the more productive and innovative companies throughout the Chinese economy.

The international financial dimension is deeply linked to internal banking reform. The extraordinary fact is that China is the third-largest trading nation, with an economy wide open to $50 billion to $60 billion per year of foreign investment, and yet its currency is nonconvertible on capital account. This is a formula for resource misallocation and corruption on a grand scale. It is also a reverse sequence from the international economic history of the past half century, beginning with West Europe after the Second World War, when currency convertibility was a normal early step to facilitate the progressive liberalization of trade and foreign investment. Current Chinese international financial relationships are further complicated by the long-standing maintenance of a fixed exchange rate to the dollar far below a market-

---

[6] "Banking sees transformation from Chinese economy, weakest link to tower of strength," *Financial Times*, November 18, 2004; and "Chinese banks line up to meet global standards on level of capital reserves," *Financial Times*, November 18, 2004.

based level, which has required the Chinese Central Bank, since 2001, to buy $100 billion to $200 billion per year in foreign exchange, in order to prevent a sharply higher black market rate for the yuan. Again, this performance is fundamentally different from the early fixed rate period of international finance through 1971, when major trading nations periodically adjusted their fixed rates by 10 percent, 20 percent, or more when they drifted out of line.

The subject of the undervalued yuan as related to IMF and WTO strictures on currency manipulation is discussed in detail in Chapter 8. The relevant point here is that a major revaluation to a market-based level would have a strong positive impact on needed structural change within the Chinese economy. The resulting lower prices for imports would reduce inflationary pressures and increase consumer purchasing power. A major financial shift to the domestic economy would result from the reduced need for the Central Bank to absorb $200 billion of domestic savings, as it did in 2004, to buy low-interest foreign securities. As for trade, and advanced technology trade in particular, a market-based exchange rate would tend to reduce or eliminate the overall trade surplus, but the adjustment would also accelerate the transition of Chinese exports away from labor-intensive industries, such as textiles and footwear, toward even greater concentration in advanced technology products. This was the earlier experience of Japan, South Korea, and Taiwan, and China has been delaying the transition through an undervalued currency, to the detriment of lower income textile exporters in particular.

The structural reforms are a lot easier to explain than to implement, and the adjustment process will include pockets of especially harsh adjustments for some industries and regions. These adjustments should not cause major disruption in the overall economy, however, given the high rate of national growth and a reasonably well-managed policy course. One result, in any event, of direct relevance to this study, is that adverse effects on the advanced technology sector should be relatively mild, within the context of a structural shift in demand toward greater concentration on the domestic market. As for a well-managed policy course, much will depend on the direction of social and political change within China in the decade ahead.

Directions of Social and Political Change

The course ahead for social and political change in China is a far more speculative subject, but there should be no doubt that there will be far-reaching changes as China moves rapidly to become a more affluent, advanced technology superstate, and to become, in effect, a fully engaged information age society. The likely directions of change, for the most part, are also fairly evident, even if the form and pace of change cannot be specified. For presentational purposes, it is useful to discuss the social and political forces separately, although in many ways they are interacting.

Social Changes Ahead

The Chinese society is in the process of fundamental change in a number of respects, and the commentary here is limited to a brief enumeration of the principal changes, with particular reference to how such change will impact on the further development of advanced technology industries. One central and obvious change is the rapid rise in education levels, from the tripling of university graduates in less than ten years to the more technical information age curricula at the primary and secondary school levels. The result is an ever-more knowledgeable population, with improved technical training for higher skill and professional jobs.

Closely related to a more highly educated population is the veritable explosion of communications throughout the country through cell phones, e-mail, satellite TV, films, magazines, and contact with foreigners through travel abroad, as well as through the burgeoning tourism trade within China. The expanding knowledge base of the Chinese people is a mutually reinforcing process of extended formal education and constant communication on wide-ranging subjects. The era of the isolated, inward-oriented peasant community, with low levels of education and exposure to the outside world, is fast becoming history.

The higher education levels, together with the creation of higher skill jobs in the industrial sector, now spreading to service industries and agriculture, are producing not only higher income levels, but greater economic independence. Professionals, skilled workers, and small business owners are living better lives and are keenly aware of alternative opportunities to improve their circumstances further. Lower skill and unskilled workers are also becoming able to choose between alternative job opportunities, as evident in hiring difficulties and work stoppages over higher pay and benefits in factories that formerly had captive labor forces at rock-bottom wages.

Higher income levels and greater knowledge about the overall course of the economy are also creating public interest and concerns beyond immediate material needs. The relatively poor quality of health care and serious degradation of the environment are areas that are receiving greater scrutiny and demands for improvement from the better-informed and more affluent population.

All of the foregoing leads to a revised set of values wherein material progress in one's lifetime is both feasible and subject to further upward movement, to the extent one works hard and is productive. Conspicuous consumption is admired today in China as it was a century ago in the United States. This belief in economic progress carries over to children, where education related to future job opportunities becomes a top family priority.

Finally and most broadly, the rapidly expanding, relatively affluent middle class is moving to center stage in Chinese society. About 300 million today, the middle class could expand to 500 million to 600 million in another decade, and thus play a decisive role in everything from consumer preferences to decisions about health care and the environment to criticisms of public policy more broadly.

These are truly momentous social changes, and as for direct impact on the continued momentum for advanced technology development, they constitute an unqualified plus. They all support upgraded technical skills, incentives to innovate and be more productive, and burgeoning consumer demand for advanced technology products throughout the Chinese economy.

Political Changes Ahead

Political changes in China are far more difficult to project, with the outer limits ranging from even more severe authoritarian rule, to a relatively peaceful transition to democratic government to civil war. The likely outcome will probably fall somewhere inside these limits and involve more contained periods of political turbulence or a relatively peaceful and nondisruptive process of step-by-step democratization. Two principal areas of possible change need to be considered with respect to the impact on advanced technology industry development: democratization and nationalism.

A process of democratization within China, whatever the pace and modalities, is almost inevitable as China progresses toward becoming an affluent, more highly educated, information-based society with a dominant middle class. Forces for democratization stem from the whole process of market-driven investment and job creation assessed in Chapters 2-4, as well as from the structural changes in the economy and the social changes under way described in the foregoing parts of this chapter. Recent historical experience has been that an advanced industrialized economy is simply too complex and subject to change to be governed by an authoritarian central command. This has been the general story throughout the newly industrialized grouping of countries over the past two decades, whereby authoritarian rule, step by step or more abruptly, has given way to private sector and civil-society decision making. External pressures for democratization and respect for individual rights have also been building in recent years, including throughout East Asia. In view of the enormous size and dynamism of current Chinese economic and social development, such a democratic transition will be put to its most demanding test in China, with greatest global consequence.

The democratization process thus far has focused heavily on the shift to market-oriented decisions within the economy, most dramatically in the manufacturing sector, with large participation by foreign companies. As a practical matter, government control is becoming more and more decentralized, with approval of private investments of up to $100 million now left to provincial or local governments. The rule of law is initially being strengthened, as in many developing countries, in the area of contract and property rights, leaving individual rights to follow in the wake, as the commercial rule of law generates institutional roots. The fundamental reform of the banking system will be another important step toward reduced government control over the economy.

In more political terms, democratization through greater free-dom of communication, albeit within strict guidelines, is apparent in the press, films, and most importantly the Internet. Public complaints and protests over many issues are becoming more common, and the government has to listen. Finally, elections are taking place, with strong public appeal, at the grassroots, village level, although thus far limited to the election of communist party-approved candidates. This is a camel's nose under the tent worth watching.

The most difficult political challenge for continued Chinese authoritarian rule is corruption. The challenge is officially acknowledged, and the government takes frequent actions against corruption, with harsh penalties, including capital punishment. But it is a losing battle, as has always been the case under authoritarian rule. Lord Acton warned that power corrupts and absolute power corrupts absolutely. A corollary to this dictum is offered here with respect to the scope of corruption: the broader the financial resources controlled by the power, the higher the absolute levels of corruption. In this context, the second-largest national economy, growing at 9 percent per year, has an unprecedented potential scope for corruption under existing authoritarian rule. The only feasible antidote is checks and balances on public power, which is a potent instrument of democratization.

President Hu Jintao, since assuming power in 2004, has disappointed observers hoping to see some democratic initiatives, however modest in scope, from this new generation of leadership. Instead, a harder line has been taken to suppress individual freedoms of speech and religion, in particular. The underlying forces for democratic change nevertheless continue to build, and may come to a head as parallel political pressures are stoked with respect to Chinese nationalism.

Nationalism has deep roots in China back through its history as the Middle Kingdom, and including pervasive xenophobia related to the many invasions and exploitations of China by foreign powers. The issue now is how this nationalist feeling will play out as China rises to become a superstate in economic terms and, to an increasing extent, a major military power as well.

In some forms, national pride and patriotism can be a positive force, as, for example, when they inspire defense against foreign enemies. The Chinese hosting of the Olympic Games in 2008 should be another positive rallying point for national pride and achievement. In the scientific and technology fields, nationalism is also engaged as a justification for committing resources to raise productivity and encourage innovation. A more prominent role for basic research at leading universities and a high-visibility space program are initiatives driven, in large part, by a sense of national pride.

The dark side to nationalism, however, has a long and sorrowful history dating from the creation of the nation state. The most insidious use for nationalism is as justification for authoritarian rule. This justification is being offered now in China, with the demise of communist ideology as the rationale for a one-party dictatorship. The nationalist card was played strongly against Japan in early 2005, largely in reaction to Japanese support for U.S. Taiwan policy, and both governments have appealed to nationalist sentiment in historical terms. Thousands of Chinese in the streets and millions by e-mail protesting Japanese transgressions, however, can be a threatening precedent for continued authoritarian rule, and it was widely reported that at the same time, independently, thousands of Chinese were in the streets in an outlying province, protesting over economic grievances.

The impact of political change on the continued expansion of advanced technology industry is unclear, but it could be significant. The possible use of nationalist appeal to discriminate against foreign investors has already been noted. A broader indirect adverse impact would result if the Chinese government were to resist economic reforms because those groups adversely affected during the transition might spill out into the streets for lack of an alternative democratic way to be heard.

The Chinese Versus the
Japanese Superstate

Skeptics of an emerging Chinese superstate like to make a comparison with the rising Japanese superstate during the 1970s and 1980s that stalled out in the 1990s and is now in a state of relative decline within East Asia. Can or will this not happen to China as well once it reaches a certain plateau of near parity with the United States and Europe? The assessment here is that the Japanese and Chinese paths to technology-driven modernization and economic growth have been different in critical respects, and that the rise of China to advanced technology superstate status is far more assured today than was the case earlier for Japan.

The emerging Japanese superstate projected by Herman Kahn in 1970 was based on continued very high economic growth driven by an export-oriented manufacturing sector, which led him to conclude: "It is now almost inevitable that at some point in the 70's or early 80's the Japanese economy will obtain a level entitling it to such descriptions as 'giant' or 'super.'"[7] Allowing for some overstatment, this is what happened through the 1980s, with growing concern in the United States that Japan would overtake it in terms of advanced technology leadership. The Japanese superstate image reached its apogee in 1988 with the best seller, *Trading Places: How We Allowed Japan to Take the Lead*, by Clyde Prestowitz, in which he explained: "Whether in disk drives, robots, printers, optical fiber electronics, satellite ground stations, or advanced industrial ceramics, the Japanese have come to dominate. . . . Even the U.S. level in such areas as aircraft and biotechnology is rapidly being whittled away. . . . Even more important, the United States is losing basic leadership in technologies. . . . The National Academy of Engineering reviewed the competitive situation in thirty-four critical areas such as artificial intelligence, optoelectronics, and systems engineering and control, and concluded Japan to be superior to the United States in twenty-five of the technologies."[8]

---

[7] Herman Kahn, *op.cit.*, p. 87.
[8] Clyde V. Prestowitz, Jr., *Trading Places: How We Allowed Japan to Take the Lead* (Basic Books, 1988), p. 11.

The reasons for the peaking out of Japanese technological advance in the early 1990s can be traced to the Kahn analysis, which articulated 13 positive characteristics of Japanese economic performance and 10 possible arguments for expecting an economic slowdown or downturn. Most of the positive characteristics, such as a high savings rate, superior education and training, and adequate capitalization were clearly sustained and are, indeed, similar to current circumstances in China. The ten arguments for a possible slowdown were each examined and dismissed as either overstated, uncertain, or subject to being negated. With the benefit of hindsight, however, three fundamental weaknesses emerged in the subsequent Japanese experience that were wrongly assessed by Kahn, and for which, in each case, the current Chinese prospect is far more favorable.

The first weakness in the Japanese assessment was the demographic projection. Kahn recognized that Japanese population growth would decline, and that the average age of the population would increase, putting a two-way squeeze on the labor force. In 1970, however, he was unable to predict the very rapid decline in birth rates that has taken place in Japan, as elsewhere, to the point where Japan is beginning to experience an absolute decline in population, and thus an actual contraction in the labor force. The Chinese population of 1.3 billion, in contrast, still has hundreds of millions of underutilized workers that can be progressively absorbed into a more highly educated and productive labor force. Chinese population policy has been to restrain population growth, in part through its highly criticized policy of one child per family sustained by forced abortion. This extremely harsh policy is on the way to relaxation, mainly because, as in other emerging market economies, the birth rate is dropping through individual choice, especially in urban areas, where the Chinese rate is already approaching 1.5 births per childbearing woman, compared with a national rate of about 2.0. Inadequate population size, however, will not be a constraint on Chinese advanced technology industry development within the coming ten years or for long beyond.

The second weakness in the Kahn analysis was the highly positive assessment of the Japanese company in terms of work-oriented, loyal, and enthusiastic employees, within an organizational framework based on lifetime employment and seniority in rank. These relationships have turned out to be overly rigid and less adaptable to the constant change necessary to respond to the rapid technological advances driving industrial development over the past 15 years. Seniority-based management has also tended to be risk averse, with little incentive for younger employees to think independently, not to mention disagree with their superiors. This rigid Japanese corporate structure carried over to one of Kahn's projections about the declining growth in the Japanese labor force. He saw an Asian "hinterland" of 100 million workers that could be incorporated into the Japanese superstate through international trade and investment. Japanese investment in Southeast Asia did grow in the 1980s, but the highly structured Japanese companies, with all control retained in Japan and by Japanese managers in the field, worked only for labor-intensive industries and not for the more advanced technology manufacturing that has been thriving in East and Southeast Asia during the past 10 to 15 years. Again, comparison with the new generation of companies in China, both Chinese and foreign, shows sharp contrast—with organization based on the need for constant restructuring and innovation and on incentives for younger, more productive, and creative workers to advance quickly.

The third and all-encompassing weakness in the Kahn analysis was his captivation by the "excellent management of the economy—by government, by business, and to some degree, by labor; this results in a controlled and, to some degree, collectivist (Japan Inc.) but still competitive and market-oriented (but not market-dominated) capitalism."[9] Indeed, the decisive chapter in the book is entitled "Japan Inc.: The Future of the Economic Miracle," which is followed by the chapter titled, "The Emerging Japanese Superstate." The recent history of Japan Inc., in contrast, has been unkind. Financial resources have been misallocated, structural imbalances have developed, the workforce has lacked flexibility, and, in general, competition has been stifled through the collusion of companies, banks, and government regulatory powers. In the international sector, manufactured imports have been highly restricted through informal controls and foreign direct investment has been almost absent until recently. The continuing success stories for Japan, in fact, have been those large companies, particularly in the automotive and consumer electronics sectors, that have broken out of the control culture of Japan Inc. and become strongly competitive on their own, at the technological forefront and of multinational scope. And once again, the recent advanced technology experience of China has been, in most respects, the antipode of Japan Inc.

The conclusion is that Japan in the 1970s-1980s was a flawed model for rise to superstate status, particularly in the era of fast-moving technological change that began in the mid- to late-1980s.

---

[9] Kahn, *op. cit.,* p. 5.

China, in contrast, by opening its economy to trade and investment and creating a highly competitive market environment in the manufacturing sector, is, despite an overarching "socialist" political orientation, far more advantageously positioned to continue its momentum toward becoming an advanced technology superstate.

The Net Assessment

The net assessment is that China is, indeed, an emerging advanced technology superstate, and that all of the economic circumstances are favorable for its rising to full superstate status by 2015. This is most evident within the advanced technology sector, in terms of resources for R&D, university training, and infrastructure, for private sector competition, investment, and exports, and, most importantly, for the central focus on technology innovation.

The outlook for necessary broader economic reforms is less clear, but the reform strategy is self-evident, and ample financial resources are available for implementing them. The basic objective is a relative shift from export-led industrial growth to more balanced growth, with a relatively larger role for domestic demand. This would be beneficial to the Chinese people while reducing the structural imbalance in the global economy, particularly the unsustainable large U.S. current account deficit. A major revaluation of the yuan would be a key component for the restructuring of Chinese economic growth, and would have the added benefit of freeing up $200 billion per year of Central Bank purchases of foreign exchange for domestic expenditures, including for health care, energy development, and improved environmental standards. The economic reforms should include adjustment assistance for groupings of the population adversely affected during the transition, but this could readily be done in an economy which should continue to grow at 7 percent to 9 percent per year if the reforms are upheld, and with $660 billion of available foreign exchange in the Central Bank.

The biggest question mark concerns political change, which centers on how the authoritarian communist government will respond to the growing pressures for democratization and the decentralization of power to the provinces, to the private sector, and to civil society more broadly. Democratic change need not be disruptive or violent. Within East Asia, peaceful change from authoritarian rule to multiparty democracy with full individual rights has taken place in South Korea and Taiwan over the past two decades, and like China is today, both were emerging advanced technology economies (if not superstates) 20 years ago.

The potential for political confrontation, economic disruption, and violence nevertheless exists, and some would say is probable. The principal responsibility for the outcome rests with the Chinese government, but much will also depend on Chinese relationships abroad, most importantly that with the United States. But before turning to these relationships, which are the subject of Chapters 7-10, two other dimensions of the emerging Chinese advanced technology superstate, the geopolitical and geostrategic, need to be considered.

Chapter 6

The Geopolitical and Geostrategic Dimensions

The analysis of the emerging Chinese advanced technology superstate, up to this point, has focused on the economic and commercial dimensions, on the achievement, that is, of giant economic, technological, and financial status for the Chinese economy, and on how this status is strengthening Chinese competitiveness in international trade and investment. There is also the second half of the superstate definition, however, of China's becoming financially and politically powerful in international affairs, and, in the not too distant future, a military superpower as well. This latter half has major foreign policy and national security implications, which are wide-ranging and will influence significantly many aspects of international relations in the decade ahead and beyond. The two most important and immediate issues addressed here are China's rise as economic hegemon in East Asia and the impact of advanced technology industrial development on the modernization of China's military capability.

China as Economic Hegemon in East Asia

China has now become one of the four dominant participants in the global trading system, and will become one of three key currency financial powers soon after the yuan becomes convertible. The implications of these very recent or approaching developments for the international trade and financial systems—the WTO and the IMF—are addressed in Chapters 8 and 9. There is also a regional economic development, however, that is moving forward at an even more rapid pace, largely outside the multilateral frameworks, and which has major geopolitical and foreign policy implications: the rise of China as economic hegemon in East Asia.

Hegemony is defined as "leadership, predominant influence, or domination, especially as exercised by one nation over others."[1] There is no question that China is moving quickly to become the predominant economic influence within East Asia, taken here to include Southeast Asia. The critical question is how China will use this influence in terms of leadership or dominance in political as well as economic terms.

China's rapid emergence as the dominant economic power in East Asia can be dated from 2003-2004. Both Chinese exports and imports grew by 35 percent in both years, the inflow of direct investment (mostly from East Asians) reached record highs of $54 billion in 2003 and $61 billion in 2004, and Chinese Central Bank foreign-exchange holdings rose from $286 billion in December 2002 to $612 billion in December 2004. This astonishing growth in international economic engagement, moreover, has been strongly oriented to advanced technology industry. Eighty-four percent of total merchandise exports by Asian nations are in manufactures, of which two-thirds is in the information technology, machinery, transportation, and chemical sectors, compared with only about 20 percent in apparel, textiles, and other consumer goods.

As a result, China has risen to become the largest trading nation and, by far, the largest recipient of FDI in East Asia, and is heading to become the largest individual trading partner throughout the region. Unfortunately, there are no readily available, up-to-date data to track this course of events in terms of individual East Asian trade and investment relationships, steadily gravitating toward the Chinese center. Such analysis would involve assembling national trade and investment accounts, adjusted to a comparable basis, as they are issued, and could usefully be done by the Asian Development Bank, in view of the deep linkages between the economic impact of China throughout the region and decisions on many projects in the Bank's lending program. From the U.S. perspective, the East-West Center in Honolulu, a recipient of substantial federal funding, might be tasked to do an annual assessment as well.

One broad snapshot of the relative rise of Chinese trade among East Asians, derived from information available in the WTO *International Trade Statistics*, is presented in Table 6-1. When China is taken to include Hong Kong, its share of total East Asian merchandise exports rose from 15 percent in 1995 to 27

---

[1] Random House *Webster's New College Dictionary*, 1997.

percent in 2003, and stood at $458 billion in 2003, while the import share was up from 17 percent to 28 percent, and stood at $437 billion in 2003. The big loser in market share was Japan, down from 37 percent to 27 percent for exports, and from 30 percent to 24 percent for imports. By 2003, China had reached parity with Japan for exports, at 27/27, and was ahead for imports, at 28/24. With growth in trade in 2004 of 35 percent for China, compared with 13 percent for Japan, the Chinese number-one regional trade position increased significantly in 2004, and will continue moving up in subsequent years.

Table 6-1
East Asian Exports and Imports
Total Merchandise Trade

	Value ($ billions) 2003	Share	
		1995	2003
A. Exports			
1. China	438	13	26
2. Hong Kong (domestic exports)	20	2	1
3. China / Hong Kong	458	15	27
4. Japan	472	37	27
5. South Korea	194	11	11
6. Taiwan	150	10	9
7. ASEAN (10)	451	27	26
B. Imports			
1. China	413	13	26
2. Hong Kong (domestic imports)	24	4	2
3. China / Hong Kong	437	17	28
4. Japan	383	30	24
5. South Korea	179	12	11
6. Taiwan	127	9	8
7. ASEAN (10)	451	32	29

Source: WTO, *International Trade Statistics*, 2004, Table III-72

The impact of this upward movement toward an economically dominant position by China in East Asia is having substantial geopolitical and foreign policy impact on all others in the region. The situation of Taiwan was described in Chapter 3 with respect to the deepening integration of the two economies through Taiwanese direct investment in China and the related rapid growth in Taiwanese exports to China, particularly since 2001, shown in

Table 4-11. The result is a much greater dependency of Taiwan on China for its economic well being, and hence greater political leverage by China over the issue of Taiwanese political independence and sovereignty.

The most important geopolitical consequence of Chinese regional economic hegemony is the fundamentally changed and diminished relative role of Japan. The displacement of Japan by China as the number-one East Asian trading nation was shown in Table 6-1. Table 6-2 breaks down Japanese trade by principal trading partner, with a similar picture. The share of Japanese exports to China increased from 8 percent in 1995 to 13 percent in 2004, while the import share rose from 11 percent to 21 percent. The United States remains the single largest export market for Japan, at $128 billion in 2004, compared with $75 billion for China, but given that the Chinese market for Japanese exports is growing two to three times faster than the U.S. market, China will almost certainly be number one by about 2006. For Japanese imports, China was already number one in 2004, at $95 billion, compared to $63 billion of imports from the United States. Taking imports and exports together, total Japanese trade with the United States in 2004 was $191 billion, compared with $170 billion for China, and $142 billion for the EU. For total trade, therefore, China is headed to become Japan's largest trading partner in 2005 or 2006 at the latest.

Table 6-2
Japanese Trade With Principal Trading Partners

	United States	China	EU (15)
A. Exports			
2004 Value ($ billions)	128	75	85
2004 Percent of total	22	13	15
1995 Percent of total	28	8	16
B. Imports			
2004 Value ($ billions)	63	95	57
2004 Percent of total	14	21	12
1995 Percent of total	23	11	16

Source: Japanese Ministry of Finance

The changed role of Japan in East Asia resulting from these rapid changes in the patterns of trade, deeply linked to the very large foreign direct investment into China, is truly extraordinary, with only a 15-year historical perspective. In the late 1980s, Japan appeared to be the rising economic hegemon in East Asia, stimulating political concerns throughout the region that were fueled by studies within the Japanese Ministry of International Trade and Industry (MITI) foreseeing some form of latter-day "East Asian Co-Prosperity Sphere." The analogy of the flying geese, with Japan as the lead goose, trailed by others following the Japanese model of government–private sector partnership, or Japan Inc., was frequently cited and seriously discussed. And then came the stalling out of Japanese economic growth during the 1990s, the Asian financial crises of the late 1990s, largely the result of "Crony Capitalism, Inc.," and since 2000 the emergence of China as the regional economic superstate.

Attitudes in Japan have changed dramatically. No one any longer speaks of Japanese primacy in the region, and almost everyone acknowledges, at least in private, that China will soon become the dominant economic power in the region. In November 2004, the biannual macroeconomic report of the Japanese Cabinet Office Economic and Social Research Institute projected Japanese economic growth to average only 1.5 percent per year from now until 2030, while the Japanese population, now at 126 million, will decline to about 100 million in 2050.[2] This does not mean that the current level of affluence in Japan will decline. To the contrary, 1.5 percent annual economic growth, together with a 0.5 percent decline in the population means a plus 2 percent annual increase in per capita income. But in relative terms, in comparison with China, it means falling far behind.

In foreign policy terms, Japan has to balance the prospect of primary economic dependence on China with the long-standing military alliance and dominant economic relationship with the United States. For example, Japanese preferential free trade and investment agreements with China and other East Asians, discussed in Chapter 9, would accelerate the shift in the economic balance toward China. In broader terms, the issue is whether it is in the Japanese interest to have an East Asian political as well as economic grouping—with China at the center—as a counterweight to the United States and the EU lead positions in North America and West Europe. Japan is, in fact, becoming more concerned that China's growing economic power poses a security risk to Asia. Prime Minister Junichiro Koizumi expressed concern about the large increases in the Chinese military budget, and has moved

---

[2] *Daily Report for Executives*, 0148-8155, November 10, 2004.

closer to U.S. support for Taiwan, including permission, despite Chinese complaints, for the former Taiwanese President Lee Tenghui to visit Japan in December 2004. In January 2005, Japan supported the United States in opposing the planned lifting of the arms embargo against China by the EU. China, in response, condoned if not encouraged anti-Japanese street demonstrations and announced it would oppose a permanent UN Security Council seat for Japan. Where the political relationship between the two largest East Asian economies is headed, and how its direction will impact on U.S. relationships with both countries, is thus ambiguous. Japan is largely on a conflicted course of deepening economic engagement with China and closer foreign policy collaboration with the United States in disagreement with China.

The situation of South Korea is distinct and important in a number of respects. China will become South Korea's number-one trading partner in a year or two, and the surge of Korean investment into China since 2000 is integrating the two economies further. South Korea also has aspirations to become a regional financial and economic "hub," but this will happen only to the extent that South Korea is fully engaged, in financial as well as trade and investment relations, with China. Another major concern within South Korea is the prospect of economic normalization with and an opening up of the North Korean economy. These could have a disruptive economic impact on South Korea, and would largely play out in terms of cross-border trade and travel among the two Koreas and China. The principal issue for South Korea, however, like Japan, is the balancing out of a primary economic relationship with China, on the one hand, with the U.S. alliance, including a U.S. troop presence in South Korea, on the other. In this respect, South Korea could play a catalytic role in bridging FTAs within East Asia and across the Pacific, by being the first major trading nation to have FTAs in both directions through an FTA with the United States. This issue is addressed more fully in Chapter 9.

The evolving Chinese economic relationship with the ASEAN grouping will hinge largely on the negotiations for a free trade and investment agreement begun in November 2004 and scheduled for full implementation for trade by 2012, and on related Chinese financial support. The substantive content of the individual country relationships, however, varies greatly. Singapore, Malaysia, Thailand, and increasingly Vietnam are in the "newly industrialized" grouping, balancing manufactured exports to China with similar imports, and they have concerns about FDI going to China at their expense. Indonesia, in contrast, is more heavily dependent on primary and agricultural commodity exports, which can benefit from Chinese investment and long-term export contracts.

The Chinese deepening economic relationship with the poorest ASEAN countries—Cambodia, Laos, and Myanmar (or Burma)—could have the greatest relative impact. The Chinese trade and investment relationship could be accelerated through sorely needed long-term loans at concessionary rates from China to these countries. Myanmar, in particular, is a nation of 50 million people, rich in natural resources, and of interest to China. China has an historical interest in penetrating Myanmar as a route to the sea for its southwest provinces, and a bilateral financial agreement in 1997 was designed to build a road, rail, river, and port network through to the deep-water Myanmar port of Kyaukpyo on the Bay of Bengal. The unilateral U.S. and other Western embargoes on Myanmar have further facilitated the rise of Chinese influence. For example, a Chinese firm won the Yangon port development project when the U.S. bidder withdrew because of the embargo.[3] In 2003, Myanmar imports from China were $900 million, compared with $170 million of exports, which presumably reflects very large Chinese financial support for the struggling Myanmar economy. In November 2004, ASEAN leaders abandoned—as ineffective—attempts to censure human rights abuses by the Myanmar government because Myanmar receives strong financial and political support from China.[4]

The other major geopolitical change caused by the rise of China to economic hegemon is the relative decline in U.S. economic influence in the region. Over time, the U.S. market will become relatively less important for overall East Asian growth. The rate of relative decline, moreover, will accelerate when the unsustainably large U.S. trade deficit, largely with East Asia, is reduced through exchange rate adjustment or otherwise. As a consequence, the United States will have relatively smaller economic leverage over East Asians, compared with China, in the pursuit of U.S. foreign policy objectives.

The underlying geopolitical question for East Asia, in light of the rise of China to be the central and soon dominant economic power in the region, is how China will use the increasingly asymmetric economic power relationships to pursue its foreign

---

[3] For a fuller discussion of the Chinese relationship with Myanmar, including the impact of the U.S. embargo, see Ernest H. Preeg, *Feeling Good or Doing Good With Sanctions: Unilateral Economic Sanctions and The U.S. National Interest* (CSIS, 1999), pp. 111-146.

[4] *Financial Times*, November 30, 2004.

policy as well as commercial interests. China repeatedly denies any intention to become a regional hegemon bent on using its economic influence to achieve political or other objectives. When it comes to disputes over fishing rights or borders, however, China is prone to insinuate its superior power position, even through the display of military forces.

In more positive terms, China can offer economic benefits, such as trade financing and enhanced market access, to its dominant regional market, to achieve its noneconomic objectives. Zheng Bijan, dean of the Chinese Communist Party School, explained: "If China does not provide economic opportunities for the region, it will lose the opportunity for a peaceful rise. . . . This is by no means a bid for hegemony." In response, U.S. Assistant Secretary of State James Kelly commented that China's bilateral agreements mean little in economic terms, "but they serve notice of how China is using its newly won economic power to expand its presence and political influence among its southern neighbors."[5]

China's status as a regional economic hegemon invites an analogy with the situation in North America, where Canada and Mexico are economically dependent, to a very high and asymmetric degree, on the United States, but the analogy, more importantly, also highlights the critical difference between the United States and China as regional hegemons. The United States has a democratic government, where disputes are resolved internally through the rule of law or popular vote, and this basic approach generally carries over to regional relationships. China, in contrast, has an authoritarian government which rules through political coercion and police force at home, with the tendency to approach international relations in a similar manner. An important exception is Chinese accession to the WTO, with all of the ensuing rules-based commitments, subject to third party dispute settlement procedures. No such rules and commitments yet exist, however, in the emerging economic and geopolitical relationships within East Asia. The subject of regional advanced technology hegemons, including the United States and China, is addressed in far broader terms in Chapter 11.

Chinese Military Modernization

The performance capability of the Chinese People's Liberation Army (PLA) from the 1970s through the 1990s was dismal, a fact

---

[5] *Wall Street Journal*, June 16, 2004.

that was clearly recognized both within China and by foreign observers in the United States and elsewhere. In 1979, China launched a punitive attack on Vietnam, and suffered enormous casualties against the smaller but more experienced Vietnamese defenders. Chinese command and communications were un-coordinated and many casualties were from "friendly fire." The huge gap with the United States in modern weapons systems was demonstrated dramatically by U.S. performance in the 1991 Gulf War, through U.S. "surgical" bombing and electromagnetic warfare, and was further displayed in 1996 when two U.S. aircraft carrier battle groups off the coast of Taiwan upstaged Chinese missile exercises with flight combat maneuvers and the monitoring of PLA activities on the ground. During the 1990s, the U.S. Department of Defense consistently assessed the Chinese military capability as being at least 20 years out-of-date across the board, a view shared by most independent analysts.[6]

The reasons for this failure of the PLA to develop combat readiness and modern weapons systems have been analyzed extensively.[7] In 1978, Deng Xiaoping delegated military modern-ization to fourth priority among the Four Modernizations, and it stayed at the bottom into the 1990s. A continuing series of "reforms" within the military establishment were frustrated by vested interests in the status quo, the lack of incentives to improve performance, and the general isolation of highly secret defense facilities even from one another, including the relocation of defense enterprises to remote interior areas known as the "Third Line." R&D institutes were separated from manufacturing facili-ties, which prevented cost-benefit analysis at the development stage related to production costs and ultimate weapons per-formance. There was also massive corruption, stemming mainly from the large-scale production by defense industry enterprises of goods intended for commercial markets with weak accounting procedures.

Finally, in 1997-1999, a fundamental restructuring of the Chinese defense industry complex did take place, and it is having a major impact on the development of modern weapons systems.

---

[6] David Shambaugh, *Modernizing China's Military: Progress, Problems, and Prospects* (University of California Press, 2002), p. 328.

[7] See, for example, *The People's Liberation Army in the Information Age*, James C. Maulvenon and Richard H. Yang, eds. (Rand Corporation, 1998); *The Chinese Armed Forces in the 21ˢᵗ Century*, Larry M. Wortzel, ed., (Strategic Studies Institute, 1999); *China's Growing Military Power: Perspectives on Security, Ballistic Missiles, and Conventional Capabil-ities* (Strategic Studies Institute, 2002); and Shambaugh, *op. cit.*

The restructuring, moreover, is deeply interrelated with the rapid development of advanced technology civilian industries beginning in 1995, described in Chapters 2-5. The National Defense Law of 1997 essentially subordinated the armed forces to state or civilian government control, asserting that "the State Council shall direct and administer the building of national defense" in nine categories of responsibilities, including, most importantly, fiscal appropriations. The 1998 National Defense White Paper elaborated this shift in control, with the State Council given responsibility for deciding the size, structure, and location of defense assets. With regard to defense industry, which is most directly related to this study, three basic changes were implemented: (1) control of the very large state-owned defense enterprises was shifted from the military to the civilian government; (2) these defense industry enterprises became more integrated with other advanced technology enterprises for weapons development, including through joint R&D programs at universities and elsewhere; and (3) defense projects were subjected to competitive bidding among defense and other enterprises, based on price and performance. The restructuring of Chinese defense industry as related to the development of advanced technology industry was summed up in this way: "The divestiture of the PLA's commercial operations took place at the same time as far-reaching reforms to curb and separate the state's involvement in business was being implemented. . . . This was a key pillar of Zhu Rongji's overall efforts to develop a robust market economy."[8]

This fundamental restructuring of Chinese defense industry constitutes, in effect, a rejection of the failed Soviet model, where military facilities operated by administrative decree in isolation from the rest of the economy, and movement toward the U.S. model of civilian defense companies competing on the basis of price and performance, with considerable interaction between primary defense contractors and many other advanced technology companies engaged in everything from R&D to dual-use components.

The decisions of 1997-1999 were nevertheless generally met with skepticism if not dismissal by U.S. and other foreign observers. This was a reaction based largely on the consistent failure of previous PLA reforms, and thus the cautious view that several years of credible implementation would be required before a

---

[8] See Tai Ming Cheung, China's *Entrepreneurial Army* (Oxford University Press, 2001). The restructuring process is recounted in detail in Chapter 10, "The PLA's Divestiture from Business, 1998-1999," with the quote from p. 258.

positive assessment could be made. For example, a 1999 assessment concluded, "Whereas the PLA's ambitions were clear, the gap between ambitions and capability could well be growing with the continuing advance in military technologies. . . . What should be anticipated is a slow and sometimes erratic expansion of CMIC [i.e., Chinese military industrial complex] capabilities in technologies applicable to the areas viewed as critical in future warfare."[9] The 2002 study by David Shambaugh reached a similar conclusion: "One overarching thesis—namely, that although the PLA has embarked on a systematic and extensive modernization program . . . a combination of domestic handicaps and foreign constraints severely limits both the pace and the scope of China's military progress."[10]

Even as recently as May 2004, the Department of Defense FY04 annual report to Congress on Chinese military power devoted relatively little attention to reforms within the Chinese military industrial complex.[11]   Only one page out of 54 was devoted to "Domestic Defense Industry," and the conclusion was that "Chinese defense industries have taken near-term steps to address deficiencies, but Beijing realizes that long-term modernization will take time and entail a variety of measures." More specifically, with respect to advanced technology development, the report explains that "with few exceptions, such as ballistic missile research, development, and production, most of China's domestic defense industries are inefficient and remain vulnerable to dependencies on foreign suppliers of technology." Nevertheless, the net assessment of the report is guarded and somewhat vague: "Self sufficiency will continue to be China's long term defense goal, with plans to achieve weapon quality levels approaching those of the industrialized world within the next 5 to 10 years. At best, we expect China to meet with uneven success meeting this goal." This is nevertheless a far cry from the DOD assessment five years earlier of China's being at least 20 years out of date across the board. The FY 2005 DOD report has been delayed over interagency debate about rising Chinese military influence and capability, and the final version will likely devote more attention to the modernization of Chinese defense industry,

---

[9] Bernard D. Cole and Paul H. B. Godwin, "Advanced Military Technology and the PLA: Priorities and Capabilities for the 21st Century"; and Wortzel, op. cit., pp. 209-210.

[10] Shambaugh, op. cit., p. 10.

[11] Annual Report on the Military Power of the People's Republic of China, at www.defenselink.mil/pubs/d20040528prc.   The quotes that follow are from pages 28, 19, and 5, respectively.

with more specific commentary on the narrowing gap in capability with the United States.[12]

Despite this continuing hesitancy to assess the results of the 1997-1999 restructuring, recent reports clearly indicate that some basic change and more productive results are under way. A path-breaking paper by Evan Medeiros of the Rand Corporation which was presented before the U.S.-China Economic and Security Review Commission in February 2004, lays out the changed circumstances:

> In the last five years, China's defense industry has become far more productive than in past decades. The defense industrial reforms implemented in the late 1990s, unlike the ones adopted in previous years, were substantial and have positively influenced the quality of China's defense industrial output. . . . Chinese defense firms have improved their R&D techniques, production processes, and, thus, the quality of their output.

With respect to the operations of the largest defense industry enterprises, Medeiros continues:

> These firms are not controlled by the Chinese military. . . . They are civilian entities under the authority of the State Council and its subordinate organ, the State Commission on Science, Technology, and Industry for National Defense. . . . Current estimates of the amount of civilian production in each of the eleven large defense corporations range from 65 percent to 90 percent. . . . Thus, even though these enterprises are officially considered by the government as defense industrial firms, they are also primarily involved in producing civilian goods and services, and thus are intertwined with China's huge civilian economy. In addition, there are a growing number of firms that do not belong to the eleven defense-industrial conglomerates (especially in the information technology [IT] sector) which produce goods under contract for the military. The line between defense industrial firms and civilian firms in China is increasingly blurred.

---

[12] *Wall Street Journal*, June 3, 2005. The DOD report, due March 1, had still not been released in mid-June 2005.

More specifically:

> In the last two years alone, Chinese defense factories
> have produced a variety of new weapons systems based on
> novel Chinese designs. Many are highly capable weapons
> platforms. The development of these weapons im-
> portantly reflects improvements in R&D techniques,
> design methods and production processes, especially com-
> pared to the 1980s and the 1990s. Not only are the new
> systems more advanced, but China's production of them is
> faster and possibly more efficient.

Medeiros goes on to explain how progress has been mixed
among defense industry sectors and that systemic weaknesses
remain. The extent and effectiveness of competitive bidding for
defense contracts is probably still limited. He nevertheless concludes that "A new paradigm is needed to analyze China's defense
industrial capabilities."[13]

The linkage between accelerated military modernization and
the advanced technology commercial sector is most intense for the
Chinese navy. China has a 9,000-mile coastline and a long history
as a maritime power dating back to the Ninth Century. Current
naval strategy is to achieve short-term national security objectives
related to Taiwan and the South China Sea and longer-term
regional maritime dominance through both combatant and
merchant ships. By 2010, China plans to build about 70 modern
surface ships and 20-30 submarines.[14] Over the past four years,
for the first time, four new 7,000-ton destroyers were built, based
on modern stealth design and improved air defense and anti-
submarine capability. The Chinese submarine fleet continues to
be upgraded, and in July 2004, ahead of schedule, the new 094-
class submarine was launched. It is capable of launching medium
to large range nuclear missiles judged by the U.S. Department of
Defense as a major improvement over China's current ballistic-
missile submarines.[15]

The commercial maritime counterpart is even more impressive, and is strongly supportive of the navy modernization

---

[13] Evan S. Medeiros, "Analyzing China's Defense Industries and the
Implications for Chinese Military Modernization" (paper presented
before the U.S.-China Economic and Security Review Commission,
February 6, 2004). The quotes are from pp. 1, 3, and 9.
[14] See Bernard D. Cole, *Waterways and Strategy: China's Priorities*
(Jamestown Foundation, February 2005).
[15] *Washington Times*, December 3, 2004.

program. China already has one of the largest merchant marines, and its shipbuilding industry will soon surpass that of Japan to become second to South Korea. In 2004, China State Shipbuilding Corporation, the largest shipyard, produced 3.6 million tons of ships, a 65 percent increase over 2003. In August 2004, the Huadong Shipyard contracted to build five advanced-design liquefied natural gas (LNG) carriers, related to a policy requiring Chinese-built ships to participate in LNG import contracts. Chinese merchant shipping is, of course, linked to the rapid rise in Chinese trade, with container traffic through Chinese ports growing 29 percent per year from 1998 to 2003. Shanghai is spending $10 billion to expand its port so as to pass by Hong Kong and become the world's largest container port. The rise of China to become the dominant maritime nation in the Pacific, as the United States was a century ago, has profound geopolitical as well as national security implications.[16]

China's aerospace industry for short-range ballistic missiles is also improving its output in terms of accuracy and destructiveness, including the development of anti-ship cruise missiles with satellite-aided navigation. The development of eight new road-mobile DF-31 long-range missiles, reported in January 2005, goes beyond the predictions of the DOD FY04 report cited above.[17]

And, finally, and most deeply integrated with Chinese advanced technology industry development are the Chinese defense electronic systems, defined in terms of command, control, communications, computers, and intelligence, or C4I systems for short. Thousands of kilometers of buried fiber-optic cable, connected by modern switches and routers, now provide secure communications to nearly every unit of the Chinese armed forces, while large computer networks are dedicated to operational command and control.

These are some of the results of the revised Chinese defense industry complex. The more efficient and competitive industry structures are supported by major increases in defense budget allocations for weapons procurement, up from 5 billion yuan in 1990 to 57 billion yuan in 2002, which represents an increase in

---

[16] See Tai Ming Cheung, *Chinese Defense Industrial Reform and the Navy* (Jamestown Foundation, February 2005), and *Financial Times*, December 17, 2004.

[17] *Washington Times*, January 21, 2005, with reference to an assessment by the International Institute for Strategic Studies.

the share of the aggregate defense budget dedicated to weapons procurement from 16 percent to 34 percent.[18]

No attempt is made here at a net assessment of Chinese military modernization prospects over the coming decade. New reports of military developments in China continue to surface.[19] Certainly it is warranted to call for a new paradigm, one which integrates fully the advanced technology development process under way in civilian industry, described in this study, with the parallel and conceptually similar strategy being pursued for modernizing Chinese military systems. Further analytic and intelligence-gathering work is in order, and an expanded study by the Rand Corporation, building on the work of Medeiros, is scheduled for completion in 2005. In any event, it is fair to say that the military dimension of China's emergence as an advanced technology superstate appears to be on track.

---

[18] Medeiros, *op. cit.,* p. 5. Part of the budget increases reflect lost commercial revenues from the shift of defense industry to the civilian sector.

[19] *Washington Times,* June 9, 2005, reported that U.S. intelligence agencies have missed a number of Chinese military advances, including a new attack submarine, precision-guided missiles, and surface-to-surface missiles for targeting U.S. aircraft carrier battle groups.

Part II

The U.S.
Policy Response

Chapter 7

A Fundamentally Changed Policy Relationship

The discussion of Chinese military modernization concluded that a new analytic paradigm was needed. For U.S.-China policy, the emergence of China as an advanced technology superstate quickly leads to the same conclusion writ large. The U.S.-China policy relationship is undergoing fundamental and far-reaching change, although, as often happens, there is a considerable time lag on the part of governments to adjust to the new circumstances.

The new U.S.-China relationship centers on a deepening bilateral economic engagement of wide-ranging mutual benefit, together with a far less engaged set of mutual national security interests. These mutual interests, however, are overlaid with a largely conflicted political relationship, tending toward an adversarial relationship in broader, geopolitical terms. China's emergence as one of the three principal participants in the international economic system together with the United States and the EU, as the second-largest national military power, and as the economic hegemon in East Asia extends greatly U.S.-China bilateral interests to the multilateral arena, both for the international economic system and the world political order. The most important medium to longer term U.S. interest in play is the maintenance of U.S. leadership in advanced technology industry in the face of rapid Chinese development in this area, including the impact of this development on military modernization in both countries. The loss of U.S. leadership, as the President's Council of Advisors on Science and Technology concluded, "would have serious detrimental effects on the Nation's economic security and the citizens standard of living."[1]

This study focuses on the changed U.S.-China economic policy relationship, and Chapters 8-10 present a forward-looking U.S. policy response in the areas of international finance, trade and investment, and related U.S. domestic policies. Such

---

[1] President's Council of Advisors on Science and Technology, *op. cit.*, January 30, 2004.

123

economic policy formulation, however, cannot be developed in isolation from the other elements of the overall policy relationship, and must take into account the relative importance of the various U.S. interests involved, interactions among them, and differing time sequences for policy implementation. This chapter, therefore, provides a brief assessment of the overall, fundamentally changed U.S.-China relationship as the basic framework from which the subsequent economic policy conclusions are derived. Five dimensions of the new U.S.-China policy paradigm are presented: economic interests; national security interests; political-ideological conflicts; geopolitical objectives; and cultural-ethnic affinities. These individual policy strands are then brought together to form a few basic conclusions, relating the role of economic policy to the overall bilateral relationship.

The Paramount Economic Relationship

The substance of U.S.-China relations, at this stage, is overwhelmingly economic in operational content, through trade, investment, and financial engagement. Almost every large U.S. manufacturing company and bank is significantly engaged in China, and other service sectors, including transportation, communications, and even retailing—as highlighted by the much-publicized launch of Wal-Mart China—are increasingly engaged as well. The immediate result is very large mutual economic benefits in terms of higher productivity and lower prices for consumers in both countries. The shift of Chinese production and trade from lower to higher technology industries increases these mutual benefits further, through the "dynamic gains" from trade generated by investment in new trade-related industries, the restructuring of existing industry, and applied new technologies throughout. Of particular policy relevance, these mutual economic benefits are concentrated in manufacturing and related services that account for 80 percent to 90 percent of bilateral trade.

This "positive sum game" of major proportions from expanding trade and investment, however, is subject to important qualifications with respect to U.S. interests. Most fundamentally, the U.S. advanced technology global leadership role is being seriously challenged by China, and this requires a substantially changed U.S. policy response. This response should not involve import protection or, with limited defense-related exceptions, export sanctions, which would have adverse impact on the U.S. economy while being largely ineffective in restraining Chinese technological advance. Rather, the U.S. policy response should head in three other directions.

The first direction of policy change, within the context of the free trade and investment relationship that exists with China, would be to place much higher priority on, and to pursue more forcefully, a "level playing field" for trade and investment, one based on fair competition and market forces. Most importantly, Chinese exchange rate policy since 2001 has been used to increase substantially the Chinese export surplus in manufactures, with adverse impact on U.S industry, most sharply felt by advanced technology industry. Such "currency manipulation" is in violation of Chinese IMF and WTO obligations, and needs to be terminated. In addition, there are elements of Chinese trade and investment policy that are trade distorting, to the detriment of U.S. exports, and that also need to be brought into compliance with Chinese WTO obligations. These areas of policy are addressed in detail in Chapters 8 and 9.

The second direction for a restructured U.S. policy response pertains to domestic economic policies. For macropolicy, a higher national rate of savings is needed to reduce the trade deficit, 83 percent of which was in manufactures in 2004, with a growing share of the deficit in advanced technology products. A number of other policy initiatives would provide greater incentives and resources for technological innovation and applied technology investment, including improvements in publicly supported R&D and education, tax reform, tort reform, and adjustments in other regulatory policies that put American advanced technology production at a disadvantage *vis-à-vis* China and other foreign competitors. This domestic policy agenda is the subject of Chapter 10.

The third change of direction for U.S. economic policy relates to broader international economic policy relationships stemming from the rise of China to become an advanced technology super-state, including a presumptive Chinese leadership role within the international financial and trading systems, principally the IMF and the WTO. A central and active Chinese role in these institutions would have far-reaching impact, although the need for change in response to China's new role is not widely recognized. Both the IMF and the WTO need a fundamental policy re-orientation, the former to a market-oriented floating-rate relationship among major currencies, and the latter to a consolidation of the burgeoning bilateral and regional free trade agreements into a multilateral framework. These changes, however, will happen only with full Chinese participation and leadership, and, in fact, joint leadership by the United States and China will be decisive for the outcome. It is no exaggeration to state that if the United States and China agree on basic changes in the international economic system, they will almost certainly take place, while if the two do not agree, the changes will, with equal certainty, not take place. This somewhat Delphic assertion is explained in detail in the latter parts of Chapters 8 and 9.

Mutual National Security Interests

A truly new world order of national security interests emerged during the post–Cold War 1990s. The previous four decades centered on bilateral rivalry and conflict between the two nuclear superpowers, the United States and the Soviet Union, maintained in balance through the terrifying strategy of "mutually assured destruction," and played out in diplomatic, economic, and, at times, military terms in all corners of the world. This configuration has now been replaced by a new order of national security interests, wherein the advanced and emerging industrialized states, which comprise the large majority of the global population and over 90 percent of global economic and military power, are faced with increasing security threats from the proliferation of weapons of mass destruction and high-casualty terrorist acts by so-called rogue states and independent terrorist groupings. The rapid pace of advanced technology development in the former grouping, moreover, tends to facilitate the clandestine acquisition of weapons of mass destruction and the capacity for terrorist acts by the latter grouping.

In this new configuration of national security interests, the United States and China have a fundamental mutual interest to contain the proliferation of weapons of mass destruction and to destroy terrorist groupings. The increasing pace of Chinese military modernization, including C4I capability and the beginnings of a special police force capability for international peacekeeping, could complement the dominant U.S. role in global actions to these ends. Unfortunately, however, although the two nations state their common objectives in these areas, there has been relatively little bilateral diplomatic initiative or positive collaborative results. Much of the U.S. exchange with China has consisted of diplomatic damage control in order to obtain a positive Chinese vote, or at least an abstention, in UN Security Council votes, or to pressure China to desist in actions that would violate or weaken international nonproliferation and antiterrorist programs. Military coordination for international peacekeeping has been nonexistent, while cooperation for intelligence gathering and exchange has been meager.

The one major exception involves North Korea, where the United States and China are mutually engaged to achieve a Korean peninsula free of nuclear weapons. Even here, however, the engagement has produced mixed results, with China considerably more sympathetic to its long-standing North Korean ally. China has often tried to get the United States to weaken its stance for complete elimination of the North Korean nuclear weapons program, subject to full verification, as the basis for normalization of relations. In fact, U.S.-Chinese collaboration is the key to elimination of the North Korean nuclear program. There is much commentary about the six-way talks under way (involving the two Koreas, the United States, China, Japan, and Russia), but the decisive relationship is between the United States and China on one side, and North Korea on the other side, in view of the critical economic and political support given by China to the North Korean government. This opens the way for a more forceful U.S.-Chinese collaboration that would successfully resolve the impasse, while setting a path-breaking precedent for further U.S.–China cooperation in national security affairs. Thus far, however, there are few signs of such serious collaboration.

The U.S.-China national security relationship is thus developing in the direction of more concerted actions toward mutual objectives, but on a hesitant track with very limited results to date. This is in stark contrast with the heavily engaged economic relationship, based on clearly established mutual interests. The contrast reflects the fact that to the extent China becomes more forthcoming in collaboration with the United States on national security objectives, it will be because China comes to see it is in its national security self-interest, unrelated to economic interests, to do so. And this observation, in turn, leads to the largely conflicted political and ideological bilateral relationship.

The Conflicted Political and
Ideological Relationship

The conflicted U.S.-China bilateral political and ideological relationship is long-standing, dating from the communist takeover of China in 1949. It is also a complex relationship, and is becoming more so as a result of the now dominant and deepening economic relationship. There remains a fundamental political difference between the U.S. democratic system, based on individual rights and the rule of law, and Chinese authoritarian rule, harshly enforced by the communist party and military leaderships. There is a process of democratic change under way in China, described in Chapter 6, emanating principally from the economic strategy oriented toward greater personal freedom and the rule of law in business relations, but authoritarian government rule, with widespread suppression of individual and private group freedoms, remains dominant.

In broader international terms, China is not pursuing ideological conflict with the United States, as did the Soviet Union in its quest for the global triumph of communism over capitalism. Chinese relations with the three remaining communist regimes in Cuba, North Korea, and Vietnam are of minor political significance, excepting China's concern for the North Korean nuclear weapons program, while the relationship with Vietnam is decidedly reserved in view of historic Vietnamese concerns about Chinese geopolitical intentions.

U.S-Chinese ideological differences over democracy and respect for human rights will continue, and the United States, as the global champion for such rights, will continue to play an active role, both bilaterally and multilaterally, in pressing for greater respect for basic human rights in China. Time, in any event, appears to be on the side of the United States, and China is often on the defensive over violations of basic human rights as contained in international covenants. U.S. support for democratic nongovernmental organizations in China is clearly justified, as are active contacts with reform-minded private Chinese groupings. Support for individual freedom and democracy in China, moreover, is consistent with current U.S. initiatives in the Middle East and elsewhere to foster freedom and democracy over authoritarian rule throughout the world. Last but not least, the United States can make its case by example at home, increasingly communicated to the Chinese people through the ever more powerful telecommunications products of advanced technology industry. In sum, the future track of the bilateral political and ideological relationship can be viewed in hopeful terms, with gradual convergence toward more democratic governance through peaceful, nondisruptive change within China—except for Taiwan.

Taiwan constitutes the critical and most threatening issue in the U.S.-China political relationship. It involves a unique three-way relationship, with the rest of the world largely disengaged. There is a serious risk of confrontation through a Chinese military attack on Taiwan, most likely triggered by a Taiwanese declaration of independence, which could lead to a U.S. military response, or at least major economic sanctions against China. Chinese military modernization is geared heavily to achieve an asymmetric advantage over U.S. forces, most particularly *vis-à-vis* U.S. aircraft carriers that protect Taiwan. The existing relationship, which allows Taiwan to develop on an independent course within a vaguely defined one-China framework, has worked well, but important changes are taking place. The rapid deepening of economic integration between China and Taiwan was described in Chapters 3 and 4. In international economic terms, a modus vivendi was established for independent Taiwanese participation in the APEC in 1993, and as a full member of the WTO in 2001, relationships that will be examined further, with policy recommendations, in Chapter 9. Most importantly, in political terms, Taiwan started down the path of rapid advanced technology industrialization in the 1970s, 20 years before China, a move that fostered the circumstances for a political transition in Taiwan from authoritarian rule to democratic government with respect for individual rights in the 1990s. This has to be viewed as a disturbing precedent by the Chinese government and a potentially difficult subject to address—if more serious political dialogue should develop between Beijing and Taipei. All that can be said here is that serious disruption of the U.S.-China bilateral relationship over what should be a manageable political course in Taiwan would amount to a small tail wagging two very large superstate dogs.

These are the basic elements of the mixed and largely conflicted bilateral political relationship, which is evolving favorably in some respects, largely as a result of deepening economic engagement based on market forces and open trade, while remaining troubled in other areas, most importantly over Taiwan. The overarching conflict is the ideological divide between American democracy and Chinese one-party dictatorship. The Chinese government defends its authoritarian rule in terms both of Confucian values, which give primacy to group and national interests over individual interests, and of deep-seated Chinese nationalist aspirations as described in Chapter 5. The result, in foreign policy terms, is for China to view the U.S. superpower as its political adversary, and to pursue policies that will diminish U.S. power and influence in all parts of the world, and within East Asia in particular. Moreover, the current rivalry, apart from the conflict over Taiwan, is being played out more in geopolitical than geostrategic terms.

Geopolitical Objectives

China and the United States both have legacies of "manifest destiny." Both are major powers with strongly felt national identities, motivated to extend their political and cultural influence, particularly within their regions. China's understanding of itself as the "Middle Kingdom," dates back a millennium, while the American expansionist experience began in the 19th Century, through the Louisiana Purchase, the Monroe Doctrine, and wars with Mexico and Spain. Such regional hegemonic ambitions have also formed part of broader geopolitical power relationships to defend against foreign incursions and exploitation, experienced to some extent by the United States through the Civil War, and more frequently and to much more harmful effect by China. Regional geopolitical objectives were relatively dormant through most of the 20th Century, as China was consumed by internal civil war, invasion by Japan, and the difficult early decades of communist rule, while the United States was drawn into global conflicts, first against fascism and then through the Cold War conflict with the Soviet Union.

Since the 1980s, however, a new configuration of regional geopolitical interests has emerged from the rapid deepening of economic interdependencies, driven principally by the development and application of new technologies within the dominant regional economic powers. This economic globalization process can have important political and foreign policy content, although the political orientation varies greatly among the three principal advanced industrialized regions of West Europe, North America, and East Asia. West European regional economic integration began in the 1950s, as an historic initiative to contain conflict between France and Germany, which had triggered three wars in less than a century, and it has now proceeded the furthest in terms of economic, monetary, and partial political union. European regional integration, however, is essentially self-contained, bounded in scope by Central Europe and the Mediterranean Basin, and it is moving at a restrained pace in the face of complex adjustment to recent expansion of EU membership and the political challenge of absorbing large numbers of culturally distinct Muslim immigrants. The United States, in contrast, after the path-breaking creation of NAFTA, a free trade and investment agreement with its two largest trading partners, continues to extend its preferential economic links south through the Caribbean Basin and South America, as well as across the Pacific. The U.S. foreign policy interest in such free trade relationships is less deep than that of the European Union, but the intent is clearly to consolidate market-oriented democracies, supportive of broader U.S. economic and foreign policy interests. The interacting forces of economic integration and geopolitical interests in East Asia have already been introduced in Chapter 6, which looked at China's rapid rise to become the "Middle Advanced Technology Superstate," with important foreign policy implications.

The critical relationship in how these intensifying yet disparate regional interests will play out over the coming decade is between the United States and China. Within the Asia Pacific region, in particular, U.S. strategy for responding to the Chinese geopolitical challenge should be a major, if not the top, foreign policy priority of U.S.-China policy. The current state of play is one of proliferation of free trade agreements within East Asia, driven largely by Chinese initiative and heading toward some form of broader East Asian economic arrangement, as well as a more hesitant, selective U.S. approach for free trade agreements across the Pacific. Overarching the various bilateral free trade agreement initiatives is the 1994 summit-level APEC Declaration of Bogor, which calls for an Asia Pacific free trade and investment agreement, though this has yet to materialize in specific form.

A decisive issue for the future course of Asia Pacific trade, more specifically, is whether and how there will be free trade between the United States and China, the two largest economies and trading nations involved. Thus far, both governments have scrupulously avoided public comment on the subject and apparently have never engaged in serious private discussion of it, for understandable reasons. U.S. domestic support for free trade with China would be lacking as long as the lopsided trade deficit with China, fueled by Chinese currency manipulation, continues. As for China, all indications are that the Chinese leadership does not want free trade with the United States, but rather a dominant economic power position within a preferential East Asian economic grouping, for foreign policy as well as economic reasons, with the United States viewed as an adversarial, if not hostile, power within the region.

As of early 2005, the Asia Pacific geopolitical scenario is playing out along such Chinese lines of thought, toward separate and, to a certain extent, competing East Asian, North American, and West European regional groupings. The argument can be made that it is as much in the Chinese as the American foreign policy and economic interests to pursue multilateral rather than regional free trade objectives, as it is argued in Chapter 9. But if such a course change is to be realized, it will require sustained and very high level preparatory discussions between the two governments, which has not yet occurred.

Ethnic and Cultural Affinities

One important dimension of the U.S.-China bilateral relationship that receives very little attention, and almost no serious analysis, is the deepening ethnic and cultural ties between the two countries. The only prominent recent issue in this area, one directly related to advanced technology development, is the large number of Chinese students in American universities, particularly in the math, science, and engineering departments, thousands of whom return to China each year, while even larger numbers remain in the United States to populate university faculties and American advanced technology companies.

Ethnic and cultural ties between Americans and Chinese, however, are far broader and long-standing. In the United States, they stretch prominently from New York to San Francisco and date back 150 years. There are approximately two million Chinese-American U.S. citizens and a further large number of student, nonimmigrant visa, and illegal Chinese residents. Chinese-American communities have assimilated to become highly pro-ductive parts of American society, while retaining much admired Chinese values and culture. A number-one U.S. best-seller in 2000[2] recounted the building of the transcontinental railroad in the 1860s, wherein the many Chinese workers at the Pacific end were the consistent heroes, working the hardest in the face of constant danger and fatal accidents, while enduring harsh racial discrim-ination, and then going on to settle and prosper in the United States with their carefully saved wages. In China, the American historical presence consisted largely of traders and missionaries— primarily engaged in mutual economic gain and spiritual enrich-ment rather than foreign imperial incursions on Chinese sover-eignty—and has thus also been viewed in a generally favorable light.

These embedded ethnic and cultural affinities, like almost all other aspects of the U.S.-China bilateral relationship, are now expanding at a rapid rate as a result of the new era of advanced technology economic engagement and the related revolution in communications. The tens of thousands of Chinese students who have returned home after several years in the United States form an influential grouping within the Chinese power structure, with a full knowledge and sympathetic understanding of the United States and the American way of life. Likewise, Chinese students who have remained in the United States are opening new channels of communication with relatives and friends in China, through e-mail, cell phones, and travel in both directions. Extended travel or residence in China by U.S. senior management is now the norm for multinational American companies, including follow-on communications with Chinese contacts. The expansion of English language training in Chinese schools, together with 24-hour English language television channels, is yet another positive development for improved understanding between the two peoples.

---

[2] Stephen E. Ambrose, *Nothing Like it in the World: The Men Who Built the Transcontinental Railroad 1863-1869* (Simon and Shuster, 2000).

A further important dimension of deepening cultural affinity, still at the beginning stage, is personal contact through vacation and other travel. The U.S. tourist flow to China has been growing and will likely soon be overtaken by reciprocal visits by Chinese to the United States, stemming from the hundreds of millions of increasingly affluent middle-class Chinese with a strong penchant for foreign travel. The burgeoning Chinese tourist outflow went initially to Southeast Asia and is now shifting to European capitals, where it is overtaking the Japanese level of tourists. Chinese travel to the United States has been restrained by U.S. visa regulations, tightened after September 11, but, with time, the Chinese professional and managerial classes should easily qualify for nonimmigrant visas, and the lure of Honolulu, San Francisco, and New York, not to mention the western states and New England with their physical beauty, will become top Chinese travel destinations, encouraged by the millions of family and other Chinese-American contacts in the United States, who far outnumber those in Europe and Japan.

The question raised here is whether this almost entirely positive area of deepening ethnic and cultural affinities should be supported through initiatives by the two governments and private sectors, and the answer is clearly "yes." An immediate issue for the United States is more forthcoming visa approval, which should be facilitated by the virtual absence of Chinese nationals in international terrorist groupings. The number of Chinese students in the United States, for example, has declined from 100,000 to less than 50,000 since September 11, and there are now more Chinese students in the United Kingdom than in the United States. A broader issue for both countries is the great asymmetry in language capability and numbers of ethnic residents in each other's country, overwhelmingly favoring China. This is particularly noteworthy for advanced technology industry, including university-based R&D. Very large numbers of Chinese have attended U.S. schools and worked for American firms, either in the United States or in China, and almost all R&D professionals in China can read and follow the American technical literature in English. In sharp contrast, very few Americans have gone to school in China, have worked in Chinese firms, or can read Chinese.

There are various ways this asymmetry in professional experience and language capability can be reduced, at least somewhat, through public sector, university, and private sector initiatives. Chinese language training in the United States, starting at the secondary school level, could be expanded, with emphasis on basic conversation and reading of technical literature.[3] University junior-year-abroad programs in China, for science and engineering majors, with prerequisite study of Chinese and bilingual instruction in China, could be developed through sister university relationships. Two-year contracts for young Americans to teach English in China while receiving training in Chinese could be organized jointly by the two governments. The placement of mid-level American professionals for tours in Chinese companies, with intensive prior Chinese language training, could be a sound mutual investment for bilateral joint venture relationships, and might start with Lenovo and IBM.

An ambitious and especially high visibility U.S. initiative would be a federally funded, three-year doctoral program for Americans in Chinese universities, following intensive Chinese language training, with fields of concentration shared between science and engineering to prepare Americans in advanced technology industry for work in China and Chinese history and culture to develop highly qualified American university faculty in these subjects. The precedent for such a program was the National Defense Education Act (NDEA) of the 1960s for graduate training in science and other advanced technology fields, as a response to the Soviet space launch of Sputnik, which parallels the current Chinese challenge to U.S. advanced technology leadership.

American society has thrived on cultural diversity and the assimilation by immigrants of U.S. values based on individual freedom and opportunity. Recent priority attention to the assimilation of Hispanic immigrants is well justified in support of this integrating experience. The large Chinese-American community, especially in light of the deepening political, economic, and national security relationships between the two advanced technology superstates, now also deserves cultural programs of international scope to foster better understanding and communication between the two nations.

Concluding Observations

These are the principal dimensions of the new, rapidly deepening U.S.-China bilateral relationship, heavily oriented to the

---

[3] The author is a graduate of the Brooklyn Technical High School, where he took three years of French, strongly oriented to reading technical literature, which served him well over the years. He encourages his *alma mater* to get out front now with an even more ambitious four-year Chinese program focused on basic conversation and the reading of technical literature.

mutual economic interests of—and rivalry between—the advanced technology superstates. Before summing up with a few broad policy conclusions, however, two other observations are offered to give perspective to the historic setting of the new relationship.

The first observation is a comparison of the current U.S.-China relationship with the U.S.-Soviet relationship in the late 1940s. The basic observation is that, apart from the earlier Soviet and the current Chinese rise to superstate status, the sharp differences in the content of the U.S. bilateral relationships far outweigh the similarities. Most importantly, there was no significant economic relationship between the United States and the Soviet Union. The Soviet economy was isolated and never a functioning part of the global economy. U.S.-Soviet trade was minimal, and U.S. trade policy was concentrated on export sanctions to deny products of use to the Soviet military. The operational relationship with the Soviet Union consisted mainly of an arms race between the two countries, together with very large financial subsidies to gain political support in the developing world. The net result was a massive "negative sum game," which finally bankrupted the Soviet Union. There was also very little personal contact between Russians and Americans, aside from official exchanges. There were relatively few Russian-Americans and minimal private travel or language capability in either direction.

In fundamental contrast, which cannot be overstated, the U.S.-China relationship is, or at least should be, a predominantly "positive sum game," stemming principally from the gains from open trade and investment, while personal and private sector contacts are large and growing. More troubled parts of the new bilateral relationship with China, such as Chinese geopolitical objectives in East Asia and the Chinese challenge to U.S. advanced technology leadership, which is related to the pace of Chinese military modernization, are principally economic in content as well. Even for national security interests, there is mutual interest with respect to the proliferation of weapons of mass destruction and international terrorism, in sharp contrast to the direct military confrontation, based on mutually assured destruction, which existed between the United States and the Soviet Union. These definitive contrasts, almost entirely negative in character for the U.S.-Soviet relationship while predominantly positive for the U.S.-China relationship, are particularly relevant to official U.S.-Chinese relations at this time because many, if not most, of the foreign policy and defense cadres in both governments received their formative training and professional experience as "Cold War warriors," with deeply ingrained negative sum mindsets.

The second observation to help adjust to the new realities of the U.S.-China relationship concerns the question of which now is the single most important U.S. bilateral relationship. A recurring debate during the Cold War, at least within the State Department, was over which bilateral relationship was number one. Some opted for the Soviet Union, others for Germany in its pivotal position between East and West, and still others for the United Kingdom and its "special relationship" with the United States. The usual winner, however, was Japan, and a favorite line for American ambassadors to Tokyo was to refer to Japan as the most important U.S. bilateral relationship. This has now all changed. Russia does not come close to being number one, Germany has faded into a largely neutral Central European nation, and the United Kingdom, while the key U.S. ally in Iraq, does not have the global reach to top the list. This leads to a choice between Japan and China and, on every count, from economic to geopolitical to national security interests, China emerges as the more important. It may be premature for the U.S. Secretary of State to state this new reality publicly, but at least the long habit of referring to Japan as the single most important relationship should be quietly ended.

This summary assessment of the new U.S.-China policy relationship leads to three basic conclusions, which form the framework for the more detailed economic policy discussion that follows.

First, *economic interests dominate the bilateral relationship*. Expanding mutual gains from trade and investment need to be developed within a policy relationship of fair trade and competition, based on market forces. Longer term interests in the evolving international financial and trade systems should be managed through collaborative U.S. and Chinese leadership roles. Most importantly for the United States, U.S. leadership in advanced technology industries should be maintained, for the reasons given by the President's Council of Advisors on Science and Technology. All of these policy objectives are elaborated in Chapters 8–10, with recommendations for a more assertive, forward-looking, and, in some respects, restructured policy response.

Second, *the political relationship with China is troubled, but it is likely to move in the right direction, largely as a result of the deepening bilateral economic engagement*. There is no global ideological struggle between communism and capitalism, as during the Cold War, but rather basic differences with respect to democratic process, respect for individual rights, and the rule of law within China. U.S. direct involvement in Chinese internal affairs is limited principally to pressing for compliance with international political norms and obligations. Much of the U.S. response should be by example at home, now greatly facilitated by expanding contacts between the two peoples, which should be encouraged. In parallel, U.S. companies engaged on the ground in China are having the broadest direct impact on positive political change in China through their productive, competitive enterprise and their observed respect for individual rights and opportunities for Chinese employees.

Finally, *mutual national security interests are less significantly engaged and, in any event, should not be pursued at the expense of U.S. economic interests*. This is the most controversial conclusion in view of criticisms of recent U.S.-China policy favoring national security over economic interests. The basic conclusion drawn here is that, almost entirely, the two sets of interests should be treated independently, on their respective merits, with economic actions related to national security limited to directly targeted sanctions, such as for specific U.S. exports of military use or against Chinese firms in violation of international covenants. The broader conclusion not to trade off U.S. economic interests to achieve national security objectives is not argued further here, but recent experience points to the need for serious debate on the subject, within the executive branch and the Congress, as well as by nongovernmental public policy organizations and the private sector.

Chapter 8

International Financial Policy

The most important and immediate U.S. policy conflict with China is in the area of international finance, that is, the issue of "currency manipulation," whereby China is maintaining its exchange rate to the dollar far below the market-determined level, and thus gaining an unfair trade advantage, including substantial adverse impact on U.S. advanced technology industry. Another important and related international financial issue is that, over the next five to ten years, China will rise to center stage as one of three key currency financial powers and as the financial center of East Asia. The two issues are related in that the resolution of the currency manipulation conflict will open the door for the rapid realization of the Chinese global financial role. In fact, the great anomaly, up to this point, of the Chinese economic strategy for market-based industrialization through open trade and foreign investment has been the maintenance of a nonconvertible currency on capital account, rigidly linked to the dollar. Almost all less developed and even the least developed countries have some form of currency convertibility and exchange rate flexibility to avoid the economic distortions and corruption that result from a nonconvertible currency that is fixed well above or below its market-based level. Change by China to a flexible, market-oriented exchange rate is long overdue in order to resolve conflict with trading partners over currency manipulation, provide a more productive financial sector within the Chinese economy, and pave the way for China to assume its proper role as an international financial power.

This presentation deals with currency manipulation at considerable length in view of its complexity and the gravity of the current situation.[1] It is first defined in terms of IMF and WTO

---

[1] The presentation here draws on the author's tracking of the currency manipulation issue since the late 1990s, including: *The U.S. Trillion Dollar Debt to Foreign Central Banks* (Institute for International Finance, 1998); *The Trade Deficit, The Dollar, and The U.S. National Interest* (The Hudson Institute, 2000), especially Chapters 3 and 7; "Chinese Currency Manipulation" (statement before the Senate Committee on

obligations and then assessed with respect to the degree of undervaluation of the yuan and the impact this is having on international trade and the internal Chinese economy. From this assessment, a more forceful and effective U.S. policy response to curb currency manipulation is recommended. The final section of the chapter moves beyond the immediate issue of currency manipulation to broader systemic change under way within the international financial system, with a focus on the role China will play in it.

Currency Manipulation: IMF and WTO Obligations

Currency manipulation can be described as a deliberate policy to keep the exchange rate below its "equilibrium" rate so as to gain an unfair competitive advantage in trade through lower export and higher import prices. This definition leads to the questions of what is an equilibrium exchange rate and what policy instruments are being used to manipulate a currency down.

The equilibrium exchange rate cannot be defined quantitatively over time because it is constantly changing. In the case of China, in particular, the rapid expansion of foreign investment and exports in newly created advanced technology industries over the past five years has changed significantly whatever the equilibrium rate was in the late 1990s, in the direction of a stronger yuan. The market-oriented benchmark for a fair or equilibrium rate is a free-floating rate, such as currently exists among the dollar, the euro, and a number of other currencies. Another basic indicator of equilibrium for currencies not freely floating is the degree of "basic balance" in external accounts, measured as the aggregate of the current and long-term capital accounts. A sustained large basic balance surplus, for example, is an indication of under-valuation. Yet another, less direct indicator of equilibrium is that of purchasing power parity (ppp) indices among trading nations. All of these measures are examined in the following section, especially as they relate to the degree of current undervaluation of the yuan and other East Asian currencies.

Banking, Housing, and Urban Affairs, May 1, 2002); "Exchange Rate Manipulation To Gain an Unfair Competitive Advantage: The Case Against Japan and China," C. Fred Bergsten and John Williamson, eds., *Dollar Overvaluation and the World Economy* (Institute for International Economics, 2003), pp. 267-284; and "Currency Manipulation and the U.S. Trade Deficit" (statement before the U.S.-China Economic and Security Review Commission, September 23, 2003).

The question of policy instruments utilized for currency manipulation is more straightforward. The only policy instrument used solely for the purpose of influencing the exchange rate is Central Bank intervention in financial markets to buy or sell foreign currencies. As for currency manipulation to gain an unfair competitive advantage, this means Central Bank purchases of foreign exchange, which work to hold a currency below its market-oriented level. These purchase figures are readily available in the monthly IMF *International Financial Statistics*.

These basic points about currency manipulation were well understood by the framers of the international financial and trading systems, the IMF, and the General Agreement on Tariffs and Trade (GATT), now incorporated in the WTO. The term "currency manipulation" derives from IMF Article IV, and is appropriately defined in terms of measurable policy actions through Central Bank intervention, in particular. Article IV, Section 1, states that members should "avoid manipulating exchange rates . . . in order . . . to gain an unfair competitive advantage over other members." Section 3 then elaborates "the right of members to have exchange arrangements of their choice consistent with the purposes of the Fund and the *obligations under Section 1 of this Article*." (Italics added.) In other words, member exchange-rate policies, whether a floating rate, as now exists for the Japanese yen, or a fixed rate, as for the Chinese yuan, must all be implemented in a way that does not entail currency manipulation, as proscribed under Section 1.

This leads to the official definition of currency manipulation, which is contained in the IMF surveillance provision related to Article IV, referring to it as "protracted large-scale intervention in one direction in the exchange market." "In one direction," again, means Central Bank purchases of foreign currencies, since this is the way to maintain an undervalued currency in order to gain an unfair competitive advantage.

Thus the question of whether China has been manipulating its currency in violation of its IMF Article IV obligations is determined by the three adjectives—protracted, large-scale, and one directional (i.e., purchases) related to intervention by the Chinese Central Bank. Before examining this in terms of recent performance, however, it is useful to relate the IMF currency manipulation obligation to counterpart obligations under Article XV of the GATT, now incorporated within the WTO. This article deals with "Exchange Arrangements," and stipulates that members should not take exchange rate actions that "frustrate the intent of the provisions of this Agreement." The intent of the agreement, as stated in broadest terms in the Preamble, is the objective of "entering into reciprocal and mutually advantageous arrangements directed to the substantial reduction of tariffs and other barriers to trade." Clearly, "exchange rate manipulation to gain an unfair competitive advantage," as defined by IMF Article IV, meets the "frustrate the intent" test. Moreover, GATT Article XV also provides for full consultation with the IMF, including the stipulation that members "should accept all findings of statistical fact presented by the Fund relating to foreign exchange." Thus, there is a direct link between IMF proscribed currency manipulation and WTO obligations under GATT Article XV.

This IMF-WTO linkage is important in terms of policy recourse for countries suffering the adverse trade effects of currency manipulation. Even if China were to be found in violation of its IMF Article IV obligations not to manipulate its currency, no significant IMF penalties are available if China were to continue currency manipulation. The most the IMF could do would be to make China ineligible for IMF stand-by loans, which is frivolous in view of Chinese foreign exchange holdings of $660 billion, as of March 2005. A counterpart finding of violation of GATT Article XV, however, opens the way to WTO dispute settlement procedures, with ultimate recourse to trade sanctions.

Turning to the three adjectives that define currency manipulation, an assessment of whether the Chinese Central Bank purchases of foreign exchange were "protracted" and "large-scale" can best be viewed in relation to the Chinese external basic balance, that is, the current account together with the long-term capital account, which is approximated here by the inflow of foreign direct investment. If this basic balance is in substantial surplus, there will likely be a net inflow of foreign currencies, which will put upward pressure on the exchange rate. Central Bank purchases under these circumstances, however, take this foreign currency inflow off the market, thereby keeping the exchange rate below a fair or market-determined level. In the current context of a fixed and nonconvertible yuan, the Chinese government does this by requiring almost all incoming foreign exchange, which is not used to purchase imports or for other current account expenditures, to be sold to the Central Bank at the fixed rate.

Within this analytic context, Chinese Central Bank purchases from 2001 through 2004—related to the current account surplus and the inflow of foreign direct investment, which together are an approximation of the basic balance—are presented in Chart 8-1. Central Bank purchases were $57 billion in 2001, rising steadily to $118 billion in 2003, and then skyrocketing to $207 billion in 2004. The basic balance, in parallel, rose steadily from $61 billion in 2001 to $130 billion in 2004. For the three-year period 2001-2003, Central Bank purchases totaled $249 billion, compared with a cumulative basic balance surplus of $222 billion. In other words, Chinese Central Bank purchases during these three years more than offset the entire net inflow of foreign exchange from the current account surplus plus the inflow of FDI. As for 2004, the surge in Central Bank purchases to $207 billion greatly exceeded the $130 billion basic balance surplus, but many of these purchases were made to offset the inflow of short-term capital in anticipation of a yuan revaluation which, incidentally, would have put further upward pressure on a market-based or floating yuan. The enormity of these Central Bank purchases over four years, related to what were also extraordinarily large basic balance surpluses, surely qualifies as "protracted" and "large-scale." Nothing comes remotely close during the 60-year history of the IMF, except recent Japanese Central Bank purchases, which also clearly qualify as currency manipulation. There could be mitigating circumstances for occasional large-scale purchases, such as to replenish an inadequate level of foreign exchange holdings or to mitigate a large trade deficit which is having a negative impact on economic growth. The opposite circumstances currently prevail in China, however, with $660 billion in foreign exchange holdings, roughly equal to annual imports, while the trade account has consistently been in surplus. Thus there should be no question that China has been manipulating its currency in gross violation of its obligations under IMF Article IV and, by extension, GATT Article XV of the WTO.

The Degree of Chinese Undervaluation

There has been considerable analysis and commentary about how far the Chinese yuan is undervalued, with estimates ranging from 20 percent to over 50 percent. All of the estimates are, at best, rough approximations, but this does not change the basic assessment that the yuan is greatly undervalued, thus giving China a substantial unfair competitive advantage in trade. If the yuan were undervalued by 40 percent, for example, that would equate to an across-the-board tariff of 40 percent on all Chinese imports, together with a 40 percent subsidy on all exports. The resulting price adjustments, favoring Chinese export- and import-competing industries, would far outweigh those from reductions in Chinese trade barriers resulting from WTO membership.

Chart 8-1
Chinese Currency Manipulation: Central Bank Purchases and the Basic Balance

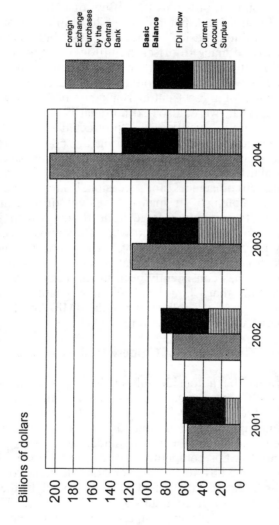

Sources: IMF, *International Financial Statistics*, and Chinese government sources

High-end assessments of the undervaluation of the yuan include that of financial guru Henry Kaufman, who estimates that China would have to revalue its currency upward by 50 percent to 70 percent in order to realign its economic and financial relationships.[2] This is consistent with World Bank estimates of a more than 50 percent undervaluation based on differences in national purchasing power parity indices. Jeffrey Frankel made similar ppp estimates suggesting that the yuan, in 2000, was undervalued by 45 percent in logarithmic terms and 36 percent in absolute terms, and that it is undervalued by at least as much in 2005.[3] *The Economist* magazine's Big Mac survey which, in similar fashion, compares the price of Big Macs around the world, finds the yuan is undervalued by 58 percent, the largest spread of the 30 countries surveyed.[4]

Morris Goldstein of the Institute of International Economics estimated an undervaluation of the yuan in 2004 "in the upper half of the 15 to 30 percent range," but this range substantially understates the degree of undervaluation for two reasons.[5] The first reason is that Goldstein underestimated the Chinese trade surplus and the U.S. trade deficit in 2004. Based on trade data for the first few months of 2004, he estimated a major decline in the Chinese trade surplus and a corresponding decline in the current account surplus from 4.5 percent to 5 percent of GDP in 2003 to only 2.5 percent in 2004, while the Chinese trade surplus actually increased moderately from $26 billion in 2003 to $34 billion in 2004, and the current account surplus rose from $46 billion in 2003 to $69 billion in 2004.[6] Likewise, Goldstein estimated a U.S. trade deficit in 2004 of $495 billion, about the same as in 2003, while the actual U.S. deficit rose sharply in 2004 to $618 billion.

The second reason why the Goldstein estimate is on the low side is because of his estimated "normal" capital account surplus of only about $20 billion, or 1.5 percent of GDP, based on the

---

[2] *Financial Times*, December 9, 2004.
[3] Jeffrey Frankel, "On the Renminbi: The Choice Between Adjustment Under a Fixed Exchange Rate and Adjustment Under a Flexible Rate" (NBER working paper No. 11274, April 2005).
[4] *The Economist*, December 18, 2004, p. 162.
[5] Morris Goldstein, "China and the Renminbi Exchange Rate," C. Fred Bergsten and John Williamson, eds., *Dollar Adjustment: How Far? Against What?* (Institute for International Economics, 2004).
[6] The Chinese trade balance is seasonal, with any trade deficits in the early months offset by large surpluses later in the year, related to Christmas season exports.

period 1999-2002, which excludes Central Bank purchases of foreign exchange as capital inflows. If such purchases were included for 2003, for example, the capital accounts surplus would rise to 7 percent to 8 percent of GDP, with a correspondingly much higher calculated undervaluation of the yuan.

A more appropriate measure of the degree of yuan under-valuation would be the external "basic balance," that is the current account surplus plus the surplus or net inflow of long-term capital, principally the inflow of FDI. This is a more direct measure of the total net inflow of foreign exchange that the Central Bank needs to offset through official purchases in order to maintain the lower fixed exchange rate, a relationship confirmed by Chart 8-1, where Central Bank purchases during 2001-2004 exceeded the basic balance surpluses, as explained above. An estimate by the author, for the years 2001-2002, based on the basic balance surplus related to Central Bank purchases, was a yuan undervaluation in the order of 40 percent.[7]

These are the most widely cited estimates of the degree of yuan undervaluation. Up to this point the 40 percent figure, re-lated to the basic-balance measure, has appeared to be a reason-able benchmark, perhaps put within a range of 30 percent to 50 percent. Even more important, however, looking ahead, there will likely be a major increase in the Chinese trade and current account surpluses in 2005-2006. Chinese exports of textiles and apparel alone, as a result of the elimination of quotas, could rise $50 billion to $100 billion per year, based on WTO projections. China has also recently shifted from being a net importer to a net exporter of steel, and the very large trade deficit in semiconductors should decline sharply as a result of the rapid expansion of semiconductor production in China as described in Chapter 3. As a result, the trade surplus of $34 billion in 2004 could rise to $100 billion to $150 billion by 2006. As for the current account surplus, in addition to the larger trade surplus, interest payments to the Central Bank should increase substantially. On current course, Central Bank foreign exchange holdings will increase from $600 billion in 2004 to at least $900 billion in 2006, and in conjunction with an increase in the earned interest rate from 4 percent to perhaps 5 percent, the result would be a $21 billion increase in the current account surplus from official interest payments alone, for the most part offset by a larger U.S. current account deficit. In conclusion, the degree of yuan undervaluation is estimated here, on a conservative basis, to be at least 40 percent, and perhaps significantly higher.

---

[7] Preeg, *op. cit.*, 2003.

The Trade and Economic Impact

A greatly undervalued yuan, compared with a market-based floating rate, is having substantial impact on international trade and on the course of the Chinese national economy. The trade issue that has received the most political attention has been the impact on the U.S. trade deficit with China, particularly in the manufacturing sector, but other trade effects are also important, such as that on developing country labor-intensive exports. The discussion here focuses on the three issues of the U.S. trade deficit, developing country labor-intensive exports, particularly in apparel and textiles, and the impact on the Chinese economy.

The Impact on the U.S. Trade Deficit

The adverse impact of the undervalued yuan on the U.S. trade deficit is both direct and indirect. The direct effect is from the price advantage obtained by Chinese export- and import-competing industries, which leads to a larger U.S. bilateral trade deficit with China and a loss of U.S. exports to Chinese competitors in third-country markets. The indirect effect is from other trading partners, principally Japan, South Korea, and Taiwan, who also manipulate their currencies below market-based levels in order to remain competitive with China, their principal trade competitor. This is the so-called "linchpin" position of China, with the presumption that if China were to revalue its currency to a market-based level, the others would also curtail intervention and allow their currencies to float up to market-based levels, thus eliminating their unfair competitive trade advantage as well. This is particularly important as related to the export platform issue discussed in Chapter 4. The very large majority of Chinese imports incorporated in reexports to the United States are from the other three principal currency manipulators—Japan, South Korea, and Taiwan. Therefore, if China revalues and the others follow suit, the entire content of such products exported by China would be subject to a major revaluation.

How much impact the elimination of currency manipulation by China and others, principally in East Asia, would have in reducing the U.S trade deficit, like the degree of yuan undervaluation, cannot be estimated with precision, although again even rough orders of magnitude indicate that the impact would be very substantial. There has, in fact, been considerable econometric research since the 1980s on the relationship between the dollar exchange rate and the U.S. trade deficit. The resulting rule of thumb is that a 1 percent decline in the dollar, with a one- to three-year time lag, would result in a $10 billion lower U.S. trade deficit.[8] There are two reasons, however, why the termination of currency manipulation by China and other East Asian nations would have a greater than $10 billion per percent devaluation impact on the trade deficit. First, the value of trade has expanded greatly since the $10 billion estimates were calculated. A doubling of the value of trade involved, other things being equal, would lead to a $20 billion rule of thumb. The second reason is that other things are not equal with respect to the trade relationship between the United States and East Asia, where the currency manipulation is concentrated. About 90 percent of U.S.-East Asia trade is in manufactures, the increasing majority of which is in higher technology products, directly competitive with U.S. production, and this trade has above-average price elasticities. For example, U.S. imports of petroleum, industrial raw materials, tropical agricultural products, and labor-intensive consumer goods, such as apparel and footwear, where the large majority of consumption is already imported, are "price inelastic," which is to say that a 10 percent change in the import price would lead to a less than 10 percent change in the quantity of imports. In contrast, for higher tech sectors, such as information technology and communications, machinery, and automotive products, a 10 percent change in U.S. import and export prices would lead to a much larger percentage change in the quantities of imports and exports, in the order of 20 percent to 30 percent.[9]

A 40 percent revaluation of the yuan, together with a linchpin effect of a 20 percent or more revaluation by Japan, South Korea, and Taiwan, would result in a 7 percent trade-weighted average decline in the dollar.[10] The $10 billion rule of thumb would indicate a $70 billion lower U.S. trade deficit, but for the two reasons stated above, plus the fact that there are other apparent

---

[8] This does not necessarily mean that the absolute level of the trade deficit would be $10 billion lower, since other factors, such as the income effect of differing rates of GDP growth, also influence the absolute level of the deficit. It is likely that these other effects are tending to increase the U.S. deficit, and that therefore a 1 percent decline in the dollar would lead to a less than $10 billion decline in the absolute level of the deficit. This does not change the point made here, however, that, as a result of a 1 percent decline in the dollar, the deficit would be at least $10 billion lower than it otherwise would have been.

[9] The 20 percent to 30 percent range implies price elasticities for imports and exports of minus two to minus three, a generally accepted range for these kinds of products.

[10] In 2004, these four trading partners accounted for 17 percent of U.S. exports, 28 percent of U.S. imports, and, thanks in large part to currency manipulation, a 41 percent share of the U.S. trade deficit.

currency manipulators, such as Malaysia and Singapore, who would also be pressed to desist, a rough estimate for the reduction in the U.S. trade deficit would be $100 billion to $150 billion, or upwards to a quarter of the $618 billion total deficit in 2004. Some 80 percent to 90 percent of this reduction would benefit U.S. manufacturing industry, of which about 30 percent would be in advanced technology industries, of particular interest to this study. As for additional steps to reduce the U.S deficit, there could be further dollar devaluation *vis-à-vis* other currencies, as well as U.S. domestic economic policy actions described in Chapter 10. And it may be that Henry Kaufman is right and the yuan needs to be revalued by 50 percent to 70 percent.

The Impact on Developing Country Exports of Labor-Intensive Products, Principally Apparel and Textiles

A major revaluation of the yuan would accelerate the restructuring of Chinese exports from labor-intensive to capital- and technology-intensive products, a process that is already happening, as shown in Tables 4-5 and 4-6. As Chinese GDP grows at 8 percent to 9 percent per year through rapid expansion of more advanced technology industries, labor costs also rise at a relatively rapid rate, with a resulting decline in the competitiveness of labor-intensive exports. This was the earlier experience of rapid industrialization in Japan, Taiwan, and South Korea, and more recently in Mexico. Maintaining a substantially undervalued currency, however, holds back this process of trade restructuring, with adverse consequences for other exporters of labor-intensive products.

The principal beneficiaries of a yuan revaluation impact on these labor-intensive industries would be the lower income and least developed countries, particularly in South Asia, the Caribbean Basin, and sub-Saharan Africa. A 40 percent increase in labor costs in China from revaluation to a market-based exchange rate would make the exports of these other countries substantially more competitive *vis-à-vis* China, and lead to an increase in their global market share for such products. The restructuring trade effect from Chinese revaluation would be especially powerful because Chinese labor-intensive industries, such as apparel and textiles, footwear, toys, and sporting goods, involve very high proportions of domestic value added, and relatively small amounts of imported components as often is the case for higher tech products. The change in price competitiveness in this case, involving high price "elasticities of substitution" be- tween Chinese and lower income country exporters to industrialized country markets, would be very large, to the great benefit of the lower income country exporters.

This relationship between Chinese currency manipulation and highly price-sensitive competition with labor-intensive exports of lower income countries is particularly important in 2005 because of the termination of the four-decade-old "multifiber arrangement" of apparel and textile import quotas, which worked to restrain Chinese exports, to the benefit of lower income exporters, in this largest trading sector of labor-intensive products. The WTO estimates that the termination of textile quotas could lead to a more than doubling of the Chinese global share of apparel and textile exports from 18 percent to 50 percent, or, in terms of 2004 Chinese exports of $90 billion, an increase of more than $100 billion, mostly at the expense of lower income country exports. It is in this context that an early major revaluation of the yuan could greatly ease the adverse impact of textile quota elimination on the apparel and textile exports of lower income countries.[11]

The Impact on the Chinese Economy

The effects on the Chinese economy from a major revaluation of the yuan and the termination of large-scale Central Bank purchases of foreign exchange would be substantial and, for the most part, beneficial. They were discussed briefly in Chapter 5 and have received fuller treatment elsewhere.[12] In macropolicy terms, a major revaluation would restrain inflationary pressures and support structural transition away from over-concentration on export-oriented industrial production and toward production for the domestic market, including service industries and domestic sources of energy. Banking sector reform would be greatly facilitated from currency convertibility and more effective competition in the financial services sector. As for resource allocation, the Central Bank currently absorbs about 10 percent of GDP in the form of foreign exchange purchases, earning relatively low rates of interest, while these domestic savings could be better utilized for the building of infrastructure, environmental improvements, health care, and other domestic priorities. There are also "terms of trade" benefits from a stronger currency, in terms of

---

[11] China recognized this adverse impact, in principle, by applying a 2 percent to 4 percent export tax on apparel exports, but this was a token action that will have very small impact compared with a major revaluation related to the termination of currency manipulation.

[12] For example, see Goldstein, *op. cit.*, pp. 209-228, with extensive references.

lower import prices for consumers, lower cost vacation travel abroad, and a reduced yuan price for petroleum and other imported industrial raw materials, of benefit to Chinese industry.

Despite all these benefits, however, China is now in the fifth year of currency manipulation to maintain a greatly undervalued currency that has depreciated further as a result of its link to the dollar. One reason for this is the familiar political fact of life that export- and import-competing manufacturing industries would face stronger competition and reduced profits from currency revaluation, and these industries have a relatively more targeted and powerful influence on government decision making. In broad policy terms, the result is a "mercantilist" trade strategy of setting a large trade surplus in manufactures as a national policy objective, implemented not so much through trade policy, which is subject to the constraints of WTO obligations, as through the more powerful and, up to this point, uninhibited financial modality of currency manipulation.

There is probably another more political reason, however, why China is pursuing a financially driven mercantilist trade policy, which goes to the core of the subject of this study. China sees the maintenance of a large trade surplus in manufactures as the driving force for the rapid development of advanced technology industry, and the concomitant narrowing if not elimination of the U.S. advanced technology leadership position in world trade. Chinese trade strategy can thus be further qualified as "advanced technology mercantilist" in character, with very large national interest stakes involved, particularly *vis-à-vis* the United States. Year by year, the rapid development of new Chinese advanced technology industries, thus far principally by multinational corporations, but with increasing participation by Chinese companies, is being driven by unfairly high export profits as a result of currency manipulation. The threat this poses for U.S. economic and national security interests, as noted earlier, was articulated by the President's Council of Advisors on Science and Technology. There is clearly an urgent need for a more forceful and effective U.S. policy response to currency manipulation by several trading partners, and by China most urgently of all, in order for the United States to continue its international leadership position in advanced technology industries.

A More Forceful and Effective
U.S. Policy Response

The positive point of departure for the U.S.-China financial policy relationship is agreement that the yuan should become flexible and market-oriented, which strongly implies a substantial upward revaluation. Nothing concrete happened, however, during four years of discussion on the subject through 2004, while the United States accepted, without formal complaint, the increasingly undervalued yuan, the growing Chinese trade and investment surplus, and the related doubling of the U.S. trade deficit, including a sharp decline into deficit for advanced technology products. As for the massive Chinese currency manipulation in violation of IMF and WTO obligations, the U.S. policy response can be characterized as implausible denial. This harsh policy assessment requires some background explanation.

Exchange rate manipulation to gain a competitive advantage in trade has a long history within the IMF system. During the late 1960s, various European and other currencies were pegged at low rates to the dollar, and in response to a growing U.S. trade deficit, the United States, in August 1971, ended dollar convertibility into gold and imposed a 15 percent import surcharge, which ushered in a new era of largely free-floating exchange rates among the major currencies.[13]   The more recent proliferation of protracted large-scale Central Bank purchases to maintain unfairly low exchange rates can be dated from the mid-1980s, with Japan and Taiwan as the initial principal manipulators. A lackluster response by the U.S. Department of the Treasury led to congressional initiative in the 1986 Omnibus Trade Act, whereby the Secretary of the Treasury, every six months, was required to analyze and report to the Senate Banking Committee any evidence of currency manipulation by trading partners. The reference to "currency manipulation" clearly referred to IMF Article IV obligations, since that was the source of the term and the issue of Article IV violations was discussed during the formulation of the legislation. The early Treasury reports pursuant to the 1986 Act made a few references to possible currency manipulation by Taiwan and others, but, by the early 1990s, the issue faded away as the U.S. trade deficit declined greatly, in response to a much lower dollar. The financial crises of 1995-1997 further removed currency manipulation from the picture, because all of the crisis-stricken countries, to their later misfortune, were trying to maintain

---

[13] This forceful and successful U.S. action, led by Treasury Secretary John Connolly, former Governor of Texas, and his highly able young Undersecretary for Monetary Affairs, Paul Volcker, was directed principally against key NATO allies at the height of the Cold War, and despite State Department grumbling. This is significant for the current situation, where foreign policy interests appear to take precedence over U.S. economic interests *vis-à-vis* China.

overvalued currencies, the opposite of currency manipulation to gain competitive advantage through an undervalued currency.

The current wave of currency manipulation began in 1998-1999, as countries pursued export-led economic recovery from the low growth financial crisis years, which would obviously benefit from an undervalued currency.[14] Japan and Taiwan were again out front, followed by South Korea, and, beginning in 2001, China. In fact, a broadly based shift was under way in international financial policies, away from the traditional preference for a strong currency to fight inflation and reap economic gains from lower import prices, and toward maintaining an undervalued currency to stimulate export-led growth.[15] In other words, a global shift to the mercantilist international financial strategy has taken place since 1998. The most notable exception has been the United States, with its unqualified assertion that a strong dollar is in the U.S. interest. The semiannual Treasury reports to the Senate Banking Committee have become briefer, while consistently denying any evidence of currency manipulation by others.

In this radically changed international financial policy context, and with the U.S. trade deficit up from $200 billion in 2000 to $618 billion in 2004, in large part as a result of the exchange rate induced surpluses of others, there has been a strong reaction by the U.S. private sector and the Congress against the U.S. Treasury's benign acceptance of currency manipulation. The Coalition for a Sound Dollar was formed in the spring of 2002, chaired by the National Association of Manufacturers and consisting of over 90 private sector industry, agriculture, and labor organizations, to protest currency manipulation by the four East Asians, in particular, with documentation provided in its "Monthly Asia Currency Manipulation Monitor."[16] The bipartisan U.S.-China Economic and Security Review Commission, created by the Congress in 2000, condemned Chinese currency manipulation in its 2003 report. Congressional statements of concern coalesced in

---

[14] In some cases, such as that of South Korea, initial purchases of foreign exchange were principally intended to rebuild depleted reserves after the financial crises, but the benefits to the export sector from the resulting undervalued exchange rate soon became habit forming.

[15] Examples of other countries that have recently undertaken large-scale official purchases of foreign exchange while maintaining a current account surplus are, with reserve holdings as of late 2004, India ($121 billion); Russia ($114 billion); Singapore ($110 billion); Malaysia ($59 billion); Brazil ($49 billion); and Thailand ($45 billion). The United States, in contrast, has foreign exchange holdings of only $42 billion, despite trade flows several times larger than any of these countries.

[16] www.sounddollar.org.

unanimous resolutions in both houses in September 2003, calling for urgent action against currency manipulation in violation of IMF and WTO obligations, with China and Japan the principal targets.

Confrontation between the two branches reached a climax with the appearance of Secretary of the Treasury John Snow before the Senate Banking Committee in November 2003. He presented his semiannual report with the conclusion that China did not meet the "technical requirements" of the 1986 Trade Act with respect to currency manipulation. Chairman Richard Shelby's first question was to ask what technical requirements were not met, and the Secretary's inability to answer the question led to two hours of highly critical comments and questions from 13 Senators on both sides of the aisle. Secretary Snow concluded the session by reiterating his intent to press China toward a flexible market-based yuan, although without setting a deadline for results.

This is the case for the assessment that U.S. policy toward Chinese and other currency manipulation has been in a state of implausible denial. U.S. Treasury statements every six months asserting there is no indication of currency manipulation reduce leverage against China and others to terminate currency manipulation. They also present an awkward dilemma for IMF management, faced with unprecedented abuse of Article IV currency manipulation obligations, while the largest shareholder and principal victim of the resulting competitive disadvantage in trade categorically denies currency manipulation by any IMF member, every six months.[17]

There has been widespread comment as to why the United States has not pursued China more forcefully to revalue its currency. Some American companies and banks with operations in China benefit from the stable, undervalued yuan. There is also a traditional institutional aversion within the U.S. Treasury to have open conflict over exchange rate policy, and abhorrence to the idea of allowing exchange rate policy to be adjudicated through WTO dispute procedures. The most frequently cited reason for restraint on the currency issue, however, is that priority is given to U.S. foreign policy interests for obtaining Chinese cooperation in negotiations with North Korea and for the war on terror more broadly. The conclusion drawn in Chapter 7 rejects this rationale

---

[17] Technical level U.S. Treasury officials and IMF staff are aware of the provisions of Article IV, including the surveillance criterion related to protracted large-scale purchases by Central Banks. In private conversation, their response to pointed questions tends to be a shrug of the shoulders.

for sacrificing major U.S. economic interests with China for more questionable results in the national security arena, and recommends that, in any event, each of the distinct sets of interests should be pursued on its own merits.

During the spring of 2005, there have been clear signs of increased pressure by the U.S. Treasury on China for an early currency revaluation. In part, this has been in response to increased congressional concern, as expressed in an April 7 measure in the Senate, adopted 67-33, calling for a vote in July on the application of 27.5 percent tariffs on imports from China if China does not agree to revalue its currency within 180 days. It also reflects the prospect of a substantially larger U.S. trade deficit in 2005 together with a much larger Chinese trade surplus. Secretary Snow reported to the Senate Banking Committee in May 2005 that China should move significantly toward a more flexible currency over the ensuing six months, but again denied that China was manipulating its currency.

In any event, the time has clearly come for a more forceful and effective policy response to currency manipulation by China and others, in violation of IMF and WTO obligations, which is having substantial adverse impact on U.S. trade, and especially so for advanced technology industry. The following steps are offered as the broad lines of such a policy response:

1. *The United States should make a clear statement of the adverse impact on U.S. export- and import-competing industries from currency manipulation by a number of trading partners, which is in clear violation of IMF Article IV and WTO GATT Article XV obligations.* The resulting increase in the unsustainably large U.S. trade deficit would be explained, including the especially serious adverse impact on U.S. advanced technology industry, which makes this a priority issue requiring prompt resolution.

2. *The initial designation of currency manipulators should at least include China, Japan, South Korea, and Taiwan, all of whom clearly qualify in terms of protracted large-scale Central Bank purchases of foreign exchange, while maintaining large current account and basic balance surpluses.* China should not be singled out for exceptional criticism, and equally harsh condemnation of Taiwan should temper expected anti-American reactions in Beijing. At the same time, however, it should be made clear that Chinese curtailment of currency manipulation is essential and the linchpin for broader resolution of the issue with others.

3. *The United States should state a clear preference for re-solving the currency manipulation issue through informal bilateral and group consultations, but also the intent to pursue formal dispute procedures in the IMF and the WTO if necessary.* Bilateral consultations with the four or more designated manipulators would begin promptly, while discussion would also take place within the Group of Seven (G-7) (Canada, France, Germany, Italy, Japan, the United Kingdom, and the United States) and the APEC finance ministers' forums. The G-7 finance minister grouping should be expanded to a G-8, with full Chinese participation, in view of China's rapid growth in trade, investment, and international finance. At the same time, however, the United States should emphasize the urgency of resolving the currency manipulation issue, and make clear that if informal consultations do not achieve early results, the United States will initiate dispute procedures within the IMF and the WTO, fully confident that it will prevail in justifying its grievances.

4. *The termination of currency manipulation should also be discussed in the broader context of the need for global eco-nomic adjustment from the current large and unsustainable imbalances, particularly the huge current account deficit between the United States and East Asia.* The adjustment would involve increased savings and reduced consumption in the United States, together with corresponding lower savings and higher domestic consumption in the surplus countries of East Asia and elsewhere. The termination of currency manipulation and the resulting currency revaluations *vis-à-vis* the dollar, in this context, would facilitate the global adjustment process.

5. *The consultation process for resolving the currency manipu-lation issue should be up through the summit level, both bilaterally and in group summit meetings, such as the annual G-8 and APEC summit meetings.* This issue is simply too important to be left to finance ministers alone. The current G-8 summit meetings, which now include Russia, should be expanded to a G-9 summit with full Chinese participation. The November 2005 APEC summit meeting would likewise have the currency manipulation issue, and the related need for adjustment in the transpacific trade imbalance, high on the agenda.

These are the specific steps that should lead to a resolution of the currency manipulation issue and end its adverse impact on U.S. trade. Overall resolution would be multilateral in content, and related to the necessary global economic adjustment. The critical relationship, however, is between the United States and China. If the two agree on resolving the issue, it will happen, and if they do not, it will not. In terms of financial diplomacy, the currency manipulation linchpin designation for China should thus be extended as the "linchpin U.S.-China financial relationship."

As for what China should do, specifically, to end its currency manipulation, the decision should be left to China. Any course of action would have some transitional disruptive impact on the domestic Chinese economy, especially when the currency has been permitted to drift so far out of line. There are two basic options that China would have to consider. The first is to move directly to a flexible, market-oriented rate, presumably a floating rate with the currency convertible on capital account. There is ample experience among developing countries of such a direct move from a fixed to a floating rate, often realized *in extremis* as market forces overwhelm the Central Bank's capability to resist. Under these circumstances, there can be an abrupt impact on certain sectors of the economy and a temporary overshooting of the equilibrium exchange rate by financial markets, but the adjustment would be prompt and comprehensive, while policy instruments can then be directed towards taking positive steps forward rather than holding together a partial solution to past problems.[18] The second alternative would be a substantial revaluation of the yuan, for example by 25 percent, together with a limited exchange rate band, that would continue to be heavily managed by the Central Bank. This could be less disruptive in the short run, but the implied partial convertibility, within a progressively widening band, raises questions as to how financial markets will react. In any event, the Chinese government has an ample supply of highly able financial experts, and it should be left to make its own decisions, as long as they lead to the early termination of IMF-proscribed currency manipulation.

---

[18] Some observers are concerned that a free float and convertibility on capital account could lead to large net outflows of capital from China and a further devaluation of the yuan, but this appears extremely unlikely. Some Chinese savings would be progressively invested abroad, but the huge net currency inflow from the current account surplus and FDI of over $100 billion per year, likely to increase substantially in 2005-2006, plus the anticipated initial speculative inflow of capital to reap the gains from a revaluation, should overwhelm any initial outflow of private savings, which will likely require time to become institutionalized.

U.S.-Chinese Leadership in a Changing
International Financial System

The discussion thus far has been about the immediate issue of currency manipulation and its impact on U.S.-China trade and investment, which is the most important problem currently facing the bilateral relationship. Looking ahead five to ten years, however, an equally important international financial issue, with even broader implications for the global economy, is how the United States and China will interact in shaping the fundamental changes under way within the international financial system. Once China achieves its stated objective of a flexible, market-oriented currency, presumably in the form of a floating rate, the yuan will relatively quickly rise to become one of three principal international currencies, along with the dollar and the euro. Beijing, Shanghai, and Hong Kong will become major East Asian financial centers, and regional trade and investment will increasingly be denominated in yuan, in view of China's preeminent regional economic position. This not very distant rise of China as an international financial power, moreover, will unfold in parallel with a fundamental restructuring of international financial relationships that is already well advanced, although not fully recognized within the financial system centered on the IMF. It is in this context that the U.S.-China financial relationship would become a critical element of the leadership needed to shape and improve the future order of international financial relations.

The international financial system has been essentially undefined for over three decades. The fixed-to-the-dollar, but adjustable, rate system created at Bretton Woods in 1944 ended in 1971 when the United States closed the window on dollar convertibility into gold. This precipitated a potpourri of exchange rate relationships from fixed to floating rates, with various forms of adjustable pegs and currency bands in between. The lack of systemic definition was highlighted in 1994, at the 50-year anniversary of Bretton Woods, when a Bretton Woods Commission of 47 distinguished financial leaders and experts, chaired by Paul Volcker, called for the "establishment of a new system . . . [because] the alternative to the new global system is to continue the present non-system." The Commission report had little to offer, however, as to what form the new system should take, except to note that the "system could possibly involve flexible exchange rate bands."

Five months later, the Mexican peso crashed through the bottom of its dollar exchange rate band, and financial markets assumed the lead role in pushing governments toward a truly new, post-dollar, floating rate system. Subsequent financial crises in Thailand, Indonesia, South Korea, Russia, Brazil, Turkey, and Argentina all resulted in shifts from some form of dollar-linked currencies to managed floating rates. Moreover, as noted earlier, all of these countries tended to manage their floating currencies downward through large-scale Central Bank purchases of foreign exchange, in order to stimulate export-led economic recovery and growth.

These developments since the mid-1990s have been redefining international financial relations in fundamental ways, although the existing IMF system has been far behind the curve in adjusting to the new realities. Four principal characteristics define the new financial order, summarized to highlight the key roles to be played by the United States and China.

1. *The IMF lending program is largely history.*—IMF stand-by loans were central to the early decades of the Bretton Woods system, as financial assistance to members for maintaining fixed rates during periods of cyclical adjustment. During the first 25 years, most IMF loans were to the industrialized countries, including the United States, but with the 1971 shift toward floating rates, such loans declined sharply, and the last major IMF loans to industrialized countries were in 1976. Now, for close to 30 years, the industrialized countries, which account for about 65 percent of global trade and investment, have been "graduates" from the IMF lending program. Similarly, as a result of the floating rates that emerged from the financial crises of the late 1990s, together with subsequent large Central Bank purchases of foreign exchange, almost all of the crisis-stricken, newly industrialized economies will no longer need IMF loans. Only Argentina remains engaged in protracted IMF loan negotiations, largely because the earlier IMF loans critically delayed financial adjustment and caused an even more serious ultimate crisis, together with default on foreign loans.[19] Other major trading nations, including China and India, now also have very large foreign exchange holdings and therefore no future need for IMF loans. As a result, nations comprising 90 percent or more of global trade and investment are now IMF loan "graduates," and the remaining 10 percent or less consist mostly of poorer countries, where official development assistance through concessionary loans and grants by the multilateral development

---

[19] An irony of this last hurrah of major IMF loan negotiations is that new IMF loans to Argentina are used principally to repay old IMF loans at full value plus interest, which involves a serious conflict of interest for the IMF negotiators.

banks and bilateral donors is usually more appropriate than three-year IMF loans at close to market rates of interest.

The future roles of the United States and China in managing this phase-down of the IMF lending program will be modest, consisting mainly of guidance to avoid excessive IMF loans to the poorest countries. More important will be related joint efforts to provide adequate development assistance to the poorer countries. China, with $660 billion in foreign exchange reserves, should greatly expand its economic assistance programs which, in some areas, could be done in collaboration with the United States.[20] Disaster relief to poorer countries would be one area for closer collaboration, in terms of delivery capability and financial resources, with the disappointing response of China to the tsunami disaster in Southeast Asia in December 2004 a case study for future improvement.

2. *The management of floating rates, including proscribed currency manipulation, is now the most important international financial policy instrument.*—This recent story was recounted in the previous sections of this chapter. The management of floating rates, and its impact on international trade and investment, should become the focus of future international financial policy deliberations. There are also underlying questions about excessive levels of international reserves and the reasons why Central Banks intervene to buy or sell foreign exchange. For example, foreign exchange requirements are zero for a freely floating currency and much lower for any form of floating rate compared with earlier fixed or dollar-linked rate policies. Unfortunately, none of these questions, including the immediate issue of unprecedented currency manipulation, have been seriously addressed within the IMF framework over the past five years. The lack of discussion about IMF Article IV obligations, which is now at the center of the new international financial order, further detracts from the relevance of the IMF during this important period of fundamental change in international financial relations.

The roles of the United States and China will be critical in determining how the predominant floating rate relationships are or should be managed in the years ahead. The first step, of course, is for China to adjust to a market-based, floating rate, which, in turn, will greatly influence how other East Asian floating rates are managed within this high-growth, highly dynamic economic

---

[20] World Bank and Asian Development Bank loans to China are an anachronism that should be terminated. China has no need for such loans, while loans to China deprive poorer countries of financial support from limited multilateral development bank resources.

region. The United States and China, together with the European
Monetary Union (EMU), Japan, and a few others, will also
determine the extent to which the IMF becomes more or less
directly engaged in floating rate management, and how this
relationship relates to meetings outside the IMF, as currently
prevail in bilateral U.S.-China and G-7 discussions.

3. *Monetary unions are a limited but potentially larger
"second corner" component of a new international financial
order.*—The most viable alternative to a floating rate policy is a
monetary union, whereby currencies are merged or smaller
countries adopt the currency of a dominant neighboring economy,
such as the dollar, the euro, or, at some point ahead, the yuan.
This basic dual policy choice between floating rates and currency
unions has led to the term "two corner financial system," with the
choice of corner derived, in part, from long-standing economic
analysis in terms of an "optimum currency area."[21] Small open
economies, highly trade dependent on a large neighboring
economy, are the most likely to reap greater economic benefits
from monetary union with the currency of the large neighbor than
from a floating rate. Thus far, the monetary union alternative has
been adopted by most of the EU (15) members through creation of
the euro, and is in process of implementation by a few Caribbean
Basin nations and Ecuador that are moving towards dollarization.
The future of the monetary union corner is unclear, but it could
well be extended to additional smaller Mediterranean Basin
economies through euroization and to Caribbean Basin economies
through dollarization.[22] As for "yuanization," the most likely eco-

---

[21] Monetary unions involve the loss of national monetary and exchange
rate policies, with the demise of the central bank, and the potential benefits of more stable rates of inflation and greater access to long-term loans
at lower interest rates. The recent transition toward a two corner international financial system is explained in Preeg, *op. cit.*, 2000, especially
Chapters 2 and 9. Those who dislike the "two corner" term because all
geometric relationships have at least three corners are captives of plain
geometry; in the world of economic globalization, spherical trigonometry
prevails, wherein many configurations have only two corners. A more
substantive point is that a "currency board" constitutes an interim policy,
at best, because it does not give financial markets the assurance of
permanency. Its reputation has also suffered from the conspicuous
failures of dollar-linked currency boards in Indonesia and Argentina,
economies that did not meet the basic criteria for optimum currency areas
in the first place.

[22] The case for dollarization by smaller Caribbean Basin nations is made
in Ernest H. Preeg, "Dollar Rising Over the Caribbean" (*American
Outlook*, Winter 2000), pp. 42-43.

nomic candidates would be Hong Kong, Taiwan, and Myanmar, but all three would have great political reluctance despite the potential economic benefits.

The future U.S. and Chinese roles in the development of monetary unions would be as two of the three major regional currencies, along with the euro, that could form the centers of monetary unions within the three industrialized regions—North America, East Asia, and West Europe. China might be the most important of the three in terms of broader economic and political impact. Dollarization and euroization around the Mediterranean and Caribbean Basins would have little economic or political significance outside the regions, while discussions already under way for some kind of financial integration or monetary union in East Asia, potentially centered on the yuan, would involve much larger trade, investment, and foreign policy interests, including across the Pacific with the United States. U.S.-China bilateral and APEC discussions on this subject could therefore become important for defining future relationships between floating rates and monetary unions within the Asia Pacific region, and for the international financial system more broadly. The IMF role in the monetary union component of financial relations has been minimal, and once monetary unions are formed the IMF becomes of little relevance for financial relations among members. The extent to which the IMF becomes involved in the future will depend most importantly on whether the United States and China choose to bring their regional monetary-union and financial-integration initiatives within the IMF consultative framework.

4. *Financial relations will become even more oriented toward bilateral and group relationships among the major currency countries and away from multilateral IMF engagements.*—This has long been the trend among the major industrialized countries, and was also criticized by the 1994 Bretton Woods Commission, although again without specific proposals to reverse the direction. The subsequent shift to floating rates by the newly industrialized countries and the resulting decline in their need for IMF loans further diminishes the operational role of the IMF multilateral system. The course of the global economy, in any event, is determined by a relatively few large economies and financial powers, represented in large part by the G-7, whose central position would be reinforced by the inclusion of China in a G-8 finance minister grouping. At the regional level, the financial role of APEC is likely to grow in view of the concentration and interaction of managed floating rates within the Asia Pacific region, and the need for adjustment in the U.S.-East Asia trade imbalance over the next several years.

The future role of the IMF will thus likely be reduced further in relative terms, but it will still be important if it is reformulated with foresight. Graduation from IMF loans for economies comprising over 90 percent of the global economy should be an occasion for celebration. At the same time, the IMF should remain a useful forum for deliberations about the course of the global economy and appropriate macropolicies by members, with analytical support provided by IMF staff. There will likely remain some form of IMF financial support for poorer countries, in conjunction with the multilateral development banks, including technical assistance for financial sector reform. The biggest question is whether the multilateral IMF can or should play a central institutional role for the issue of floating rate management, or whether this can better be handled principally within a G-8 (including China) and on an informal, bilateral basis. Experience to date has been to avoid the IMF, as in the U.S. preference to deal bilaterally with China on exchange rate policy rather than through IMF Article IV consultations. There is also the institutional weakness of the IMF in dealing with currency manipulation from not having at its disposal significant sanctions for noncompliance, although this could be rectified through a more structured linkage to GATT Article XV.

Much of what will happen in the IMF, as elsewhere in international financial relations, will depend on the bilateral relationship between the United States and China, and this relationship will likely become the most important for determining the future course of the international financial system. The U.S. exchange rate and other financial relationships with Japan will remain important, but the growing economic role of China in East Asia has already made the yuan more important than the yen in policy terms, as in the current currency manipulation debate. The U.S. relationship with the EMU will also continue to be of major importance, but transatlantic decision making in international finance is hampered by the unclear decision-making process within the EMU.[23] In any event, the discussion here need go no further than to conclude that the United States and China will both have global leadership roles to play in international finance, and therefore need to become more closely engaged in policy collaboration. A more structured bilateral financial consultative

---

[23] In particular, the respective roles of the EMU board and member finance ministers for dealing with intervention in currency markets, the principal policy instrument for managing floating exchange rates, are unclear. This ambiguity complicates the U.S. identification of financial *interlocutors valables* within the EMU.

framework, heavily analytic in content, and with regular meetings between finance ministers and Central Bank presidents, would be a good first step in the long financial march ahead.

Chapter 9

International Trade and Investment Policy

The U.S. trade and investment relationship with China is the broadest and deepest part of the overall relationship in content, and will almost certainly continue to grow at a rapid rate over the coming five to ten years. Once the international financial issue of currency manipulation is resolved, trade policy should become an even more central focus of the bilateral policy relationship, in terms of both problems and opportunities to pursue mutual interests. This policy focus will involve specific issues of direct commercial impact and broader issues influencing the future course of the international trading system. Moreover, more than commercial interests are at stake. Geopolitical and national security interests have an important trade policy dimension, and, more fundamentally, international trade and investment are the driving forces for the development of advanced technology industries in both countries.

The United States and China begin with a shared commitment to open, market-oriented trade within the rules-based WTO system of market-access commitments. In one sense, this is similar to the shared commitment in international finance to the goal of flexible, market-oriented exchange rates. The crucial difference, however, is that whereas China has not yet made any movement toward the flexible exchange rate goal, China's open trade policy was already well advanced before its 2001 entry into the WTO, which is currently the vehicle for implementing a comprehensive set of open trade obligations contained in the WTO accession agreement. The mutual benefits from free trade are recognized by both governments, and are supported by the majority of industries in both countries, which have increasingly global business horizons. The future pursuit of this mutual free trade interest is seriously constrained by other factors, however, in the United States by the unsustainably large trade deficit, and in China by ideological conflict and institutional inertia. The free trade opportunity is nevertheless real and substantial.

In this broad context, a presentation of the U.S-China trade and investment policy relationship is wide-ranging and needs categorization by principal issues and objectives. The discussion here begins with a commentary on the U.S. trade deficit, globally and with China, to explain, in particular, why trade policy is not the principal cause of or solution for what is a major problem for the United States. The discussion then turns to specific issues under current discussion, principally related to WTO obligations by China. The following section addresses the "two track" path to further trade liberalization, multilaterally through the WTO and bilaterally and regionally through FTAs, with emphasis on the distinctive paths currently being pursued by the United States and China. The final section examines, within a longer five- to ten-year timeframe, what is referred to as the "Big Option," namely a multilateral free trade agreement in manufactures, the realization of which will essentially be decided by the United States and China.

The U.S. Trade Deficit

The U.S. trade deficit has spun out of control, rising from $165 billion in 1998 to $618 billion in 2004, of which $550 billion, or 83 percent, was in the manufacturing sector.[1] The trade balance for advanced technology products declined even more sharply than for other manufactures, from a surplus of $30 billion in 1998 to a deficit of $36 billion in 2004.

During this six-year period, China surpassed Japan to record the largest bilateral deficit at $162 billion, or 20 percent of the total U.S. deficit, in 2004, as shown in Chart 9-1 and Table 9-1.[2] The trade balance, moreover, is extremely lopsided, as shown in Chart 9-2, with U.S. imports from China five times larger than U.S. exports in 2004. This imbalance is overstated somewhat by the "export platform" production in China, principally by Taiwanese, South Korean, and Japanese companies, as discussed

---

[1] The global deficit figures include both merchandise and services trade. Ensuing figures related to U.S.-China trade are limited to merchandise trade because services trade is not broken down by country.

[2] These U.S. figures on the bilateral deficit are much larger than the $70 billion Chinese bilateral deficit figure. The principal difference is that Chinese exports to Hong Kong and third countries, for processing and reexport to the United States, are recorded as imports from China in the U.S. figures. There is also the standard asymmetry in that imports, but not exports, include the costs of insurance and freight, which makes trade surpluses smaller and deficits larger.

in Chapter 4. The aggregate deficit of all four East Asians also increased sharply, however, from \$143 billion in 1998 to \$270 billion in 2004, although the share of the total U.S. deficit for the four East Asians declined from 58 percent in 1998 to 48 percent in 1999, and to about 40 percent in 2002-2004, largely because of the leveling off of the deficit with Japan at about \$70 billion and an increase in the deficit with the EU. The Chinese share of the deficit, meanwhile, increased from 19 percent in 2000 to 24 percent in 2004, and accounted for 60 percent of the aggregate East Asian deficit in 2004.

This unprecedented U.S. trade deficit, with China at the forefront, results in considerable job loss in the United States, and corresponding protectionist pressures to reduce imports. Likewise, U.S. initiatives to reduce trade barriers further, particularly for U.S.-China trade, face strong opposition as long as the deficit remains at record levels. A major reduction in the U.S. trade deficit, in any event, has become both a national priority and the central challenge for adjustment within the global economy, as discussed in the G-7 finance ministers group and the IMF. The principal means for achieving this objective are not, however, in

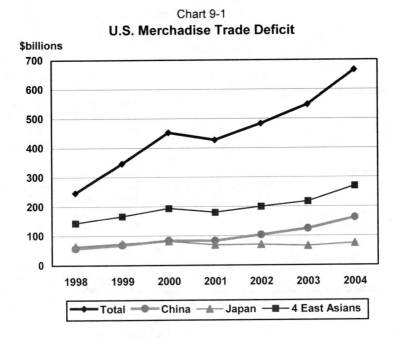

Chart 9-1
U.S. Merchadise Trade Deficit

Source: U.S. Bureau of the Census

Chart 9-2
U.S. China Merchandise Trade

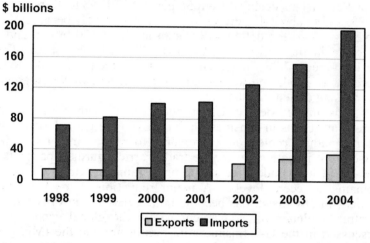

Source: U.S. Bureau of the Census

Table 9-1
U.S. Merchandise Trade Deficit
(\$ billions)

	1998	1999	2000	2001	2002	2003	2004
A. Absolute Level							
1. Global	-246.7	-346.0	-452.4	-427.2	-482.9	-547.6	-666.2
2. China	-56.9	-68.7	-83.8	-83.1	-103.1	-124.1	-162.0
3. Japan	-64.0	-73.4	-81.6	-69.0	-70.0	-66.0	-75.2
4. Four East Asians*	-143.4	-166.4	-194.0	-180.4	-199.9	-217.5	-270.0
B. Percent of Total							
1. Global	100.0	100.0	100.0	100.0	100.0	100.0	100.0
2. China	23.1	19.9	18.5	19.5	21.4	22.7	24.3
3. Japan	25.9	21.2	18.0	16.2	14.5	12.1	11.3
4. Four East Asians*	58.1	48.1	42.9	42.2	41.4	39.7	40.5

* China, Japan, South Korea, and Taiwan

Source: U.S. Bureau of the Census

the trade policy field. Unilateral increases in import barriers by the United States would be met by retaliation abroad against U.S. exports. The most important action to reduce the U.S. trade deficit would rather be to increase the U.S. domestic rate of savings, as discussed in Chapter 10. The other major related area for urgent action is the currency manipulation issue, already addressed in Chapter 8.[3]

Trade policy can have a significant positive effect for reducing the U.S. deficit, but it is more limited in scope and usually relatively long-term in effect. Specific issues of improved market access for U.S. exports, related to Chinese WTO obligations, need to be pursued forcefully, as addressed in the following section. Bilateral FTAs can also bring net gains to U.S. exporters because tariffs and other import barriers are generally higher in the other countries. However, as long as the U.S. trade deficit remains at current excessive levels, with China as the conspicuous number-one deficit country, a heavy dark cloud hangs over the trade liberalization process in general, and over the U.S.-China bilateral trade relationship in particular.

Bilateral Trade Issues and WTO Obligations

China applied for WTO membership in October 1986,[4] which led to 15 years of negotiations and final Chinese accession on December 11, 2001. The negotiations involved market-access commitments for goods and services and wide-ranging rules that would govern trade with China, with obligations related to more than 20 existing WTO agreements covering all areas of trade. The lengthy negotiating process involved multilateral discussions within a WTO working party and bilateral negotiations with individual working party members, prominently including the United States. This major undertaking became an important component of the fundamental restructuring of the Chinese economy to market-oriented open trade, described in Chapters 2-4.[5]

---

[3] This can involve the ultimate threat of import sanctions against currency manipulators. Such a threat, however, is not protectionist in a unilateral sense, but rather the normal ultimate recourse for issues addressed by WTO dispute settlement procedures.

[4] An historical footnote is that the Chinese application came just one month after the GATT ministerial meeting in Punta del Este, which launched the Uruguay Round of negotiations. The author, who was a member of the U.S. delegation to that meeting, recalls various informal discussions with members of the Chinese observer delegation about GATT accession, but with little thought of China's becoming an export powerhouse within 10 years, and an advanced technology superstate within 20 years.

[5] A full and fascinating account of the Chinese WTO accession negotiations is contained in Nicholas R. Lardy, *Integrating China in the Global Economy* (Brookings Institution, 2002).

The three years since Chinese accession to WTO membership have likewise entailed a comprehensive consultative and negotiating process over implementation of the commitments contained in the accession agreement, which is to be completed by 2007. This process, in fact, is far more detailed than the WTO accession negotiations, and is directed at wide-ranging specific issues of technical and legal complexity. It is also being carried out both at the multilateral and bilateral levels. The WTO established a ten-year Transitional Review Mechanism for monitoring compliance, with annual status reports. Bilaterally, the U.S.-China Relations Act of 2000 requires the U.S. Trade Representative (USTR) to report annually to the Congress on Chinese compliance, within an oversight compliance program, currently carried out through the bilateral Joint Commission on Commerce and Trade. The agenda and activities of this bilateral mechanism are comprehensive and include consultations with thousands of U.S. companies. It is by far the most intensive area of bilateral negotiations between the two governments, and will remain so at least through 2007. The 2004 report to the Congress[6] covers nine broad categories of WTO commitments undertaken by China: trading rights and distribution services; import regulation; export regulation; internal policies affecting trade; investment; agriculture; intellectual property rights; services; and legal framework. Within these nine broad categories, 24 specific areas of policy commitments are recorded in detail. The 88-page single-spaced report is a timely briefing on the status of implementation and the scope and complexity of the issues engaged.

The 2004 USTR assessment is mixed, with implementation in some areas moving forward on schedule and in other areas facing major problems. The problems involve administrative and technical difficulties in bringing the Chinese governmental structure into effective compliance, political or protectionist resistance, and the pervasive threat or reality of corruption. The course of progress over the first three years is summarized in the December 2004 report:

> China deserves due recognition for the tremendous efforts made to reform its economy to comply with the requirements of the WTO. . . . The first year of China's WTO membership saw significant progress as China took steps to repeal, revise or enact more than one thousand laws, regulations and other measures to bring its trading system into compliance with WTO standards. . . . [The

---

[6] December 11, 2004, available at www.ustr.gov.

second-year report] concluded that China's WTO implementation efforts have lost a significant amount of momentum, and we identified numerous specific WTO-related problems. As those problems mounted in 2003, the Administration responded by stepping up its efforts to engage China's senior leaders. . . . This new approach was exemplified by the highly constructive Joint Commission on Commerce and Trade meeting in April 2004. . . . [where] the two sides achieved the resolution of no fewer than seven potential disputes over China's WTO compliance. . . . U.S. stakeholders were significantly more satisfied with China's WTO performance in 2004 than in the previous two years.

No attempt is made here to summarize or critique the content of this comprehensive bilateral trade policy consultative mechanism, and readers are encouraged to read the full USTR report. Commentary is, instead, offered on a selective basis for seven issues most relevant to trade and investment in advanced technology industries. Other policy areas, such as market access for agriculture and financial services, are also very important, but less directly germane to this study.

1. *Intellectual property rights.*—China agreed to overhaul its legal regime to ensure the protection of intellectual property rights in accordance with the WTO agreement, which sets minimum standards of protection for copyrights, trademarks, geographic indicators, industrial designs, patents, and integrated circuit layout designs. It also requires enforcement through civil and, in some areas, criminal actions. This is by far the number-one problem area of noncompliance to date with WTO obligations, and is deeply integrated with the trade and investment relationship in advanced technology products.

The 2004 USTR report states that the Administration "places the highest priority on improving the protection of IPR in China," and observes that "counterfeiting and piracy in China are at epidemic levels and cause serious economic harm to U.S. businesses in virtually every sector of the economy." The problem centers on lack of effective implementation of existing Chinese laws: "Enforcement . . . remains ineffective in 2004. Indeed, some U.S. rights holders reported that IPR infringements worsened in 2004 . . . IPR enforcement is hampered by lack of coordination among Chinese government ministries and agencies, local protectionism and corruption, high thresholds for criminal prosecution, lack of training, and weak punishments. . . . Cases brought by the administrative authorities usually result in low fines. . . . The infringers consider the seizures and fines simply to be a cost of doing business, and they are usually able to resume their operations without much difficulty." Secretary of Commerce Donald Evans, before his final trip to China in January 2005, commented that "you've got to start putting people in jail."[7]

The annual quantitative costs to U.S. business from IPR infringement run in the billions, if not tens of billions, of dollars. The 2004 USTR report states that current estimates of U.S. losses due to the piracy of copyrighted materials alone range between $2.5 billion and $3.8 billion. The market value of total counterfeit and pirated goods in China was estimated in the report at between $19 billion and $24 billion in 2001, and these figures could have doubled by 2004 simply because Chinese trade has doubled during the ensuing three years. One U.S. trade association is cited in reporting that "counterfeiting and piracy rates in China remain among the highest in the world, exceeding 90 percent for virtually every form of intellectual property." Another source estimates that China accounts for nearly two-thirds of counterfeit goods worldwide.[8]

The qualitative dimension of this out-of-control piracy of intellectual property is pervasive for advanced technology industry production in and trade with China, with increasingly adverse impact on Chinese as well as multinational firms. R&D is inhibited, especially in such fields as software design, biotechnology, and pharmaceuticals. It is a major reason why multinational companies with substantial R&D activities in China still maintain the most advanced, leading-edge R&D in the home country.

Some steps are being taken to begin to make progress in the protection of intellectual property in China. In October 2004, the United States launched the Strategy Targeting Organized Piracy (STOP!) program, which intensifies the blockage of imported counterfeit goods of worldwide origins, with China accounting for two-thirds of the counterfeit goods seized to date. USTR undertook an out-of-cycle Special 301 review of Chinese violations of IPR, to be completed in 2005.[9] The Chinese Supreme People's Court, in December 2004, issued an interprettation of Chinese law that extends criminal penalties, including through lower threshold values of piracy for jail time, but only

---

[7] *Washington Trade Daily*, January 10, 2005, p. 5.
[8] *Business Week*, February 7, 2005.
[9] The "Special 301" section of the 1986 Omnibus Trade Act deals with infringements of U.S. IPRs. See the letter to industry from USTR Ambassador Josette S. Shiner, at www.ustr.gov.

time will tell how much difference this will make in actual enforcement.

IPR will remain as the number-one problem area for U.S. trade relations with China, with especially severe adverse impact on U.S. advanced technology companies. More forceful actions by the United States are clearly in order, and recurring complaints from U.S. industry that the United States is going slow on IPR enforcement for foreign policy reasons should be negated by demonstration effect. Two pending significant cases before the Chinese courts that bear watching involve a complaint by General Motors that the Chinese Chery automobile company illegally cloned a GM car, and the suspension of the Pfizer patent for Viagra. The findings of the Special 301 review could warrant selective trade sanctions, for example against advanced technology imports from Chinese companies using pirated software and advanced technology components. The STOP! program could be extended to embargo all imports from companies whose pirated products have been seized. Perhaps most important, the WTO dispute settlement procedure, not yet utilized for IPR complaints, should now be utilized for selective cases where IPR enforcement is grossly ineffective.

2. *Investment.*—China accepted the provisions of the WTO Trade-Related Investment Measures Agreement, which includes the elimination of measures that require foreign investors to use local imports ("local content requirements") or limit imported components to a stipulated share of exports or foreign exchange earnings ("trade balance requirements"). In its accession agreement, China went further and undertook to eliminate all export performance local content and foreign exchange balance requirements, and, even more specifically, *to no longer condition importation and investment approvals on requirements such as technology transfer and offsets*.

The italicized commitment is of particular importance to U.S. advanced technology industries, and the assessment in the USTR 2004 report is discouraging and somewhat misleading. It states that "some of the revised laws and regulations continue to 'encourage' technology transfer, without formally requiring it. U.S. companies are concerned that this 'encouragement' will in practice amount to a 'requirement' in many cases, particularly in light of the high degree of discretion provided to Chinese officials reviewing investment applications. In addition, according to U.S. companies, some Chinese government officials in 2004 still consider factors such as export performance and local content, when deciding to approve an investment." This assessment is an understatement at best. Examples of "encouragement" amounting to a "requirement" abound, for example the GE case cited in Chapter 3. As for advanced technology industry, in particular, the official Chinese foreign investment policy statement of June 14, 2004, quoted at length in Chapter 3, explicitly seeks "to encourage foreign investors to introduce, develop, and innovate technology and to invest in technology-intensive projects." As for WOFEs, which now comprise the majority of foreign direct investment in China, they "must adopt international advanced technology" and/or "most of the products must be export-oriented." This amounts to more than "some of the revised laws and regulations," and applies to all foreign investors, while the conditions for WOFEs amount to a formal "requirement" rather than "encouragement."

U.S. negotiations within the joint commission for implementation of the investment commitments also appear less comprehensive than for IPRs. Attention has focused on industrial policy in the automotive sector, where limited progress was reported with respect to distribution channels for foreign companies. As for "encouragement" or "requirements" for technology transfer, the 2004 report concludes that "the United States will continue to follow this situation closely in 2005," which essentially means a passive approach until at least 2006.

A more forceful response to the coercive transfer of technology should be undertaken on an urgent basis. In view of the Chinese practice of forcing foreign firms to compete against one another to meet technology transfer demands, the United States could, in addition to direct bilateral pressures on China, take an initiative within the OECD, with reporting requirements from member companies, which could lead to a joint WTO complaint by OECD governments of the principal investors in China.

3. *Standards, technical regulations, and conformity assessment requirements.*—This is another important area of concern for American advanced technology companies, and it received extensive coverage in the USTR 2004 report. Under the WTO Agreement on Technical Barriers to Trade, China agreed to establish rules and procedures for the development, adoption, and application of product standards, including testing and certification. The aim is to prevent the use of technical requirements as barriers to trade.

The administration of these commitments is highly complex and wide-ranging throughout the Chinese government, involving such issues as transparency, fees, processing permits, and complaint procedures, all in the context of equal treatment for imported and domestic goods. In 2001, China created the Standardization Administration of China, charged with unifying Chinese standards and aligning them with international practices.

As a result, the USTR 2004 report notes that China has made "significant progress" toward its goal of having 70 percent of its nearly 20,000 technical regulations based on international standards by 2006. The United States has provided technical assistance to China for carrying out this massive undertaking, and the Department of Commerce will soon open a U.S. private sector standards office in Beijing.

The threat or practice of Chinese use of technical standards to gain unfair commercial advantage nevertheless remains real and pervasive. USTR reports that, in a number of sectors, including autos, telecommunications equipment, wireless local area networks, radio frequency identification tag technology, audio video coding, whiskey and other distilled spirits, and fertilizer, concern has been growing that China is actively pursuing the development of unique requirements, despite the existence of well-established international standards, which will create barriers to entry into its market. These potential standards barriers include major areas of the advanced technology sector and could result in substantial adverse impact for American companies *vis-à-vis* Chinese competitors.

The United States has been actively challenging such developments, with success in targeted cases. The dispute over proposed Chinese encryption techniques for secure telecommunications was resolved in April 2004, through the indefinite suspension of the proposed standards. At that time, China also announced that it would support technology neutrality regarding 3G (i.e., third generation) telecommunication standards, but implementation of this commitment is open to doubt, and the USTR continues to monitor it closely.

Technical standards will remain a major and complex component of the bilateral trade relationship for many years to come, and a continuing example of how deeply engaged the two governments are becoming in dealing with commercially sensitive issues, heavily oriented to advanced technology industries.

4. *Taxation.*—China has committed to most-favored-nation and national treatment (i.e., the same treatment for all foreign and Chinese companies) for taxes and other levies on imports and exports, fundamental obligations under GATT Articles I and III. This issue came to a head with respect to differential application of the Chinese value added tax (VAT) for semiconductors and fertilizer. China rebated a substantial portion of the 17 percent VAT on semiconductors for domestically produced but not imported semiconductors, affecting $2 billion of U.S. exports in 2003. The United States, in March 2004, after two years of fruitless bilateral discussions to end the discrimination, initiated a

WTO dispute settlement procedure, which led to a resolution of the problem in July 2004, whereby China agreed to eliminate the rebate. This was a striking example of how the WTO dispute procedure can be useful for obtaining Chinese compliance with WTO obligations.

The similar domestic rebate problem continues for fertilizer production, and in other sectors the VAT payments are often not collected for domestic producers while they always are for imports. There are also problems with certain consumption taxes that treat domestic and imported products differently. In other words, tax treatment remains a significant area for continued negotiation on Chinese implementation of WTO commitments.

5. *Subsidies.*—China agreed to eliminate all export and certain import substitution subsidies, in accord with the WTO Subsidies Agreement. China also agreed to accept indirect, market-based criteria for measuring subsidies under certain circumstances, particularly with regard to state-owned enterprises, which is related to WTO enforcement, including the possible application of countervailing duties. China has still not fulfilled one of the key requirements of the subsidies agreement, however, which is to notify the WTO with basic information about its subsidy program on an annual basis. The United States has requested detailed information regarding several programs which appear to constitute subsidies, including for various high technology products. Another likely area of subsidies is unpaid bank loans from state-owned banks. In November 2004, China committed to submit its subsidies notification information in 2005. Thus, subsidy policy has not yet been fully engaged and needs further strong pressure from the United States and other interested WTO members.

6. *Telecommunications services.*—China agreed both to the WTO General Agreement on Trade in Services, which provides a legal framework for addressing market access and national treatment affecting trade and investment in services, and to a substantial market opening for a broad range of services industries. Implementation has thus far been uneven or unrealized in some areas, with excessive requirements for market entry a frequent problem. USTR reports that "progress was made on some fronts in 2004," but much remains to be done. The sectoral commitments are wide-ranging, with eight individual sectors assessed in the 2004 report. Only telecommunications services are commented on here, as the most directly related to advanced technology industry, and as a good example of the kinds of

difficult issues that are involved. The other sectors, however, are also important to U.S. commercial interests.[10]

China committed to permit foreign suppliers to provide a broad range of telecommunications services, with up to 49 percent ownership of ventures with Chinese companies, including domestic and international wired services, mobile voice and data services, value-added services (such as electronic mail, voice mail, and online information and database retrieval) and paging services. China also became obligated to adopt procompetitive regulatory principles, and to separate the regulatory from the operating functions of the government, formerly combined within one ministry. Progress to date has been small and a number of major problems have emerged during the implementation process. Excessively high capital requirements have been established, which pose a barrier for foreign suppliers, compared with no or low requirements in many other WTO members. A truly independent telecommunications regulator has not yet been established. The application process for foreign companies is complicated and slow-moving, with no applications to provide value-added services approved through the end of 2004. Several telecommunications services have been reclassified out of the value-added category, where market access commitments apply, contrary to widely accepted international practice. A long-awaited draft of a new telecommunications law was circulated among Chinese ministries in 2004, but it was not made available for public comment. The telecommunications services sector will continue to be a problem-plagued area for effective WTO implementation, and may warrant a U.S. initiative, together with concerned EU, Japanese, and other members, for WTO dispute resolution.

7. *Biotechnology regulations.*—This is the one among six categories within the agricultural sector that comes closest to the interests of advanced technology industry.[11] Biotechnology regulations were cited by USTR as one of the most troublesome problems in the agricultural sector in 2002 and 2003, but some progress was reported for 2004. The rules adopted in 2001 for safety, testing, and labeling did not provide adequate time for scientific assessment related to approval of safety certificates for biotechnology products, and U.S. exporters, most importantly of

---

[10] The other seven sectors are financial, legal, express delivery, construction and related engineering, aviation, maritime, and other services.
[11] The other five categories are tariffs, tariff-rate quotas, sanitary and phyto-sanitary issues, inspection-related requirements, and export subsidies.

genetically modified soybeans, were adversely affected or put at risk. As a result of bilateral negotiations, application of the new rules was delayed, and then, in early 2004, final safety certificates were issued for U.S. biotech soybeans and other products, including corn and cotton. Other U.S. concerns about biotechnology regulations and implementing rules remain, and a bilateral group of experts was formed to continue work during 2005 on specified technical issues.

These status reports and commentary on selected trade policy issues related to Chinese WTO accession indicate not only the importance of this bilateral policy engagement for U.S. export and investment interests, but also the scope and complexity of the issues involved. Progress towards full WTO implementation has clearly been made, but a long list of significant problems remains. Moreover, after three years, the need for definitive resolution of problem issues has become more urgent, again in the context of the rapidly widening U.S. trade deficit with China during these same three years. The U.S. negotiators should press more rigorously for full compliance within the bilateral Joint Commission on Commerce and Trade. Greater recourse to WTO dispute procedures, which worked well for the discriminatory VAT on semiconductors, is also more justified after three years of initial discussion, and should be utilized more frequently for selective issues where a strong case of noncompliance can be presented.

Two Track Trade Liberalization

The multilateral trading system created in 1947 as the GATT, and now expanded to become the WTO, has two basic functions. The first is a rules-based system of market access commitments, subject to dispute settlement procedures through third-party panels. The Uruguay Round Agreement of 1994 expanded the scope of market access commitments to include trade in services, intellectual property rights, and some trade-related investment measures, and greatly strengthened the dispute procedures. The previous section about the comprehensive market access commitments undertaken by China with WTO accession, and how they are currently being implemented, is an outstanding example of the positive workings of this rules-based trading system.

The second function of the WTO system is to progressively reduce trade barriers on a reciprocal, most-favored-nation, or nondiscriminatory basis, through periodic "rounds" of multilateral negotiations, the current Doha Round being the ninth such undertaking. Since the 1980s, however, there have also been numerous negotiations of FTAs, permitted under GATT Article XXIV, whereby tariffs and other barriers to trade are eliminated among members, but are retained on a discriminatory basis against nonmembers. The overall current process of trade liberalization is therefore referred to as "two track," and, as pursued by the United States, as the "competitive liberalization" strategy.

Over the past 12 years, the FTA track has gained momentum and produced most of the trade liberalization results. The Doha Round of multilateral negotiations, in contrast, has made little progress after four years, and the outlook for substantial reduction in trade barriers is not promising. This shift from multilateral to FTA trade liberalization raises basic questions as to where the international trading system is headed.[12] The outcome, moreover, as has become a recurring theme throughout this study, will be determined largely by how the United States and China interact in responding to the current two track configuration. This bilateral trade policy realtionship ahead is examined first in terms of current negotiations under way or anticipated over the next couple of years on each of the two tracks—the Doha Round and further FTAs—and then, in the final section of the chapter, through presentation of a more forward-looking and ambitious "Big Option," namely a multilateral free trade agreement for the nonagricultural sector, centered on the dominant manufacturing sector.

The Doha Round Multilateral Track

The WTO Doha Round remains bogged down after four years in disagreement over the "norms," or broad guidelines for reducing trade barriers, which are preliminary to the more detailed negotiation of specific commitments to be included in or excluded

---

[12] An early analysis of the post–Uruguay Round two track orientation of trade liberalization is contained in Ernest H. Preeg, *Trade Policy Ahead: Three Tracks and One Question* (CSIS, 1995). The third track was bilateral U.S. negotiations by sector, principally with Japan, and by function for IPRs and investment with various countries, but this track was largely overtaken by implementation of Uruguay Round commitments. The "one question" referred to where the two or three tracks were headed over the longer term, and the concluding Chapter 5, entitled "Convergent Toward What?" specified the question as multilateral free trade or some enduring mix of FTAs and MFN tariffs. The question was ahead of its time in 1995, but now it should be front and center, as presented during the remainder of this chapter.

from the guidelines. The first attempt to launch a WTO round failed at Seattle in September 1999 over confrontation between industrialized and developing countries,[13] but a second attempt at Doha in November 2001 succeeded, thanks largely to a surge in international solidarity in the wake of the September 11 terrorist attack. The agreed negotiating agenda at Doha, however, was vague, and papered over the "North/South" differences which remain central to the ongoing impasse.

In substantive terms, the top priority of the Doha negotiations has been agriculture, and some positive results should make it possible to liberalize trade in agricultural products. The central position of agriculture, however, has tended to sideline the other areas of negotiation, principally improved market access for nonagricultural merchandise and services trade. Agriculture accounts for less than 10 percent of world trade, and farmers in almost all parts of the world have long benefited from very high protection through import barriers, export subsidies, and trade-distorting domestic subsidies. In sharp contrast, trade in manufactures, which accounts for over 60 percent of world trade, is subject to much lower import barriers, while export and domestic subsidies are almost all prohibited under the WTO, subject to trade sanctions if continued.[14] The Cancun ministerial meeting in September 2003 failed primarily over agriculture, with the EU resisting specific commitments to reduce export subsidies, the United States likewise resisting specific cuts in domestic subsidies, and the developing countries refusing to make any commitments to reduce their exceptionally high import barriers. The continuing top priority for agriculture thus hangs like an albatross over the entire Doha negotiation.

The agricultural impasse also highlights the broader roadblock to a successful Doha outcome, namely the principle of "non-reciprocity" for developing countries, or exemption from reducing trade barriers on a comparable basis with industrialized

---

[13] An assessment of the Seattle meeting is contained in Ernest H. Preeg, *Charting a Course for the Multilateral Trading System: The Seattle Meeting and Beyond* (Group of Thirty, 1999), and "The South Rises in Seattle," *Journal of International Law* (March 2000), pp. 183-185.
[14] The recent U.S.-EU trade disputes over the U.S. FISC tax exemption as an export subsidy and over EU subsidies for commercial aircraft are examples of how differently subsidies are treated for manufactures compared with agriculture.

countries.[15] "Special and differential treatment" for developing countries, including the non-reciprocity principle, has a long and controversial history in the GATT and now in the WTO. Developing country status has never been defined and has been simply a matter of self-designation. No member, however, has ever self-graduated, including the highly competitive newly industrialized exporters, such as Hong Kong, Singapore, and South Korea. In earlier decades, non-reciprocity was not a significant issue because almost all commitments were taken by the industrialized grouping. During the Uruguay Round, the more advanced developing countries were pressed to be more forthcoming, but at Seattle and Doha the developing countries closed ranks in opposing reciprocity, and they largely succeeded in the Doha ministerial resolution, as well as in the official name of the negotiations as the "Doha Development Agenda," which strongly implies a one-way set of commitments. Much of the impasse during the past four years over the norms for negotiation has been about exceptions to reciprocity for developing countries.

The U.S.-China relationship within the Doha Round also relates largely to differences over developing country participation. The disagreement began over whether China should have developing country status as a new WTO member. The United States opposed such status, China insisted upon it, and the issue was left mute in the final accession agreement. In the Doha negotiations, China has consistently supported the developing country positions, especially with respect to non-reciprocity. When the talks finally reach the specific negotiating stage, the commitments offered by China will thus play a significant role in how far other newly industrialized participants will go, which, in turn, will influence the overall level of achievement. China, for example, in view of its growing trade surplus and strong competitive position in manufactures trade, could make a full set of specific commitments in the manufacturing sector, without any special exemptions as a developing country, while still avoiding

---

[15] In the early years of the GATT, there was discussion of developing country status related to per capita income and the share of manufactures in total exports, but the definitional question was never resolved. An account of developing country participation in the GATT through the Uruguay Round negotiations is contained in Ernest H. Preeg, *Traders in a Brave New World: The Uruguay Round and the Future of the International Trading System* (University of Chicago Press, 1995), pp. 70-75.

the formal question of developing country status.[16]   In broader
negotiating context, the United States and China, together with the
EU and Japan, could agree on a formula or "guideline" for
reducing nonagricultural tariffs, and commit to a full set of offers
within the formula, with a minimum of exceptions.   One highly
useful procedural step for doing this and recognizing China's new
status as one of the three largest trading nations would be to
enlarge the informal yet influential G-4 consultative group,
consisting of the United States, the EU, Japan, and Canada, to a
G-5, with full participation by China.

   The overall picture for the Doha Round remains bleak, with
negotiations likely continuing another two years to relatively
modest results, at best.   More forthcoming initiatives by the newly
industrialized major exporters, and by China in particular, could
help, but except for the unlikely "Big Option" discussed below,
the outcome for this multilateral track Doha negotiation will likely
pale by comparison with previous rounds.

The FTA Bilateral and
Regional Track

   In parallel with the lackluster performance of the multilateral
Doha negotiations, momentum continues to build for FTAs,
particularly within and among the three advanced industrialized
regions of West Europe, North America, and East Asia.   Within
West Europe, the EU has recently expanded membership from 15
to 25, soon likely to reach at least 28, and is deepening its FTA
network around the Mediterranean Basin.   The most important
potential FTAs by the EU would be with Turkey and the new
government in the Ukraine, which could lead to further
agreements to the East, eventually possibly including Russia.

   U.S. FTAs have been most prominent in the Western
Hemisphere, beginning with NAFTA and then within the
framework of a Free Trade Area of the Americas (FTAA).
Negotiations for a single FTAA are stalled over differences with
Brazil and a negative political turn in Venezuela, but individual
FTAs, in addition to Mexico's within NAFTA, have been
concluded with Chile, five Central American nations, and the
Dominican Republic, and are under negotiation with Colombia,
Ecuador, Peru, and Panama.   If all of these FTAs are concluded,
almost 85 percent of U.S. exports to the Latin America/Caribbean
region would be included within the FTA track.   The United States

---

[16] It is less clear how far China can go in the Doha Round in the services
sector, where it is still heavily engaged over implementation of the
accession commitments, or for agriculture.

also concluded significant FTAs across the Pacific with Australia and Singapore, and is in negotiation with Thailand. Other FTAs around the world are of lesser trade consequence.

China has most recently entered the FTA arena, with major implications for trade within East Asia and for the international trading system more broadly. China began negotiation of an FTA with the ASEAN grouping in December 2004, for implementation by 2012, which quickly led South Korea and Japan to open free trade talks with ASEAN as well. Free trade negotiations between Japan and South Korea could be completed in 2005, while discussions about an ASEAN Plus Three (i.e., China, Japan, and South Korea) FTA, perhaps extended to include Australia, New Zealand, and India, are becoming more serious. These various free trade initiatives in East Asia would accelerate further the deepening economic interdependencies within the region, increasingly centered on the Chinese economy.

There are three reasons for this proliferation of FTAs, which will soon account for the majority of world trade. First, they can be negotiated quickly and with clearly identified positive results for export industries. U.S. FTAs in the Western Hemisphere and East Asia almost all involve higher tariffs in the partner country, and thus larger gains in market access for U.S. exports compared with imports. A China-ASEAN agreement would involve relatively high tariffs and other trade barriers on both sides, and thus substantially greater direct export opportunities among participants, not to mention the equally large preferential advantage for Chinese exports to ASEAN markets *vis-à-vis* the United States, the EU, and other third-country competitors.

The second reason for FTA success compared with the Doha negotiations is their diminution or elimination of the Doha problems in agriculture and over reciprocity for developing countries. Agriculture is generally included in FTAs, but in a more limited and less decisive way. U.S. agricultural protection consists primarily of domestic subsidies, which are excluded entirely from FTA negotiations, as is the most highly protected sugar sector. This leads to smaller agricultural commitments by others and an overall lower priority for the sector. The EU and East Asian FTAs also have either modest or no agricultural content. The issue of non-reciprocity for developing countries essentially does not exist in FTAs because all participants are pledged to across-the-board elimination of import barriers, often together with open investment commitments, which usually result in developing countries undertaking much larger rather than smaller reductions in protection compared with the industrialized participants.

The third reason for the recent surge in FTA initiatives relates to foreign policy, including geopolitical interests, as discussed in Chapter 5. With respect to China and the U.S.-China relationship, the assessment here is that China is pursuing FTAs in East Asia in large part to reinforce its central economic power position within the region, while excluding the United States, in particular, for both foreign policy and commercial reasons.

The emergence of a preferential East Asian trade and investment bloc has important foreign policy as well as economic implications for all major trading partners on both sides of the Pacific. The United States will suffer adverse commercial impact from the relatively high tariffs throughout the region that will be eliminated among members but remain against U.S. exports. The impact on U.S. foreign policy will also be negative, by casting the United States and China as the leaders of rival trading blocs, while creating conflicts between foreign policy and commercial interests for American allies in the region, particularly Japan and South Korea.

In any event, the U.S. policy objective should be to thwart the creation of a preferential East Asian trading bloc which excludes the United States. This cannot be done, however, by simply opposing its formation, since it is almost certainly moving forward in any event, while the United States would be hypocritical to oppose East Asian FTAs while pursuing FTAs of its own elsewhere. The only course that will succeed is for the United States to take decisive steps toward a broader Asia Pacific free trade agreement that will include both the United States and the East Asians. Asia Pacific free trade was, in fact, the agreed objective at the 1994 Bogor summit meeting of the APEC, with a 2020 date for full implementation. Attempts to formulate a single regional free trade agreement have not been successful, but the FTAs now being undertaken, within East Asia and across the Pacific with the United States, can be considered stepping stones to the ultimate regional free trade objective. At this stage, a comprehensive Asia Pacific agreement is still not feasible, principally because the most important component of such an agreement would be a free trade commitment between the United States and China, which neither government is now prepared to undertake. It would not be possible politically for the United States until the currency manipulation problem is resolved and the huge bilateral trade imbalance begins to decline. The reasons for Chinese opposition are less clear, and could involve differences of view within the government between free traders who would see benefits from a broader Asia Pacific free trade agreement, and the nationalist and ideological proponents of a dominant Chinese economic power position within East Asia and a reduced American presence.

Toward Asia Pacific Free Trade

The proposal offered here for a decisive U.S. initiative toward Asia Pacific free trade, as counter to the otherwise likely emergence of an East Asian trading bloc excluding the United States, consists of three parts.

1. ***The formation of a high-level U.S.-China bilateral study group to examine the economic costs and benefits of free trade between the United States and China, within the already agreed broader APEC free trade framework.***—The analysis would include the economic gains from trade, adjustment problems and how they might be handled, and the impact on third countries. It is very likely that the net economic gains from free trade for both countries would be substantial.

2. ***A U.S. three-spoke initiative for further transpacific FTAs with Thailand, South Korea, and Taiwan.***—The Thailand negotiations are already under way, as are preliminary formal talks with South Korea, while informal discussions with Taiwan have prepared the way for such an initiative. A number of difficult trade issues are involved in each case. A particularly difficult issue for the United States is that South Korea and Taiwan are among the four principal East Asian currency manipulators, and this issue would have to be resolved before final agreements could be submitted to the Congress. All of these trade issues should be manageable, however, if political commitments, within the broader transpacific political-economic relationship, were forthcoming.

3. ***A formal APEC review of progress, after the first 11 years, toward the Bogor free trade objective.***—The focus would be on the various FTA stepping stones, as the practical course up to this point, including the China-ASEAN and the new U.S. three-spoke FTA initiative, and on how all of these FTAs can ultimately be consolidated into a comprehensive regional free trade framework.

This three-part initiative integrates an immediate decisive move to make the United States an integral part of the Asia Pacific free trade framework, through the three-spoke FTA initiative, with the longer term objective of comprehensive free trade within the Asia Pacific region. It also directly engages the U.S.-China bilateral relationship in addressing the central issue of free trade between the two countries. The three-part U.S. initiative should be launched during 2005 and be a focus for discussion at the

APEC summit in December 2005, when the 11-year Bogor review could be initiated.

Reactions by others to the initiative could lead to further movement toward the long-term objective. The Philippines, with a long and deep bilateral relationship with the United States, might seek to become a fourth U.S. transpacific spoke, although this would require major changes in Philippine economic policy. Most important would be the Japanese reaction. Japan has always been very hesitant about the FTA track, including during recurring consideration, over two decades, of a U.S.-Japan FTA,[17] but in this new context Japan could see it is in its interest to join in the U.S. transpacific initiative, at which point the cumulative spokes would give distinct shape to an emerging transpacific free trade wheel.

There is also the issue of the Chinese reaction to a U.S.-Taiwan FTA. Taiwan, however, is a full member of the APEC, which includes being a full participant in the Bogor objective of regional free trade. Taiwan is also a full member of the WTO, within which FTAs are negotiated pursuant to GATT Article XXIV. The inclusion of Taiwan together with two other members of APEC and WTO, Thailand and South Korea, would further demonstrate that this is not a politically motivated U.S.-Taiwan bilateral initiative, but an integral part of the broader Asia Pacific free trade process, of which Taiwan is an important and dynamic part.

Such a U.S. initiative within the Asia Pacific region, finally, would have broader and perhaps decisive implications for the global trading system. The reaction of the EU would be most important in this respect. APEC discussions over the years have consistently highlighted that a regional FTA would be open for others to join, with particular reference to the EU. Definitive free trade movement within APEC, therefore, could be the catalyst for an APEC–EU FTA which, in turn, would set the stage for a multilateral free trade agreement. This ultimate convergence or consolidation of FTAs into a multilateral framework is referred to here as the "Big Option."

The Big Option: Multilateral Free
Trade in Manufactures

The answer to the question posed in footnote 12—to what end is the two track trading system converging—can now be answered more definitively than when it was first posed ten years ago: the

---

[17] See Ernest H. Preeg, "Next, a Free Trade Agreement With Japan?" *Wall Street Journal*, September 16, 1988.

two tracks should converge into a multilateral free trade agreement, at least for the nonagricultural sector, and to the extent feasible for agriculture as well. The proliferation of FTAs in recent years demonstrates how the complete phaseout of remaining import barriers, already at relatively low levels in the dominant manufacturing sector after progressive reductions over several decades, can be done quickly and simply, with substantial economic benefits for all participants and manageable adjustment costs. U.S.-Mexican free trade within NAFTA demonstrated how the highly protected, emerging market economy of Mexico could move to free trade with the largest industrialized nation, with a resulting doubling of trade in both directions in a few years' time. The Central American Free Trade Agreement (CAFTA) between the United States and five Central American nations, concluded in 2004, demonstrated how even smaller, lower income countries, including two "least developed," now see it in their self-interest to go to free trade with their dominant industrialized trading partner.

The FTA track, however, while positive in many respects, also has its downsides, both economic and political. The economic negatives include trade diversion from nonmembers as a result of the discriminatory tariffs against them, and costly, cumbersome rules of origin. The political negatives relate to smaller, poorer members becoming even more dependent on the dominant free trade partner, without the protection of multilateral safeguards, and the broader threat of geopolitical rivalry and conflict between inwardly directed regional trading blocs.

The logical resolution to this proliferation of bilateral and regional FTAs is therefore to consolidate them into a multilateral FTA within the WTO system. For the United States, the regional free trade objectives within the Western Hemisphere and across the Pacific would, most importantly, have to be extended across the Atlantic to the EU, which would entail the easiest economic adjustment in view of the already low tariffs on both sides of the Atlantic and the similar levels of wages and industrial development. The United States, in fact, in November 2002, proposed multilateral free trade in nonagricultural products as the Doha Round objective, which was welcomed by some participants, mostly East Asians, including Singapore, Hong Kong, Taiwan, Australia, and New Zealand. This free trade initiative was resisted by the EU and others, however, and was not pursued with any rigor by the United States. The multilateral free trade "Big Option" nevertheless remains on the Doha Round negotiating table.

The specifics of how such a multilateral free trade agreement could be structured and negotiated have been presented elsewhere and are not repeated here.[18] The agreement, as a practical matter, should be subject to a 90 percent threshold, whereby participants would have to account for at least 90 percent of world trade in manufactures, or nonagricultural products more broadly.   The APEC members plus the EU and a few other free trade-oriented countries would quickly reach this threshold, while some other more highly protected economies, such as Brazil and India, could be given extended periods for implementation.   Smaller, poorer countries could proceed at their own pace of trade liberalization, while immediately receiving the benefits of multilateral free trade for their exports.   Precedent for this 90 percent threshold approach is the 1996 WTO free trade agreement for the information technology sector, with Chinese participation even though China was not yet a WTO member.

The gains from total free trade in the manufacturing sector, which is where almost all the nonagricultural tariffs are contained,[19] would be very large, and relatively the largest for the emerging market economies of Asia, Latin America, and Central Europe. The gains would be mostly "dynamic," in that they would derive from a restructuring of existing industries and investment in new export-oriented industries, mostly involving the application of more advanced technologies. The free trade and investment policy of China since 1995 is an outstanding example of such dynamic gains from free trade. The cited study estimates economic gains from multilateral free trade in manufactures leading to an approximate $2 trillion larger global GDP over several years, split roughly in half between the industrialized and the newly industrialized groupings of countries, with relatively small gains for the many poorer countries that comprise less than 10 percent of manufactures trade. In terms of the share of GDP, these gains equate to 4 percent of GDP for the industrialized countries and 8 percent to 12 percent for the newly industrialized.[20] A more recent and comprehensive set of estimates of the gains from free trade, also with emphasis on the dynamic effects, projects a comparable increase of 5.5 percent of GDP, or $600 billion, per year.[21]

---

[18] See Preeg, *op. cit.*, 2003; an updated refinement, post-Cancun, is provided by the author in *Free Trade in Manufactures: A Forward Looking Post-Cancun Trade Strategy* (Manufacturers Alliance/MAPI, 2004).
[19] Most of the remainder of the nonagricultural sector of trade consists of already duty-free petroleum and industrial raw materials imports.
[20] Preeg, *op. cit.*, 2003, Chapter 4.
[21] Scott C. Bradford, Paul L. E. Grieco, and Gary Clyde Hufbauer, "The Payoff to America From Global Integration," in *The United States and the World Economy: Foreign Economic Policy for the Next Decade*, C. Fred Bergsten, ed. (Institute for International Economics, 2005).

This, in essence, is the "Big Option" of a multilateral free trade agreement, predominantly directed at the manufactures sector. It is languishing on the table in the Doha Round, but could be given new life through the catalyst of an expanded U.S. transpacific FTA initiative of at least three spokes, as described above. If not, a modest Doha Round result, together with a continued proliferation of FTAs, would leave further consideration of the multilateral free trade option for the post-Doha period. The only firm conclusion drawn in the context of this study is that whatever the two track road ahead, it will depend decisively on the United States and China. More specifically, if the United States and China agree that a multilateral free trade agreement is in their mutual interest, and they provide joint leadership to achieve it, it will almost certainly happen, and if they do not, it will not happen. This is why the first part of the proposed U.S.-Asia Pacific initiative presented above—a high level U.S.-China free trade study group—is so timely and important.

The reasons why the United States and China together play the decisive role for multilateral free trade have been elaborated and can be summarized in briefest terms. A U.S.-China free trade commitment would quickly lead to an APEC-wide free trade accord which, in turn, would leave the EU no option but to join in the open-ended APEC arrangement as well. Others would then also express an interest in participation, which would transform the overall process into a multilateral undertaking, with the 90 percent threshold easily surpassed. Indeed, any nations remaining outside the almost total global free trade framework would be at a considerable competitive disadvantage for attracting job-creating investment and trade. Conversely, as long as China and the United States are not prepared to undertake free trade between them, the Asia Pacific as well as the multilateral free trade objectives will never come to pass.

The issue of how and to what extent two track convergence leads to multilateral free trade thus boils down to how national self-interest in global free trade is assessed in Beijing and Washington. This involves more than an estimate of the mutual economic gains from free trade, and needs to include foreign policy and national security interests as well, all in the context of a fundamentally changing world order of nations, driven largely by the rapid pace of new technology development and application. This architectonic question is the subject of the final chapter. Before that, however, one other important policy area needs to be addressed: the U.S. domestic economic policy response for maintaining global leadership in advanced technology industry.

Chapter 10

The Domestic Economic
Policy Response

The policy prescriptions of the previous two chapters were principally directed toward achieving a level playing field with other nations, and with China in particular, based on fair competition and open trade. The other two policy dimensions for defining the course ahead for the advanced technology industry relationship between the United States and China concern economic policies within each country, wherein differences can give a competitive advantage to one or the other. The comprehensive support by China for advanced technology industry since 1995 was described in considerable detail in Chapters 2-5. This chapter examines the counterpart U.S. domestic economic policy framework as it works to stimulate or discourage continued innovation to develop and apply ever more advanced technologies. The overall context is that both China and the United States will continue to upgrade their advanced technology capability and performance, which, in turn, goes to the core question of relative performance. Will China gain comparative advantage and thus narrow or eliminate the long-standing U.S. advanced technology leadership position? The U.S. domestic economic policy response will play a critical role in answering this question.

The chapter begins with a description of the manufacturing sector as the advanced technology engine for growth within the American economy, which should be the policy focus for maintaining advanced technology leadership *vis-à-vis* China. This is followed by a policy-oriented assessment of what is termed the "macropolicy savings dilemma," which is the most stark and important "advantage China" component of the bilateral relationship. The ensuing group of seven more specific policy areas each have significant impact on the U.S.-China comparative relationship, and current U.S. policy in each area can be improved significantly. A concluding section summarizes the prospect for U.S. technology-oriented innovation and provides a commentary on public perceptions of U.S. private sector leadership and the need for a greater sense of national purpose.

The Manufacturing Sector as the Advanced
Technology Engine for Growth

The manufacturing sector is central to the development of advanced technologies, as it is to the competitive trade and investment relationship between the United States and China. Manufacturing is nevertheless often downgraded if not dismissed as a relatively small part of what is now a predominantly service sector economy, considered to be in the process of secular decline as happened in the agricultural sector a century ago. This line of thinking is profoundly misleading with respect to the Chinese challenge to U.S. leadership in advanced technology innovation, in terms of both commercial application of new technologies throughout the economy and the design of advanced weapons systems. The manufacturing sector is the lead protagonist by far in the rapidly evolving U.S.-China economic relationship, and policy makers should take fuller account of it.

The key basic facts are that two-thirds of commercial R&D in the United States, and over 90 percent of new patent applications, come from the manufacturing sector. The sector also accounts for a relatively high share of investment in plant and equipment. These figures from the traditional definition of manufacturing companies as those that produce tangible products, moreover, need to be expanded to include segments of the services sector deeply integrated with advanced technology design and production, such as engineering and software application services. There is also an important joint venture relationship between manufacturing companies and university R&D programs, increasingly directed toward technology development for commercial application. The resulting output of more advanced technology products are then marketed throughout the economy by a technology-oriented marketing component of manufacturing companies, which increasingly includes customer-oriented product design and follow-on application services. This complex of activities, involving R&D, product design, production, marketing, and application services, can be called the manufacturing sector advanced technology engine for growth.[1]

In this engine for growth context, the frequent analogy of manufacturing with agriculture as a sector in secular decline

---

[1] This process of evolution within the U.S. manufacturing sector toward more advanced technology design and application is examined in detail in Duesterberg and Preeg, eds., *op. cit*, 2003. The chapters address key components of the overall engine for growth process and were authored by six MAPI economists and one historian.

requires a rebuttal: The analogy is half true and half seriously misleading.   The true half is that the same productivity-induced decline in the shares of the labor force and GDP took place in the agricultural sector, beginning in the late 19th Century, as has been taking place in manufacturing in recent decades.   The share of U.S. employment in agriculture declined from 41 percent in 1900 to 12 percent in 1950 to 2 percent in 2000, while the agricultural share of GDP declined in similar fashion to only 1.4 percent in 2000. In parallel, however, and in spite of the massive declines in the shares of labor and GDP, American farmers continue to feed—indeed overfeed—the U.S. population, export a third or more of production, and accumulate large surpluses that the government is obliged to dispose of.   The analogy of this productivity-driven growth for manufacturing in recent decades is valid. The share of the U.S. labor force in manufacturing declined from 29 percent in 1950 to 14 percent in 2000, while the manufacturing share of GDP declined from 27 percent to 16 percent. And again, the quantity of manufacturing output through 2000 continued to rise at least as fast as growth in the overall economy, but at ever lower relative cost and with relatively less labor, as a result of much higher productivity growth compared with the services sector. The net result, in both cases, was not a "hollowing out" of American production, but rather an amazing transformation to levels of productivity inconceivable 50 or 100 years ago, derived principally, in both sectors, from more advanced technology products developed, in large part, in the manufacturing sector.

The final phrase is the link to the seriously misleading second half of the analogy.   Today, farms are larger and far more mechanized, but farmers remain farmers, devoted almost entirely to raising their on-site crops.   The R&D that led to massive productivity gains in agriculture was conducted off the farm, in government and nonfarm research centers. The application of new technologies to supply farmers with machinery, fertilizers, and new varieties of seed was likewise carried out by other businesses, principally in the manufacturing sector.   The processing and marketing of farm commodities were again the domain of other sectors of the economy. And "globalization" for farmers remains limited to selling the home-grown product to other companies for export. The manufacturing firm today, in fundamental contrast, is very different from what it was 50 years ago, and is in the process of further far-reaching change.   Production is more R&D and investment-intensive.   Production cycles are shorter, with a premium placed on innovation and the introduction of new products. The labor force is more highly skilled, with relatively few production workers.   Deeper supplier relationships up and down the production chain proliferate. New within-the-firm activities in the areas of financing, marketing, and product service broaden the scope of company value added. Many jobs previously done by manufacturing companies, such as payrolls, are now outsourced. Thus, the new economy manufacturing company is on a very different and more expansive restructuring track than was the case for agriculture. The manufacturing sector will never contract to 2 percent of the labor force or 1 percent of GDP. Rather, it will likely, over time, metamorphose into something with a larger share of labor and GDP, perhaps even with a new appellation. And, in the process, it will remain the engine for advanced technology-driven growth within the national economy.

The final characteristic of the manufacturing sector that places it at the center of the U.S.-China rivalry for advanced technology development is trade. The manufacturing sector is more than ten times more deeply engaged in trade than the much larger services sector. In 2003, U.S. exports of manufactures were 40 percent of domestic value added in the sector and imports were far higher at 73 percent. In contrast, exports and imports of services were each only 4 percent of value-added output. The principal reasons for the difference are that many services, including most of education, health care, and retailing, are not tradable; that some service sectors, such as transportation and telecommunications, are more highly protected; and that still other services, such as financial services, are by foreign investment–related operations within foreign countries with little impact on trade. The principal performance consequence of this striking contrast is that growth in trade and shifts in the trade balance have more than ten times more relative impact on the manufacturing sector than on the rest of the economy. And the principal domestic policy relationship that impacts negatively on the exceptionally high trade dependency of the manufacturing sector is what can be called the macropolicy savings dilemma.

The Macropolicy Savings Dilemma

The U.S. manufacturing sector lost three million jobs from 1998 to 2004. Relatively little of it had to do with the long-term, productivity-driven secular decline of jobs in the sector, which moves at a relatively slow pace. The large majority of the job loss was rather a result of the skyrocketing U.S. trade deficit in manufactures, up from $165 billion in 1998 to $552 billion in 2004. The rule of thumb by international economists is that a $1 billion increase in the U.S. trade deficit equates to about 10,000 fewer jobs. A $387 billion increase in the trade deficit, therefore, equates to more than three million jobs, or 20 percent of the manufacturing sector labor force. In other words, if the trade deficit had remained at $165 billion through 2004, and the level of aggregate employment had followed the same path, there would have been about three million more jobs in manufacturing in 2004, and three million fewer jobs in services. This relationship goes a long way to explain how the relatively mild recession during 2000-2003 resulted in no significant change in employment in the services sector, in conjunction with the very large drop in manufacturing jobs. Moreover, for the purposes of this study, manufacturing job losses were especially large for the information technology and other advanced technology industries.

The causes of this dramatic increase in the trade deficit for manufactures were discussed in Chapter 9. A small part can be explained by trade policy, and a larger part, perhaps a quarter of the total, by currency manipulation by East Asians, and by China most of all. The largest share by far of the increased deficit, however, was a result of the inadequate level of U.S. savings, which results, indirectly, in a comparable-size current account deficit, mostly in trade. If the United States spends an excessive share of disposable income on immediate consumption, compared to the gross savings needed to finance investment, the inadequate savings can be compensated for in two ways: reduced consumption and thus higher domestic savings, or borrowing abroad. Over the past 25 years, the United States has been consuming beyond its means and borrowing abroad to finance investment, and this savings gap increased rapidly over the past five years, causing, in turn, most of the surge in the trade deficit. Private sector savings have fallen to 1 percent to 2 percent of GDP, well below that of other major trading nations, while the federal government budget shifted from a modest surplus in 2000 (i.e., net savings) to a more than $400 billion deficit in 2004 (i.e., net dissavings). This huge increase in the savings gap required massive borrowing abroad on "capital account," which, by definition, has to be balanced with an increased deficit on "current account," mainly trade. The adjustment to a larger deficit takes place through market-driven prices, interest rates, and exchange rates, but the outcome of a larger trade deficit, 83 percent of which was accounted for by the manufacturing sector in 2004, is inevitable.

The self-evident U.S. policy response should be to take rigorous actions to increase the domestic savings rate and thus reduce or eliminate the trade deficit. One reason to do so is to staunch the accumulation of net foreign debt, currently about $3 trillion and heading toward $4 trillion to $5 trillion over the next several years. This foreign debt buildup involves a generational transfer of income, similar in concept to that used for social security accounting, whereby the interest on and perhaps ultimately the repayment of principal of the growing foreign debt will have to be paid by the children and grandchildren of current consumers living well beyond their means through borrowing abroad.[2]

More directly relevant to this study, a higher domestic savings rate and a correspondingly smaller trade deficit will result in a substantially larger manufacturing sector as the production and revenue base for sustaining high levels of R&D, innovative scientists and engineers, new product design, and investment in plant and equipment—that is, the "innovation ecosystems" described by the President's Council of Advisors on Science and Technology. Put another way, the very large U.S. trade deficit with China in manufactures results in a quantitatively larger domestic resource base for the Chinese innovation ecosystems compared with that of the United States.

The need for raising the savings rate is generally acknowledged by political leaders, but performance to date has been disappointing. Tax reforms or tax cuts often give primacy to benefits for the consuming public to consume more, rather than less, while the burgeoning federal deficit has been the largest negative swing factor for national savings over the past several years. There are some hopeful signs of change. President Bush has proposed a 2005 budget which will begin to reduce the deficit, but the Congress disposes, and presidents in recent years have gotten in the habit of requesting large supplemental budgets that become "Christmas trees" for rampant spending measures. Tax reform, discussed below, could involve greater incentives to save, but the political pressures not to restrain immediate consumption are ever-present.

There is also an international set of interests disposed to support continued very large U.S. trade deficits, because this enables others to continue export-led growth through trade surpluses, again principally in the manufacturing sector. Currency

---

[2] A common misunderstanding is that borrowing abroad to finance investment leads to a comparably higher level of gross investment, and is therefore a good thing. In fact, the foreign borrowing leads to a higher level of overall disposable income, 80 percent of which is used for immediate consumption and only about 20 percent for incremental investment. Of course, the foreign borrowing does lead to a larger *share* of investment by foreigners, which is not a good thing. This important relationship is explained in Preeg, *op. cit.*, 2000, in a section entitled "The 80 Percent Consumption Null Hypothesis," pp. 69-74.

manipulation by others is the most blatant manifestation of this manufacturing sector mercantilism, with heavy orientation toward the development of advanced technology industries. But even in higher-minded deliberations among finance ministers over the need for international adjustment to reduce the "unsustainable" U.S. trade deficit, the abstract discussion rarely leads to concrete results. Others are not disposed to take actions to reduce their trade surpluses, which could slow down overall growth and have an especially adverse impact on their manufacturing sectors, even though it would benefit their consumers. The United States, meanwhile, has been unable or unwilling to take the domestic actions necessary to restrain consumption and thereby reduce the trade deficit, which would force others to shift to a more domestic-oriented growth strategy. Thus, the term "savings dilemma" is appropriate for the macropolicy decision facing governments: a choice between equally undesirable alternatives.

The contrast between low savings/trade deficit and high savings/trade surplus countries is most striking when comparing the United States and China. The United States faces the largest trade deficit in history, an extremely low domestic savings rate, and no clear or credible policy for change. China, in contrast, has a large and growing trade surplus together with an even larger inflow of foreign direct investment, an extremely high domestic savings rate, and a highly focused set of policies to remain in a strong trade-surplus position. The regrettable conclusion is that for macropolicy management as related to maintaining U.S. leadership and international competitiveness for advanced technology industries, the current scorecard shows a striking advantage to China. The United States needs to put a much higher priority on reducing its huge trade deficit, through international actions to curtail currency manipulation and, more importantly, actions at home to increase the rate of savings.

Specific Policy Areas in
Need of Improvement

Macroeconomic policy adjustment, including a major reduction or elimination of the fiscal deficit, can go a long way to increase domestic savings and reduce the trade deficit. There is also the need, however, to address a number of more specific areas of policy that influence the development of new technologies within the U.S. economy. The objective should be to create a more favorable investment climate that will enable U.S. advanced technology industry to perform up to its full potential at home, and to meet the competitive challenges from abroad. The seven most important policy areas are presented here in summary form with, as throughout the study, the impact on the China relationship highlighted.

1. *Tax policy.*—The current federal tax structure has significant adverse impact on U.S. advanced technology industry in three ways. First, it is skewed toward stimulating consumption at the expense of savings, which leads to a larger trade deficit. Second, the rates of taxation on corporate profits are much higher than in most major trading partners, both through higher profit taxes and double taxation when after-tax profits are subject to a dividend tax. A recent study showed the profit tax alone in the United States at 40 percent (consisting of the 34 percent federal rate plus an average state rate of 6 percent), compared with about 35 percent in Canada and Mexico, 30 percent in the United Kingdom and South Korea, and 25 percent in China and Taiwan.[3] And third, the U.S. profit tax laws are a tangled skein of countless exemptions and loopholes that distort the efficient allocation of investment expenditures and create large nonproductive costs through the employment of thousands of the brightest American minds as corporate tax lawyers and Washington lobbyists, seeking new tax exemptions and favorable interpretation of the old.

Preparations now under way for basic tax reform offer an opportunity to make fundamental changes, in response to all of these problems, to the significant benefit of advanced technology industry performance. For example, the shift, in whole or in part, from an income tax to some form of consumption tax would stimulate a higher rate of personal savings and thus reduce the trade deficit. Broader provisions for tax-exempt retirement accounts would have a similar effect. The corporate profit tax could be reduced to at least the Chinese level of 25 percent, perhaps together with eliminating at least some exemptions. Even better, the corporate profit tax could be eliminated entirely, thus ending the double taxation of profits, while the revenue loss would be compensated through tax increases elsewhere. The main point for whatever tax reform takes place is that it should result in greater incentives for domestic savings and the reduction or limitation of the tax disadvantages faced by American advanced technology companies compared with their foreign competitors.

2. *Education.*—The needs for improvement in education, related to advanced technology industry, are familiar. The achievement levels in math and science at U.S. primary and secondary school levels are substantially lower than in many other countries. American undergraduate students tend to avoid math,

---

[3] Leonard, *op. cit.*, p. 11.

science, and engineering courses, in part because rampant grade inflation does not apply well in these areas, where students can actually fail courses. U.S. graduate studies programs remain the best in the world, but the numerical output in science and engineering shows little or no growth, while a large share of graduates are foreigners who return home after graduation. In contrast, as described in Chapter 2, China has placed the highest priority on increasing the quantity and quality of science and engineering graduates, and already far surpasses the United States for awarding engineering degrees.

Some steps in the right direction are being taken, but much more can be done to upgrade skills for advanced technology industry. Performance standards in primary and secondary schools, as provided by the No Child Left Behind Act, are an important first step for these schools. More targeted upgrading of curricula at the local school level can have even more striking impact, such as the adoption of Singaporean math textbooks, with more selective but also more thorough learning material, already being used with success in 200 American schools.[4] Singapore, incidentally, is number-one ranked internationally for math achievement, compared with 19th place for the United States. The aversion of undergraduates to math and science is more difficult to assess. Increased math and science requirements could be part of a strengthened core curriculum. A bolder response to the grade-inflation problem would be to restructure course grading toward relative performance, such as by limiting A and B grades to 20 percent or 25 percent of the class. The most ambitious and high visibility government initiative would be a national scholarship program for graduate studies in areas most directly useful to advanced technology industries, patterned, as noted earlier, on the National Defense Education Act of the 1960s. Certainly the current Chinese challenge in advanced technology industries is of comparable if not greater consequence for the U.S. national interest as was the Soviet Sputnik.

Some of the most promising responses to the need for higher skilled workers have been through joint collaboration between the private sector and state education systems. The most active programs are at the junior college level, where curricula are designed to the job needs of technology-intensive firms, and students are offered part-time work while pursuing their studies and a full-time job upon graduation. More ambitious collaboration could take the form of cofinanced undergraduate scholarships, with majors in designated advanced technology fields. Even more

---

[4] *Wall Street Journal*, December 13, 2004.

broadly, education no longer ends with college graduation, but is a career-long process of training and upgrading of skills, especially in advanced technology industries. Many companies have structured training programs, the company "university," often linked to formal training at universities. Such collaboration, including joint financing of career-enhancing adult education, is a wave of the future, and a mutual interest between the companies that want to upgrade the skills of their employees and state education systems that want to keep the jobs in their states. Increases in federal funding for these various programs would be a catalyst for their expansion.

3. *Research and development.*—There was considerable discussion in Chapter 2 of the comparative trends in R&D expenditures in China and the United States. China places highest priority on the rapid growth of R&D in the public and private sectors, with a 22 percent annual growth in overall expenditures from 1995 to 2002. Chinese R&D is heavily concentrated in the manufacturing sector, and directed toward advanced technology industries in particular. U.S. R&D grew at a slower, 6 percent rate from 1995 to 2002, and is more broadly spread by sector, with health care far more prominent than in China.

The United States needs to maintain its leadership position in advanced technology R&D, in both quantitative and qualitative terms. U.S. public sector R&D funding, however, has been concentrated in defense-related programs, at $75.6 billion in FY 2005, and in the National Institutes for Health, at $28.6 billion, while the National Science Foundation, which provides the most direct support for advanced technology industry development, received only $5.5 billion, down $105 million from FY 2004. Some reordering of priorities, with a significant increase in resources directed toward advanced technology development, is clearly in order. Increased funding for basic research was strongly recommended by the President's Council of Advisors on Science and Technology. Selection of the most promising new technologies for applied R&D funding is technically complex in a fast-moving process of innovation, and can usually best be left to the companies already deeply engaged. Public R&D funding can therefore often best be utilized to jointly finance projects within broadly defined priority industry sectors.

The large majority of commercially oriented U.S. R&D, in any event, takes place in the private sector, and the incentives—and disincentives—to continued high levels of R&D that result from government policies and regulations relate to all of the other policy areas addressed here. As for disincentives, however, none is having greater adverse impact on technology innovation and R&D spending than the proliferation of tort litigation.

4. *Tort reform.*—Tort litigation in the United States has been growing at 10 percent per year for several decades, and more than 16 million lawsuits are now filed each year.[5] The direct cost to U.S. business from tort litigation is estimated to be about $250 billion per year. Additional indirect costs include expenditures by companies to avoid lawsuits and a general tendency to be risk averse, which has an especially negative impact on technology innovation. The direct costs alone amount to over 2 percent of GDP, compared with less than 1 percent in Japan, Canada, France, and the United Kingdom, and probably a much smaller share yet in China. The relative financial costs and other disadvantages to U.S. companies are thus substantial, with technology-intensive industries especially hard hit because they tend to be more vulnerable to lawsuits.

Litigation is necessary to protect against illegal or negligent corporate behavior, but the current U.S. tort system is out of control, with many lawsuits "frivolous," that is to say without merit. The lawsuits continue to proliferate, however, driven by the tort lawyers, who receive $40 billion per year in fees, and certain legal jurisdictions that are consistently anti-business in their judgments. Moreover, many frivolous lawsuits never get to court. Exorbitant multimillion or billion dollar claims are made, which, even if they ultimately fail in court, could entail years of litigation, large legal fees, and extensive bad publicity for the defendant company, and so the lesser evil for the company is to pay only a few million dollars to the lawyers and plaintiffs in an out-of-court settlement.

Tort reform is a major issue before the Congress, but definitive reform is doubtful in view of the powerful trial lawyers' lobby. In February 2005, President Bush signed the Class Action Fairness Act, which transferred many such cases from local to federal court jurisdiction, and instituted some rules for settlement more favorable to plaintiffs. Another proposed reform would limit pain and suffering payments for medical malpractice, which are driving up health costs. For example, up to one-half of the lower cost of pharmaceuticals in Canada is attributed to the Canadian

---

[5] A comprehensive assessment of the crisis in tort litigation, which is drawn on here, is contained in Frederick T. Stocker, ed., *I Pay, You Pay, We All Pay: How the Growing Tort Crisis Undermines the U.S. Economy and the American System of Justice* (Manufacturers Alliance, 2003).

cap on personal injury compensation at about $200,000.[6]   Still
another controversial piece of legislation would deal with the 20-
year saga of asbestos lawsuits that have forced 74 companies into
bankruptcy, with a loss of 60,000 jobs. Even if all of these proposed laws are finally approved, however, they will likely be
weakened during the legislative process, while American companies will continue to operate at a significant competitive
disadvantage to their foreign competitors.

With respect to China, the course ahead for the pharmaceutical
and biotechnology industries—both with very high R&D
content—bears careful watching.   A plethora of lawsuits is the
major problem for U.S.-based production, while in China
inadequate patent protection is the major problem.   China,
however, is moving to provide better patent protection for both
Chinese and foreign companies in these priority advanced
technology sectors, while tort reform being considered in the
United States would be of only limited relief at best. The United
States is thus at some risk of a shift of R&D and production in
these sectors away from the United States to China, where it
would be far less exposed to American tort lawyers.

Far better would be comprehensive tort reform in the United
States to minimize frivolous lawsuits and excessive compensation
penalties. Much would have to be done at the state level where the
jurisdiction lies. Caps on payments would be a key provision, and
any punitive payments should go to the state and not to trial
lawyers and plaintiffs. Penalties should be reimposed on lawyers
filing frivolous lawsuits, such as payment for the legal fees of
defendants.   Class action suits should have to demonstrate a
general pattern of wrongdoing and not just a few isolated cases.
At this point, political support for such comprehensive tort reform
is lacking, hampered in part by negative public perceptions of U.S.
corporate leadership, which are discussed in the final section of
this chapter.

5. *Health care.*—The number one concern of many U.S.
corporate leaders is rapidly rising health care costs, which puts the
United States at a significant international cost disadvantage. The
fact is that most health care costs are borne by companies in the
United States, while they are usually paid by the government in
other countries, and at much lower levels in places such as China.
There is no quick or easy solution to the problem since this basic
dichotomy in health care funding will not change, while health

---

[6] *Ibid,* p. 62, with reference to a study at the Fraser Institute in Van-
couver, Canada.

care costs will continue to rise faster than almost any other cost of doing business.

There can, however, be targeted changes that substantially moderate the rising cost of health care. The most important step would be tort reform for the health care sector, as described above. Most other initiatives are coming from the private sector, involving greater choice and involvement by the employees in making health care decisions, including the basic decisions about cost related to benefits. One model is the government program for federal employees, where costs are shared roughly 50-50, and a number of alternative programs are offered at varying levels of costs and benefits. More innovative approaches involve a given annual financial benefit which, if not used for health care by the employee, can be carried over to the next year or paid, in part, directly to the employee. The government role should be to encourage such innovation toward more cost-effective health care, and certainly not impede it through restrictive regulations.

6. *Regulatory policies.*—This is a wide-ranging category of government policy that can incur unjustified costs and substantially inhibit technology innovation. The magnitude of the problem is daunting. Close to 5,000 new "rules" to revise the existing regulations are in the bureaucratic pipeline at any one time, and more than 100 of them are likely to cost business $100 million or more per year if implemented.[7] The total cost of accumulated government regulations, including the voluminous paperwork involved, has been estimated at more than $800 billion per year. The first policy objective should thus be to reduce and streamline the huge accumulation of government regulations, which would involve rigorous, scientifically based cost-benefit analysis, more public involvement in rulemaking, and a more aggressive review and central decision-making process within the executive branch. In terms of advanced technology industry, companies should be surveyed to identify specific government regulations that are most detrimental to R&D funding and new product innovation, which would then be given priority for cost-benefit review.

Regulatory policy, in large part, is developed and implemented on a sectoral or functional basis, and decisions as to what serves the national interest are thus taken in such a context. Energy, telecommunications, and pharmaceuticals are among the most heavily regulated sectors, and all three involve large expenditures for R&D and new product development, which, in

---

[7] See Clyde Wayne Crews, *Ten Thousand Commandments: An Annual Snapshot of the Federal Regulatory State* (Cato Institute, 2002).

turn, require a continual updating of the regulatory framework. The most heavily regulated functional area is environmental standards. In all of these areas, strong political and special interest groups are heavily engaged, and the government role needs to be independent and as objective as possible in carrying out cost-benefit assessments. In all of these areas, moreover, regulatory decisions, where appropriate, should take account of the impact on advanced technology innovation in the United States compared with other countries.

One functional area of regulatory policy needs to be singled out in view of important recent changes and their serious adverse impact on American companies: corporate accounting requirements.

7. *Sarbanes-Oxley.*—The rash of corporate scandals at Enron, WorldCom, and elsewhere led to the Sarbanes-Oxley Act of 2002, which greatly increased the accounting requirements for publicly registered companies in the United States. Implementation of the Act has proven to be extremely costly in a number of ways, thus creating a new comparative disadvantage for American versus foreign production. In retrospect, Sarbanes-Oxley is a classic case of massive and misdirected overkill, and the Act should be fundamentally revised, based on thorough cost-benefit analysis of its initial years of implementation. The scandals were at the top level of management, and that is where the increased regulation of accounting should focus. Some provisions of Sarbanes-Oxley do this, such as requiring audit committee members of the board to be independent, and for them to hire and oversee the auditors. Restrictions on auditing firms providing consulting services to companies that they audit, which create a conflict of interest, are also well justified. Other provisions of Sarbanes-Oxley, however, do not stand up to reasonable cost-benefit scrutiny.

The exorbitant costs of compliance with Section 404 of the Act have gotten the most attention. Auditing costs have roughly doubled, and the annual external cost of compliance runs from an average of $8 million per year for large companies to about a half million dollars for smaller companies, with a relatively higher financial burden on the smaller companies. Additional internal costs are estimated at 100,000 man-hours per year for large companies, with one reporting 130 employees working full-time on Section 404.[8] A survey of 60 member companies by the Manufacturers Alliance/MAPI produced a total cost of compliance during the first year of $389 million, which amounted to 5.8

---

[8] *Economist*, December 18, 2004, *Financial Times*, February 9, 2005; and *Wall Street Journal*, March 2 and 3, 2005.

percent of net income.[9] As for the misdirected focus, the large majority of the costs are not related to revealing a "cooking of the books at the top," but extend from top to bottom, or as one beleaguered manager commented, to some remote warehouse clerk in Timbuktu.

Additional downsides of the Act include the requirement that CEOs and CFOs personally certify highly detailed quarterly reports on compliance, which can take extensive time better utilized for corporate leadership. Enormous amounts of information about corporate operations are made public that will never be read by a stockholder but that are of great value to foreign competitors. Some American companies are going private to avoid the costs of Sarbanes-Oxley, which can limit their ability to finance new investment. Some European companies are moving to de-register in the United States and move to London or elsewhere, while new foreign listings on the New York Stock Exchange were down from 50-60 per year before Sarbanes-Oxley to 16 in 2003, of which only two were European.

Sarbanes-Oxley is a disheartening example of overregulation that puts American companies at an international competitive disadvantage. Advanced technology companies are probably hurt the most because they have to be quickest on their feet to stay ahead of their foreign competitors, while Sarbanes-Oxley implementation works to slow down decision making on expenditures at all levels, and makes management generally more risk averse. The Chinese economic leadership undoubtedly enjoys reading the reports about the new financial and other burdens imposed on American companies, which can make a shift to production in China more attractive.

The Need for Greater National Purpose and Vision

The U.S. domestic economic policy response recorded in this chapter is disturbing and points to an increasingly difficult road ahead for American companies. This is confirmed by other recent assessments. The study of structural costs imposed on U.S. manufacturers cited earlier concluded that U.S. costs in areas such as corporate taxation, health care, tort litigation, and escalating regulatory costs add at least 22.4 percent to unit labor costs

---

[9] Donald A. Norman, *The Cost of SOX and the Compliance Process* (Manufacturers Alliance, April 2005). The survey covers a wide range of issues associated with compliance.

relative to major competitors.[10]   The Heritage Foundation's *2005 Index of Economic Freedom*, which is an indicator of innovation and international competitiveness, gives the top five rankings to Hong Kong, Singapore, Luxembourg, New Zealand, and the United Kingdom, while the United States, for the first time, dropped out of the top ten and into 12th place. The United States is judged to be conceding trade leadership through relatively higher government spending and some protectionist measures.[11]

One reason for the generally unresponsive U.S. policy framework for supporting U.S. advanced technology industry, faced with a serious challenge from abroad and especially from China, stems from competing priorities for public attention and political commitment. The war on terror clearly has top priority for public resources and foreign policy decisions. In terms of commitment to publicly funded R&D, health care has greater emotional appeal and thus far broader public support than the development of commercially oriented new technologies.   And the politics of economic policymaking inevitably focus on the level of consumer spending and other short-term goals.

There is also a lack of understanding and communication about the advanced technology engine for growth phenomenon, as described above.   The dominant position of the manufacturing sector in this engine, and the international battering it has been taking in recent years, tend to be rationalized away rather than debated over the realities of the marketplace and recent trends that do not bode well for the United States. There is a need for a better-informed debate at all levels about the critical national challenge to maintain leadership in the development and application of new technologies, for both commercial and national security reasons.

There is also a serious problem of public attitudes in the United States about corporate leadership. Corporate leaders are under unrelenting duress about their motives, if not their morals, while their creative and productive contributions to making the United States the most advanced and affluent society in history are often ignored.   The media strongly accentuate the negative, dwelling on the few bad apples on trial for breaking the law, while Hollywood prides itself in portraying corporate leaders as villains. Public attacks on business leaders are nothing new, and the least productive members of society tend to be outspoken critics of the

---

[10] Leonard, *op.cit.,* pp. 1-2.
[11] *2005 Index of Economic Freedom: The Link Between Economic Opportunity and Prosperity*, Marc A. Miles, Edwin J. Feulner, and Mary Anastasia O'Grady, eds. (Heritage Foundation, 2005).

most productive, but the negative public perceptions appear to be reaching new highs, and this clearly limits the ability of elected officials to take strong actions supportive of U.S. international business interests. It is indeed ironic, in this context, to compare the negative perceptions in the United States with the decidedly positive perceptions that now prevail in China. China remains a communist state, with a predominantly socialized economy, but successful private corporate leaders, whether foreign or Chinese, and especially those who undertake serious R&D and produce more advanced technology products, are viewed with great admiration and respect, if not as heroes. American corporate leaders in China, moreover, often receive the greatest admiration of all because of their leading-edge technology performance and their greater respect for labor and environmental standards.

What is lacking most of all is a sense of national purpose in responding to a rapidly changing world, driven most importantly by the development and application of wide-ranging new technologies on a global scale. The very term "globalization" is a source of great confusion and controversy, which seriously undermine the ability to formulate a national purpose and to develop a strong and concerted policy response in pursuit of it. Most fundamentally, the American challenge today to maintain advanced technology leadership requires a clearer vision as to where the world order of nations is heading. How central to this new order is the development of new technologies? And what role, in particular, will the emerging Chinese advanced technology superstate play in it? The final chapter offers some thoughts to help stimulate this "vision thing."

Chapter 11

U.S.-China Policy in Broader Historical Perspective

The rise of China to become an advanced technology superstate is having a decisive impact on the international trade and financial systems, as recounted in earlier chapters. China is also, however, having a profound influence on the course of the global political and security orders, principally as a result of its rapidly expanding advanced technology performance. The transformation of China, moreover, is only one part, albeit a very important part, of momentous changes throughout the world, driven by the amazing wave of technological innovation that began in the 1980s and that is being spread across borders through trade, investment, and a veritable explosion of technology-enhanced communications. In short, the course of history is undergoing fundamental change, and at an unprecedented pace.

In this context, the final presentation here extrapolates the Chinese advanced technology experience over the past ten years into a broader historical perspective ahead. The presentation is in three parts. The first is a survey of the main lines of thought about history in the making since the end of the Cold War. The second part outlines what is an emerging multipolar world centered on three, and perhaps later four, "advanced technology hegemonies." The third part concludes with a commentary on how the United States and China, two of the three advanced technology hegemons, will or should interact, and to what end.

History in the Making

The history of the second half of the 20th Century, through 1991, unfolded within the bipolar Cold War world of alliances and nonaligned nations, with the United States and the Soviet Union as the superpower centers of the NATO and Comecon blocs, pitting Western values of democracy and capitalism against Soviet communism. It was a somewhat unstable world in which the balance of power was maintained through nuclear weapons systems that threatened "mutually assured destruction," and many of the nonaligned nations suffered wars and civil strife as a result of the struggle for control or allegiance by the two superpowers. China played an important balancing role, as a communist state often at odds with the Soviet Union. There were minimal economic relationships, however, between the two blocs, while international trade and investment was predominantly among the Western industrialized nations, including Japan.

The sudden collapse and peaceful transition of the Soviet bloc to market-oriented democracies took almost all observers by surprise, and created an intellectual vacuum for defining the new world political order. The United States and NATO had clearly triumphed over the Soviet "evil empire," but what would take the place of the Cold War bipolar world was not clear, and the new situation was initially left undefined by the meaningless term, "post–Cold War world."

After a few years, however, two competing explanatory paradigms for the new historical course rose to prominence, which were radically different in content and became the subject of considerable debate. The first was the "End of History" paradigm, as formulated by Francis Fukuyama, which posited "an unabashed victory of economic and political liberalism," and asserted that "we may be witnessing . . . the end of history as such: that is, the endpoint of mankind's ideological evolution and the universalization of Western liberal democracy as the final form of human government."[1] Some local conflicts would continue in the developing countries, but international relations would no longer involve the war of ideas. Rather, relations would predominantly involve resolution of economic and technical problems, which Fukuyama concluded could become rather boring. Nationalism was not seen as irreconcilable with Western liberalism, in large part because nationalistic movements do not offer "a comprehensive agenda for socioeconomic organization." As for China, "the power of the liberal idea would seem much less impressive if it had not infected the largest and oldest culture in Asia. . . . The past 15 years have seen an almost total discrediting of Marxism-Leninism as an economic system. . . . The People's Republic of China continues to manifest traditional great power behavior . . . [but it] can no longer act as a beacon for illiberal forces around the world." Overall, the end of history paradigm was a highly

---

[1] Francis Fukuyama first presented his views in "The End of History?," *National Interest* (Summer 1989), and later elaborated them at book length in *The End of History and the Last Man* (Avon Books, 1992). The quotes here are from the article, pp. 1, 6, 7, and 9 at www.wesjones. com/eoh.htm.

optimistic view of global political harmony, and a clarion call for Western triumphalism.

The second paradigm painted a far more threatening picture for Western democracies. The "Clash of Civilizations" paradigm, as presented by Samuel P. Huntington, was based on the hypothesis that "the fundamental source of conflict in this new world will not be primarily ideological or primarily economic. . . . Conflict between civilizations will be the latest phase in the evolution of conflict in the modern world."[2]   A world of eight principal civilizations were presented as cultural rather than political entities, differentiated by language, history, institutions, and, most important of all, religions.   Western civilization was entering a period of decline and was threatened, in particular, from two directions: the "Asian Affirmation" and the "Islamic Resurgence."

The Asian Affirmation, which included China and Japan, was based on a distinctive cultural and political model, stemming largely from Confucianism, that was generating exceptionally high economic growth in the most highly populated part of the world. Successful economic development in Japan during the 1980s was being reinforced by high economic growth throughout East Asia, including China. It was a triumphant affirmation of the superiority of the Asian way over the Western model, and over American culture in particular. The "Singaporean cultural offensive" contrasted the Asian virtues of order, discipline, family responsibility, hard work, collectivism, and abstemiousness with the self-indulgence, sloth, individualism, crime, inferior education, and disrespect for authority of the West. Singaporean Prime Minister Lee Kuan Yew explained that "the values that East Asian culture uphold, such as the primacy of group interests over individual interests, support the total group effort necessary to develop rapidly."   Malaysian Prime Minister Mahathir bin Mohamad described the Asian philosophy more pointedly: "The group and the country are more important than the individual."   A Chinese view attributed to a Hong Kong leader spoke of a desire "to return to what is authentically Chinese, wherein democracy, in this historical

---

[2] Samuel P. Huntington also presented his views first as an article, "The Clash of Civilizations," in *Foreign Affairs*, Summer 1993, and later at book length in *The Clash of Civilizations and the Remaking of the World Order* (Simon & Schuster, 1996). The initial quote is from the article, and the remainder of the commentary here is drawn from the book, which developed the subject further, including the concepts of "Asian Affirmation" and "Islamic Resurgence."   The quotes in this and the following paragraph are from pp. 108, 110-112, and 114.

reemergence, is discredited, as is Leninism, as just another foreign imposition."

The Islamic Resurgence was even more threatening. Muslims in massive numbers were turning toward Islam as a source of identity that would provide stability, legitimacy, development, power, and hope, epitomized by the slogan, "Islam is the solution." Islamic law took precedence over democracy, oil wealth provided an economic foundation, and rapid population growth, including migration to West Europe, instilled a demographic momentum. The "core element" of the resurgence consisted of students and intellectuals, especially students in technical institutes, engineering faculties, and scientific departments. There was a political message again of triumphalism over the West. The resurgence was described as a reaction to the stagnation and corruption of existing institutions and a return to a purer and more demanding form of religion, work, order, and discipline, with "an appeal to emerging dynamic, middle class people." An observer of Muslim culture commented that "in one Muslim society after another, to write of liberalism and of a national bourgeois tradition is to write obituaries of men who took on impossible odds and then failed." A top Saudi official in 1994 explained: "Foreign imports are nice and shiny high-tech 'things.' But intangible social and political institutions imported from elsewhere can be deadly—ask the Shah of Iran. . . . Islam for us is not just a religion, but a way of life. We Saudis want to modernize, but not necessarily Westernize."

The decline of the West was a basic component of both the Asian Affirmation and the Islamic Resurgence, which was confirmed by Huntington in the chapter, "The Fading of the West: Power, Culture, and Indigenation." He concluded that the West will remain the most powerful civilization well into the early decades of the 21st Century, but the longer term trends of population, slower economic growth, more regional orientation of military power, and the resurgence of non-Western cultures all work toward a gradual decline of the West. He also lamented a more immediate and dangerous trend within the United States, wherein the historical American national identity, based on the heritage of Western civilization and the political principles of the "American Creed"—liberty, democracy, individualism, equality before the law, constitutionalism, and private property—"have come under concentrated and sustained onslaught from a small but influential number of intellectuals and publicists. In the name of multiculturalism they have attacked the identification of the United States with Western civilization, denied the existence of a common American culture, and promoted racial, ethnic, and other subnational cultural identities and groupings."[3] This pessimistic prospect for the West was reinforced in depth by the historian Jacques Barzun in his monumental *From Dawn to Decadence: 500 Years of Western Cultural Life*. His concluding section, labeled "A View From New York Around 1995," included such passages as: "If one surveyed the Occident and the World as well, one could see that the greatest creation of the West, the nation state, was stricken. . . . Bogged down in their efforts to keep welfare up to date, the democracies have lost the power to keep the governing machinery up to the same date. . . . To appear unkempt, undressed, and for perfection unwashed, is the key signature of the whole age. . . . Self-contempt was redoubled by knowing that performance was of slight value compared to Image. . . . Rights were continually being extended. Group propaganda and lawsuits by individuals did the work."[4]

Thus, the future of the West in 1995 was widely viewed with great pessimism, while the challenges from Asian Affirmation and Islamic Resurgence appeared to be gaining power and momentum. The End of History triumph of Western liberal democracy, in contrast, was being dismissed as unrealized in the short run and more and more unlikely over the longer term. The decade since 1995, however, has experienced several major developments that have substantially changed the outlook for both of the post–Cold War historical paradigms. To a certain extent, each has been reinforced in terms of immediate impact, while in the process a greater degree of interaction between the two has been taking place. Three major developments since 1995 have had the most influence on this evolving new course of history.

1. ***The Asian financial crises and Japanese economic stagnation.***—The financial crises of the late 1990s in Thailand, Indonesia, South Korea, and to a lesser extent elsewhere in East Asia, took the wind out of the sails of the Singaporean cultural offensive. The Asian values of order, discipline, family ties, collectivism, and group over individual rights devolved into Asian crony capitalism, revealing massive corruption and disastrous economic mismanagement, particularly in banking sectors, which resulted in the ruin of many companies and extensive job loss. Major economic reforms were undertaken, with great success, in restoring high economic growth, but they were all in the direction of open markets, more effective competition, the rule of law, and

---

[3] Huntington, *op. cit.*, 1997, p. 305.
[4] Jacques Barzun, *From Dawn to Decadence: 500 Years of Western Cultural Life* (Harper Collins, 2000). The quotes are from pp. 774, 780, 781, 786, and 787.

government transparency, or, in other words, the Western economic model.   Meanwhile, the Japanese superior economic performance of the 1980s gave way to economic stagnation during the 1990s and the first years of the 21st Century.

The impact of this economic turbulence on the two historical paradigms was substantial for both. The distinctive Asian culture, or civilizational, model for economic growth was seriously deflated, while the End of History Western liberal economic model became more firmly entrenched than before. At the same time, the quick resumption of high economic growth throughout East Asia, with the notable exception of Japan, reinforced confidence in a triumphant Asian economic power position with strong ethnic and nationalist underpinnings, only now with China rather than Japan in the dominant central position.   One other important gain for the triumph of Western values, however, was political change in East Asia toward democratic governance, most dramatically in the conversion of South Korea and Taiwan from authoritarian regimes to functioning multiparty democracies, with all basic individual freedoms, under the rule of law. In effect, the two paradigms were becoming mutually reinforcing.

2. *September 11 and the war on terror.*—This development has been even more powerful in its immediate impact, although more complicated to assess in historical terms. The surge in fanatical Muslim violence through terror and suicide attacks, most spectacularly in the destruction of the New York World Trade Center, the symbol of Western economic power, triggered a U.S. response that included the invasion of Afghanistan and the destruction of the radical Taliban regime and *al Qaeda* training camps, and later the invasion of Iraq. This U.S. response, in turn, fueled wide-ranging support in the Muslim world for the terrorist "freedom fighters," and hostility toward the United States. The Islamic Resurgence, in parallel, was making continued inroads into West Europe through large migration, which has led to 10 percent or more Muslim populations in the Netherlands and France, and a growing presence elsewhere.

The outcome of the war on terror is not yet clear. There are important results thus far, however, that are having a tragic and debilitating impact on the Islamic Insurgence of the early 1990s. One result is that the terrorist killing, post–September 11, has been principally Muslims killing Muslims.   Suicide bombers are blowing up innocent Muslims, including women and children. This has been happening for decades in countries such as Algeria, Egypt, and Pakistan, but it has reached alarming new heights in recent years in Afghanistan under the Taliban and now in Iraq and even Saudi Arabia. This negative turn within the Muslim world, moreover, has recently been accompanied by democratic political change, supported by strong external initiative from the United States. Elections have been held or scheduled in Afghanistan, Iraq, a fledging Palestine, and Lebanon, and smaller steps have been taken in such areas as womens' rights and freedom of the press.

The overarching reality that pervades all aspects of current Islamic culture is its poor performance, relative to the rest of the world, with respect to economic growth and modernization in general, including the almost entire absence of advanced technology industry. The historic irony is that the Islamic civilization was at the forefront of science and other human achievement 500 years ago, while now it has fallen far behind not only the West but most of Asia and Latin America as well. The eminent scholar Bernard Lewis sums up the story: "If the peoples of the Middle East continue on their present path, the suicide bomber may become a metaphor for the whole region, and there will be no escape from a downward spiral of hate and spite, rage and self-pity, poverty and oppression, culminating sooner or later in yet another alien domination."[5] Hardly the picture of a cultural resurgence.

The net assessment, as of 2005, is that the Islamic Resurgence of a decade ago is in a state of crisis and frustration. It is doubtful that students in technical institutes and engineering and scientific departments still constitute the core of what is now a brutally violent insurgence. Iran, the only Muslim theocracy, is plagued by corruption and economic stagnation, while the United States is greatly admired by young Iranians. Western political and economic values, meanwhile, are gaining ground through elections, free trade agreements, and ubiquitous West to East communication via satellite TV, DVDs, and e-mail.

3. *The Chinese 1995 decision to make advanced technology industry and military modernization top priorities.*—This development over the past ten years is, of course, the subject of this study, and it is not recapitulated here except to explain how it is having a major impact on the reformulation of the earlier paradigms for post–Cold War history. The rapid rise of China to advanced technology superstate status, in the context of a global surge in technological innovation and application since the 1980s, was not addressed directly in either the End of History or the Clash of Civilizations paradigms. Huntington came closest when, with reference to China, he observed, "the diffusion of technology

---

[5] Bernard Lewis, *What Went Wrong? Western Impact and Middle East Response* (Oxford University Press, 2002), p. 159.

and economic development of non-Western societies in the second half of the 20th Century . . . will be a slow process, but by the middle of the 21st Century, if not before, the distribution of economic product and manufacturing output among the leading civilizations is likely to resemble that of 1800."[6] In fact, China is emerging as an advanced technology superstate in the first decade of the 21st Century, with an information age economy that bears no resemblance to the subsistence farmers and lowest tech textile mills in England in 1800.

The emergence of China as an advanced technology superstate will have the most profound effects of all these recent developments on the course of history. As a last reprise for the two historical paradigms, it will become the decisive factor for the interaction between the forces for a politically distinct Asian ascendancy, prone to clash with the West, and the globalization of Western liberal political and economic values. Moreover, a more and more dominant global power position of the three advanced technology superstates—the United States, the EU, and China—in economic, geopolitical, and military terms, will present a very different configuration of global relationships that does not fit well within either of the earlier paradigms. The post–Cold War world order, largely as a result of the Chinese rise to advanced technology superstate status, is being fundamentally reordered, and this reordering can be described best in terms of the relationships among three, or perhaps later four, advanced technology hegemonies.

A final comment, before examining this new relationship among advanced technology hegemons in detail, relates to a fourth potential major development since 1995 that is more tentative, but appears to be taking on definitive shape and momentum. This is an apparent bottoming out of the decline of Western civilization as pointedly described by Huntington and Barzun, particularly in the United States. A more and more solid case can be made for a broadly based pendulum swing away from the multicultural attacks of the early 1990s on the historical American national identity and towards reassertion of the "American Creed," as defined by Huntington. This reassertion is largely from the grass roots within the American population, and certainly stronger among university students than faculty. It is reflected in the higher priority given to traditional values by both major political parties, and is highlighted in the new thrust of U.S. foreign policy to champion democracy and individual freedoms in all parts of the world. To the extent this reassertion gathers power and momen-

---

[6] Huntington, *op. cit.*, 1996, p. 88.

tum in the United States, and is shared in partnership with European nations with a common Western heritage, the historical course ahead will be influenced significantly. And in keeping with the persistent *leit motiv* of this study, the impact of such an American reassertion of Western values will be most decisive on relations between the United States and China.

A New Order of Advanced Technology
Regional Hegemonies

The new order of international relationships presented here is predominantly oriented among and around the three advanced technology superstates: the United States, the EU, and China. Each of the Big Three, in addition to internal superstate status, is the regional hegemon within the North American/Caribbean, European, and East Asian regions, respectively. As shown in Table 11-1, these three advanced technology regions comprise 52 percent of the world population, 79 percent of global GDP, and 85 percent of global merchandise exports. There is the possibility that within the next 10 to 20 years, India will rise to become a fourth advanced technology superstate, with a corresponding hegemonic position within South Asia. In this event, as also shown in Table 11-1, the four regional aggregates rise to 71 percent of world population, 86 percent of global GDP, and 86 percent of world merchandise exports.

This new predominant power orientation in the world political, economic, and military orders has many implications as to how international relations will evolve. To begin to understand these relationships, the commentary here addresses: the definition of an advanced technology superstate as regional hegemon; the distinctive characteristics of each of the Big Three hegemons; the relative roles of other parts of the world; and the relationships among the Big Three.

Advanced Technology Superstates
as Regional Hegemons

The definition of an advanced technology superstate derives from much of the discussion of China throughout this study and has several essential characteristics. There is first the need for a very large internal market, which attracts advanced technology companies to develop and market their new products and provides the resource base for the wide range of public expenditures needed to nurture technology innovation and production. Public expenditures are needed in particular for education, including a quantitatively large university system with strong capabilities in math and science, engineering, and business management, and for public sector R&D in conjunction with the university system and advanced technology companies. Large public expenditures are also needed for economic infrastructure to support manufacturing industry and related services, especially financial and telecommunications services. Finally, an open trade and investment policy is essential to attract the participation of leading-edge multinational companies and to stimulate effective competition in the fast-moving development and application of new technologies.

Table 11-1
Regional Groupings of Countries:
Population, GDP, Exports

	Population		GDP*		Exports (Merchandise)	
	Millions	%	$ Billions	%	$ Billions	%
1. North American/ Caribbean	509	8	13,279	26	1,193	21
2. EU	659	10	12,704	25	1,611**	29
3. East Asia	2,127	33	14,637	28	1,944	35
Sub-total, 1-3	3,295	52	40,620	79	4,748	85
4. South Asia	1,256	20	3,406	7	69	1
Sub-total, 1-4	4,551	71	44,026	86	4,817	86
5. Islamic Crescent	630	10	2,433	5	368	7
6. Russia	154	2	1,345	3	144	3
7. South America	367	6	2,637	5	181	3
8. Sub-Sahara Africa	679	11	1,151	2	108	2
Total	6,381	100	51,592	100	5,618	100

Sources: CIA, *The World Factbook,* and WTO, *International Trade Statistics, 2004*

*Purchasing power parity (ppp) measure.

**Excludes intra-EU exports; if these exports were included, the sub-total 1-3 would rise above 90 percent.

"Innovation ecosystems" sums up the overall process, and the United States, the EU, and China meet all the essential characteristics. The current fourth-place contender is Japan, although it lacks comparable internal market size and is not as open to competitive trade and foreign investment—particularly investment. The possible future rise of India to advanced technology superstate status is commented on below.

The role of the Big Three as regional advanced technology hegemons is defined in terms of leadership, predominant influence, or domination, especially as exercised by one nation over others. The term has been used here principally in the narrower sense of predominant influence, etc., for advanced technology industry relationships, including trade, investment, and cross-border technology transfer, but there are broader implications for political and national security hegemonic relationships as well. Importantly, the Big Three account for the overwhelming share of advanced military systems and for almost all development of new systems, especially related to cyber warfare. As for the three definitional characteristics, all three hegemons clearly have the "predominant influence" within their respective regions, while the respective leadership roles are less well defined. The most controversial characteristic is the degree of domination, or control exercised by the superstate over regional economic partners. The definition of hegemony, however, includes the proviso "or," and so a hegemon could exert leadership and predominant influence, but only a minimal domination effect. In any event, the characteristics that define an advanced technology hegemon vary greatly among the Big Three, and these distinctions require some elaboration.

Distinctive Characteristics of the Big Three Hegemons

The *United States*, as the overwhelmingly dominant economy within the North American/Caribbean region, can be viewed as a benign advanced technology hegemon. The NAFTA relationship with Canada and Mexico effectively integrates the three economies on a positive growth path, but with technology innovation for such growth emanating predominantly from the United States. Central American and Caribbean island economies are already highly trade dependent on the United States, and will become even more so through implementation of free trade and investment agreements. Colombia and post-Chavez Venezuela might also be drawn into this regional hegemonic relationship over time, but they have not yet crossed the definitive lines of American influence and leadership.[7]

U.S. predominant influence in the region is thus self-evident, and leadership, particularly in the international economic field, is now also well established with the advent of comprehensive FTAs throughout the region. American domination in broader foreign policy terms is more controversial and conditional, but nevertheless real in many respects. Western democratic values are

---

[7] Colombia and Venezuela are included in the South American region in Table 11-1. Cuba is included in the North American/Caribbean grouping, but this is clearly a post-Castro projection, and in any event the Cuban figures in the table are quite small.

shared throughout the region, which reduces the potential for conflict, and the strong U.S. international leadership role for freedom and democracy receives broad, but by no means complete, support from within the region. On important issues of U.S. national security, however, such as border security against terrorists and drug trafficking, the United States will assert its dominant power position, and others need to accept the outcome. Overall, the adjective "benign" is applicable, as the United States generally tries to be responsive to concerns within neighboring countries, a responsiveness that has increased in recent years with the rapid growth of Hispanic immigrants and voters.

The *European Union*, as an advanced technology hegemon, is a different sort of entity, because it is not a nation state but rather an economic union of 25 nations (half of which also have a monetary union) within a partial and ill-defined political and foreign policy framework. The EU basically meets the necessary qualifications as an advanced technology superstate, although structural rigidities in some member states and the lack of a single market in certain sectors, such as services, weaken the European "innovation ecosystems." Its functioning as a regional hegemon, however, is very different from that of the United States and China, and requires a stretch in the definition. West European countries that choose not to join the EU, such as Switzerland and Norway, are clearly faced with dominant economic influence from the EU, while on the large majority of political and foreign policy issues there are shared values and a minimum of conflict. The major hegemonic influence of the EU is exercised through negotiations with nonmembers seeking EU association or membership. EU membership involves wide-ranging political as well as economic commitments that are essentially nonnegotiable. This process of broadening the Brussels-based regional hegemony through expansion of membership has accelerated greatly in recent years, with an increase from 15 to 25 members, headed soon to at least 28.

The political-dominance factor for such membership negotiations is evident in the Balkans, where the arrest of fugitives from the International Court in The Hague by Serbia and Croatia is a condition for negotiations to move forward. The potential membership of Turkey and Ukraine would involve even broader political issues, especially for Muslim Turkey. Another important question about the future EU regional role as an advanced technology superstate is its leadership decision-making capability, especially as the EU expands beyond its original West European base. The long-standing debate within the EU about the trade-off between deepening and broadening has entered a new and more decisive phase, which came to a head over the French and Dutch rejection of the expanded EU constitution in May and June 2005.

China's prospect as a regional advanced technology hegemon is the most complicated, beginning with the fact that China is still an emerging advanced technology superstate. In addition, it has relationships with three even more advanced technology economies in the region—Japan, South Korea, and Taiwan—including the extensive export-platform operations of companies from the other three within China. China is already the number one economy in the region in terms of GDP, trade, foreign investment, and R&D, and its number one position will continue to grow in relative terms. Others in the region understand and accept this growing Chinese predominant economic influence, but it is not as overwhelming as it is for the United States and the EU in their respective regions.

How the other hegemonic characteristics of leadership and political domination will manifest themselves over time is far less clear and more controversial. A major barrier to Chinese leadership is the fundamental difference in political systems between the democratic governments in Japan, South Korea, Taiwan, and elsewhere in the region, and the communist authoritarian government in China. Deeply embedded historic rivalries and past conflicts create mutual suspicions, and thus there is serious concern throughout the region over rising Chinese influence and economic leverage. At the same time, there are shared cultural feelings of Asian manifest destiny through superior economic performance. The recent Chinese initiative to form FTAs within East Asia, beginning with the ASEAN, has elicited similar responses by Japan and South Korea. In broadest terms, the gestating Chinese economic hegemony within East Asia will be a central challenge for relationships within the region and with the other two advanced technology superstates.

The Relative Roles of Other
Parts of the World

The economies of the other half of the global population and their 20 percent of GDP will be greatly influenced by the course of the dominant advanced technology regions of North America, West Europe, and East Asia, but in the context of a highly dynamic positive sum game in which all ships rise with the tide of technological innovation, higher productivity, and modernization in broadest terms. Some of the other regions will likely fall further behind the Big Three regions in relative terms, but the opportunities will exist for all to gain in absolute terms. The circumstances in each of the other regions vary greatly, however, with correspondingly different prospects for their role in a new world order driven principally by the three advanced technology regions.

India has the prospect for rising to become the fourth advanced technology superstate and the South Asian hegemon extending at least to Bangladesh, Nepal, and Sri Lanka. India's market size and large university system are the starting points, and recent policy reforms to reduce barriers to trade and foreign investment and to stimulate private sector investment are producing positive results, particularly in the software and other information technology services sector, with annual exports up to about $15 billion. The most important change is in the political vision of the government to modernize and transform the nation into an advanced technology superstate. India, however, still has a long way to go. Manufactured exports in 2003 were about $40 billion and foreign direct investment was less than $5 billion, compared with $397 billion and $54 billion, respectively, in China. Infrastructure is lacking, import protection remains very high, and the burdens of suffocating government regulation inhibit investment. Nevertheless, India is on a higher growth path of 5 percent to 7 percent per year, which provides resources for further change, and the role of India in the global economy will grow in relative as well as absolute terms. A companion piece to this study might be entitled "India: An Emerging Advanced Technology Superstate?" with the question mark emphasized.

The *Islamic Crescent*, defined in Table 11-1 as stretching from Pakistan and Afghanistan through Iran and the Middle East, across North Africa, and including the central Asian republics and Sudan,[8] is caught in the dilemma described by Professor Lewis. The terrorist violence within these countries and with the West greatly inhibits economic advance, including the large amounts of investment needed for education and infrastructure to begin the process of advanced technology development. Many of these economies are maintained by large reserves of petroleum and natural gas, but even this is a mixed blessing over the longer term. Oil above $40 a barrel makes coal tar, shale oil, and nuclear power profitable, while technological advance continues to drive down the costs of alternative fuels and to create new energy-saving

---

[8] For purposes of the assessment, judgments had to be made about countries with large Muslim population, based on whether the national course was being driven principally by the "Islamic Resurgence" or by regional relationships with other non-Muslim countries. On this basis, Malaysia and Indonesia were included in East Asia, Turkey within West Europe, and Bangladesh within South Asia.

products, such as the hydrogen-fueled automobile engine. The Islamic states across the Crescent need to get their political houses in order so as to enter into more constructive political and economic engagement with the rest of the world, or face a continuing bleak economic course ahead.

Russia stands alone, with Belarus its only remaining regional partner left from the former Soviet Union and Comecon bloc— which had triple the population. The Russian economy, despite pockets of advanced technology capability, is in a state of industrial decline, and remains solvent only as a result of oil and natural gas exports, which are currently at exceptionally high prices. Economic infrastructure is crumbling, over-regulation and corruption inhibit productive investment, and highly protectionist policies do not meet minimum standards for WTO membership. A declining population presents further problems, including a large undocumented inflow of Chinese into a greatly under-populated and resource-rich Siberian peninsula. Russia, like many Muslim countries, needs to set a new political course if it is not to fall further behind the three advanced technology regions in relative and perhaps absolute terms. The most promising course for Russia would be to turn westward, with the ultimate goal of joining the EU, as the Ukraine is now doing, but this would require overcoming enormous historic and cultural baggage and involve major economic reforms.

South America is on an uncertain, mixed course with respect to engagement with the advanced technology regions. Chile has FTAs with the United States and across the Pacific, and Colombia, Ecuador, and Peru are following suit. Political change and turmoil, however, are moving the region largely in the direction of more government and less freedom for private sector investment and innovation, with Venezuela on a radically left revolutionary path. South America is rich in natural resources, which is attracting foreign investment, including from China, but the role of raw materials supplier to the advanced technology regions can work to substitute for the development of advanced technology industry within South America. Brazil is the dominant economy on the continent, and its course ahead will be decisive for the region. Recent Brazilian economic performance has been mixed, with dynamic sectors of industry heavily burdened by large government expenditures and import barriers. As one key indicator of the lag in industrial modernization, Brazilian exports of manufactures in 2003 were $37 billion compared with $135 billion by Mexico, $177 billion by South Korea, and $397 billion by China.

Sub-Saharan Africa remains the least developed region and the largest recipient of economic assistance to alleviate poverty and begin the modernization process for sustained economic growth. Political instability and violence are widespread, and democratization in broadest institutional terms is a priority for international assistance programs. The prospect is for even further concentration of foreign assistance in this region, with the potential for increased foreign investment and job creation wherever governments are able to create a reasonably hospitable investment climate. China, again, is noteworthy for recent investment initiatives in Africa, for example in Sierra Leone and Sudan, with primary interest in energy and industrial raw material development. Overall, however, sub-Saharan Africa is the least engaged region in the technology-driven globalization process, and this is unlikely to change greatly in the near to medium term.

Relationships Among
the Big Three

The reordering of global economic power relationships toward the most technologically advanced regions has not yet led to a correspondingly prominent three-way leadership orientation in international affairs. The tendency in this direction for the international financial and trading systems was described in Chapters 8 and 9, but the outlook in the political arena is far less clear. The war on terror, the containment of weapons of mass destruction, and regional conflicts outside the three advanced technology regions are interrelated in a variety of multilateral, regional, and bilateral ways, but rarely with three-way operational collaboration among the United States, the EU, and China. The three advanced technology superstates occupy four of the five permanent seats on the UN Security Council, which involves them in a close consultative relationship, but collaborative initiative is rare.

A major reason for the lack of three-way collaboration stems from basic differences among the three bilateral relationships involved. The United States and the EU share Western political and economic values and are jointly engaged in the Middle East, despite differences between the United States and most West Europeans over the invasion of Iraq, while China remains an authoritarian state not deeply involved in Middle East diplomacy for peace and democracy. The EU-China relationship is limited primarily to mutual commercial interests, with little direct engagement on political or national security issues. The United States and China, in contrast, are fully engaged in the full range of issues across the Pacific.

The prospect ahead for interaction and collaboration among the three advanced technology superstates is thus highly uncertain. Or put another way, the three-way relationship, whether it be cooperative, conflictive, or some combination of the two, is a matter for ongoing decision by the respective governments, which can be characterized as an historic opportunity and responsibility. Moreover, the lack of a unified foreign policy mechanism within the EU focuses this opportunity more sharply on the relationship between the United States and China. It is, therefore, fitting to conclude this study with a comment about how the United States and China will or should interact in the advanced technology-driven world ahead.

The United States and China: Will the East and West Finally Meet?

The alternative courses ahead for the U.S.-China relationship can be presented in terms of the familiar dichotomy of partners versus adversaries. What is new, however, is that the choice between these alternatives has now moved to center stage for the overall course of global relations, just as the U.S.-Soviet relationship did a half century ago. In addition, the specific circumstances for addressing this choice are now more clearly defined, since both countries are advanced technology superstates, regional economic hegemons, and the largest national military powers, with China headed toward becoming a formidable military adversary of the United States.

Views differ in both countries as to which will or should be the course ahead. The partnership course would reap the greater mutual economic and other benefits, but there are deeply held opinions that fundamental differences in political values and disparate cultural characteristics will prevail in creating an adversarial relationship, with each side seeking to increase its relative power position, including through weakening the other side as opportunities present themselves. The following observations make the case for the partnership alternative, in terms of mutual economic, national security, and political interests, leaving elaboration of adversarial scenarios to others.

The partnership or collaborative leadership approach in the economic area has been presented in detail in Chapters 8 and 9. In international finance, implementation of the already-agreed objective of market-based, flexible exchange rates would form the basis for collaborative leadership, while in international trade and finance, the implementation of Chinese WTO commitments will go a long way to building a mutually beneficial trade and investment relationship.   The unfolding issue of a preferential East Asian trade bloc, with China at the center, is headed in the direction of a more adversarial rivalry, and leaders in both countries and throughout the East Asian region should ponder the adage that before one builds a fence, one should consider who is being fenced in and who is being fenced out. The proposals offered in Chapter 9 for U.S. initiatives leading to transpacific and ultimately multilateral free trade in manufactures would eliminate the threatening fence.

Mutual national security threats facing the United States and China currently center on international terrorism and the proliferation of weapons of mass destruction. China has been reluctant, to say the least, to provide collaborative leadership to reduce or eliminate these threats. In large part, this reflects the elements within the Chinese power structure, and particularly within the military leadership, who are clearly in the adversarial camp with respect to the U.S. relationship. The best way to strengthen positive collaboration in these areas is through more intensive collaboration, taking advantage of confidence-building opportunities. Partnership in this area will succeed only to the extent both partners view it as in their own self-interest. And this, in turn, leads to the political relationship, which is conflicted in a number of ways.

Fundamentally different political values, expressed in terms of democratic versus authoritarian rule, separate the two governments politically, and as long as this difference prevails, it will remain a barrier to strong cooperative leadership in international affairs. The differences can be finessed, as they now are to a large extent, in order to pursue particular mutual interests, particularly economic. In any event, the two countries are not headed toward the mortal ideological conflict that existed between the United States and the Soviet Union. But the key question remains: Will China evolve, in one way or another, into a truly democratic political system, of broadly shared values with the United States?

The final observation here is that China is likely heading toward this outcome, and the United States should have a concerted strategy for supporting such democratic change.   The strategy should be more by demonstration effect and forceful friendly persuasion than by threats and sanctions, and there are many ways to do this. The whole process of transition to a highly open, market economy, subject to the rule of law, is moving China in the democratic direction.   The more highly educated Chinese population and a burgeoning middle class are powerful building blocks for this transition. Importantly, democratization should and can be viewed as a potentially peaceful and nondisruptive process, by no means necessarily akin to the Romanian experience.

The precedent for peaceful nondisruptive democratic transition is, in fact, much closer to home, within China proper as Beijing would define it. Taiwan over the past two decades made the nondisruptive democratic transition within a distinctively Chinese civilizational setting, and it is now a vibrant multiparty democracy with all basic freedoms under the rule of law. Taiwan also started earlier than China on the path of modernization to an advanced technology economy, thus demonstrating the linkages between technology-driven economic and democratic political change. Taiwan, indeed, is now something of a Trojan Horse within China, and if formal dialogue about political reconciliation were to begin between the two, the Taiwanese side would not only seek assurances for the preservation of its democratic system, but would also likely raise questions as to how mutually supporting democratic reforms will proceed on the Mainland. The U.S. role in nurturing this kind of democratic dialogue between the two politically distinct Chinas should be calibrated with great care. Democratic change within China, in any event, will likely entail a relatively long march. The ultimate U.S. objective, however, for East finally to meet West, at the end of history, can be summed up as the Taiwanization of China!

Index